CONTEMPORARY CHINA INSTITUTE PUBLICATIONS

MAO ZEDONG AND THE POLITICAL ECONOMY OF THE BORDER REGION

W9-AYQ-611

Publications in the series are:

Party Leadership and Revolutionary Power in China (1970) edited by *John Wilson Lewis*

Employment and Economic Growth in Urban China, 1949–1957 (1971) by *Christopher Howe*

Authority, Participation and Cultural Change in China (1973) edited by *Stuart R. Schram*

A Bibliography of Chinese Newspapers and Periodicals in European Libraries (1975) by *the Contemporary China Institute*

Democracy and Organisation in the Chinese Industrial Enterprise, 1948–1953 (1976) by *William Brugger*

Mao Tse-tung in the Scales of History (1977) edited by *Dick Wilson*

MAO ZEDONG AND THE POLITICAL ECONOMY OF THE BORDER REGION

A TRANSLATION OF MAO'S
ECONOMIC AND FINANCIAL PROBLEMS

ANDREW WATSON

Senior Lecturer, Centre for Asian Studies
University of Adelaide

CAMBRIDGE UNIVERSITY PRESS

Cambridge
London   New York   New Rochelle
Melbourne   Sydney

Published by the Press Syndicate of the University of Cambridge
The Pitt Building, Trumpington Street, Cambridge CB2 1RP
32 East 57th Street, New York, NY 10022, USA
296 Beaconsfield Parade, Middle Park, Melbourne 3206, Australia

First published 1980

Phototypeset in V.I.P. Melior by
Western Printing Services Ltd, Bristol
Printed and bound in Great Britain at The Pitman Press, Bath

Library of Congress Cataloging in Publication Data
Mao, Tse-tung, 1893–1976.
Mao Zedong and the political economy of the border region.

(Contemporary China Institute publications)
Translation of Ching chi we t'i yü ts'ai cheng wen t'i
Bibliography: p.

Includes index.

1. China – Economic policy – 1949–1976.
I. Title. II. Series: London. University.
Contemporary China Institute. Publications.
HC427.9.M2213 330.9'51'05 78-67434

ISBN 0 521 22551 5 hard covers
ISBN 0 521 29547 5 paperback

CONTENTS

TABLES

PREFACE

Mao's *Economic and Financial Problems* has long been neglected within China and, until this present translation, has not been available in English. In 1974, therefore, the Contemporary China Institute encouraged me to go ahead with a projected translation in the hope that it would eventually be published in the Institute's series. My transfer to Australia delayed the completion of the work and I am, indeed, grateful to the Institute for its patience in waiting for the final manuscript.

The Chinese text used for this translation was published in 1949 by the *Xin Minzhu Chubanshe*, Hong Kong. A comparison with the 1947 edition of Mao's selected works, *Mao Zedong Xuanji* (Chinese Communist Party Central Bureau of the Shanxi-Chahar-Hebei Border Region) Volume 5, pp. 1–180, as reprinted in 1970 by the Center for Chinese Research Materials of the Association of Research Libraries, Washington, shows no significant differences of text apart from typographical errors, particularly in the numerical tables. Part One was also compared with the 1953 edition of Volume 3 of the *Selected Works*, pages 893–8, where it appears under the title, *Kangri Shiqi de Jingji Wenti yu Caizheng Wenti*. Important changes introduced in that edition are noted in the footnotes. All footnotes to the translation are by the translator. Comments and observations by Mao are within brackets in the text, as are important Chinese terms.

I am grateful to David Holm for his comments on the draft translation and to the following for their comments on the introduction, Bill Brugger, John Gittings, Derek Healey, David Holm, Mark Selden and Stuart Schram. Their suggestions have helped me improve what follows. I am also grateful to David Holm for introducing me to the map in the Hoover Collection on which the map accompanying this translation is based. Finally I would like to thank Jenifer Jefferies for her painstaking work in typing the various stages of this project.

July 1978   *A.W.*

NOTE ON ROMANIZATION

The system of romanization used in this book is the official Chinese *pinyin* system introduced in 1958. A full description of this system can be found in most modern Chinese language textbooks. Most of the letters can be pronounced roughly as the sounds they represent in English spelling with the exception of the following:

$$c = ts$$
$$q = ch$$
$$x = sh$$
$$z = dz$$
$$zh = j$$

Some familiar names:

Kiangsi	becomes	Jiangxi
Mao Tse-tung	becomes	Mao Zedong
Peking	becomes	Beijing
Shen-Kan-Ning	becomes	Shaan-Gan-Ning
Yenan	becomes	Yan'an

NOTE ON MEASUREMENTS

	WEIGHT	
1 *dan*	=	300 *jin*
	=	150 Kg
1 *dou*	=	30 *jin* (standard)
	=	45 *jin* (old standard)
	=	15 Kg
1 *sheng*	=	3 *jin*
	=	1.5 Kg

1 pack of
salt = 150 large *jin* (24 ounces)
  = 225 *jin* (16 ounces)
  = 112.5 Kg

	AREA	
1 *shang*	=	3 mu (Yan'an)
	=	5 mu (Jingbian)
1 mu	=	0.0614 ha (Buck)
	=	0.06067 ha (Dingbian 1930)
	=	0.0667 ha (Current Standard)

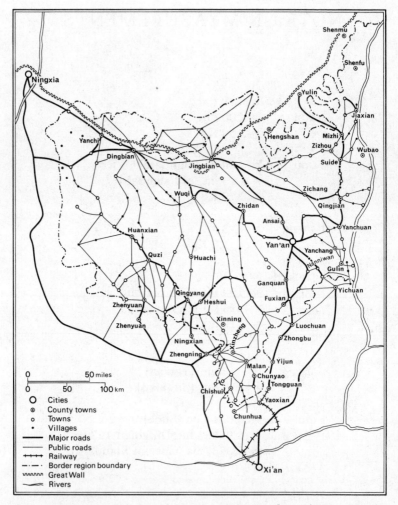

Transport routes in the Shaan-Gan-Ning Border Region. Source: *Shaan-Gan-Ning Bianqu Jiatong Ganxiantu* (Yan'an Yingong Hezuoshe, no date, probably 1944).

INTRODUCTION

The years 1941–3 were critical years for the Chinese Communist Party in its Shaanxi-Gansu-Ningxia Border Region in China's northwest.[1] It faced severe economic shortages, monetary inflation and military setback. It lacked trained and ideologically united personnel and suffered from the lingering influence of earlier political divisions. At the same time the Guomindang had withdrawn from any commitment to the second united front and was actively taking the offensive against its communist rivals. In this context the Party had to ensure its immediate survival and also rethink its methods for achieving its longer-term goals. The policies that evolved in response to this situation were not novel. In many ways they grew out of the Party's earlier experiences and the ideas that Mao Zedong had been developing since the late twenties. However, applied coherently over a wide range of activities they marked a watershed in the Party's history. Equally important, this process also saw the consolidation of Mao Zedong's position as ideological leader of the Party.

Mao's *Economic and Financial Problems* originally appeared as a report with associated reference materials delivered at the conference of senior cadres of the Shaanxi-Gansu-Ningxia Border Region held in Yan'an from 19 October 1942 to 14 January 1943.[2] Marking a high point in this crucial period of reorientation, the conference had two main goals. First, it had to confront outstanding political issues, particularly those associated with defining the historical role of 'left' and 'right' lines within the Party. While Mao's leadership was by this time secure, the debate over how to interpret the past, especially the 'left' line of the early 1930s, was by no means closed. The length of the conference and the importance of Gao Gang's report on this

1

issue underlies the explosive potential it still had. Mao and many of the key figures in the Party delivered reports dealing with this and other political and organizational problems. Secondly, the conference aimed at a clear and integrated understanding among senior cadres of the policies that were to guide their work for the rest of the war period. Thus the immediate context for Mao's report on economic questions was the need to make the case for the priorities now put forward. As is argued below, however, the lines of development proposed by Mao had implications beyond those of the expediency of the moment, and they formed part of Mao's inspiration for the initiatives he took in national development policy during the mid 1950s.

The conference took the form of reports delivered by central leaders followed by discussions during which the 267 cadres attending divided into small groups and examined the many facets of the issues raised. Study, criticism and self-criticism all formed part of the process. Eventually the conference attempted to draw the strands of the group discussions together. Much time was devoted to analysing the Party's experience in dealing with the problems it faced. Of central concern were three key interrelated campaigns, one political, one administrative and one economic. The first, and by far the most important, was the rectification campaign begun in February 1942. This campaign influenced all Party activity. Its main goal was to achieve ideological unity by resolving earlier political conflicts and by giving political education to the many new recruits who had joined the Party during the years of the united front. It also aimed to place the 'mass line' at the heart of the Party's method of leadership, insisting on principles of consultation and mass participation. On all counts this meant giving greater prominence to the role and ideas of Mao Zedong. The second campaign was that for 'better troops and simpler administration' launched in December 1941. This aimed at reducing the size and improving the quality of the army and bureaucracy, and at getting rid of excessively formal administrative and governmental procedures. In addition to any other benefits, it was intended that these reforms should help reduce the government's expenditure. The third campaign centred on economic issues. It was not developed on a large scale until 1943 when a

Great Production Movement was launched as a result of the Senior Cadres' Conference, but experience had been accumulating for a number of years. It aimed at the Party, government and army achieving economic self-sufficiency by running their own agricultural, industrial and commercial undertakings, and at encouraging the growth of the Border Region economy as a whole. Mao's *Economic and Financial Problems* was devoted to analysing the background, methods and goals of this third campaign. Many passages consist of original materials from model localities and institutions. Mao introduces these materials, endorses them, and underlines the economic principles to be derived from them.

Mao's report was published in the 1944 and 1947 editions of his *Selected Works*. It was associated with other essays and documents on economic questions that he wrote subsequently in connection with the production movement of 1943, including *Spread the Campaigns to Reduce Rent, Increase Production and 'Support the Government and Cherish the People' in the Base Areas* (October 1943), *On Co-operatives* (October 1943), and *Get Organized* (November 1943). After 1949, the report was no longer reproduced in full. The 1953 edition of Volume 3 of the *Selected Works* contains only Part I with a significant addition to the text.

This self-supporting economy, which has been developed by the troops and the various organizations and schools, is a special product of the special conditions of today. It would be unreasonable and incomprehensible in other historical conditions, but it is perfectly reasonable and necessary at present.[3]

The interpolation of this caveat reflects the changed circumstances of the Party. The re-editing of Mao's works took place at a time when the Soviet model of development commanded the stage in China. The government and Party were striving to learn from the Soviet Union, and the experience of Yan'an was neglected and downgraded. Furthermore, Mao's views on some issues had changed, particularly in respect of what were the major questions now facing the Party. Some details of policy, such as the favourable comments on the role of rich peasants and hired labour and the prominence given to material incentives, presented problems when considered in the context of a volume

3

of writings intended to guide the process of socialist construction. However, the inference that the Yan'an policies were of historical interest only is far from true. While some of the actual policies no longer applied, the dialectical approach that Mao adopted – stressing the interrelationship of economic and political issues, the importance of organizational change and political mobilization in economic development, the flexibility to accommodate various levels of ownership and various degrees of decentralization, the need for grass-roots initiative, and the crucial role played by the cadre – had an enduring quality and remained of fundamental importance. After 1955 when the Chinese path of economic development increasingly began to diverge from the lines mapped out by the Soviet Model, Mao constantly referred back to the value of the Party's experience before 1949. Mao's report thus offers us considerable insight into the foundations of his thinking on questions of political economy.

The area into which Mao led the survivors of the Long March in October 1935 was a remote, poverty-stricken region, long subject to economic stagnation and decline, its potential masked by chronically poor social conditions and lack of investment. Lying in the heart of the loess region, it was characterized by a maze of high ridges, narrow, deep rifts and gullies and abrupt light-ochre earth cliffs.[4] During the rainy season, water ate away at the ridges and gullies, and when the wind blew the air was filled with a fine yellowish dust which softened the light and hid the distance in its haze. Soil erosion was well advanced and for most of the region's history neither the means nor the organization to fight it existed. The landscape was balanced by the harsh climate. Rainfall averaging some 20 inches a year was concentrated in the spring and summer months. However, it was often unreliable, sometimes failing completely and sometimes far exceeding the average but taking the form of destructive storms. Long, cold winters with up to 150 days per year liable to frosts restricted the growing season and enforced periods of idleness on the peasant smallholders who lacked

4

resources to undertake other work. In this situation, natural disasters were frequent, prolonged drought followed by famine being the most common. During the Great Northwest Famine of 1928 to 1933 several million people starved to death.[5] Less common but similarly devastating because of their effects on the terraced fields and cave houses dug back into the soft earth cliffs, were the occasional earthquakes which shook the region. A major shock in 1920 is estimated to have led to the death of up to 250,000 people.[6] Throughout China the northwest was notorious for its hardship, poverty and backwardness. Writing in 1920 Eric Teichman recorded,

We had heard much of the terrible bitterness of this road, and certainly what with the ravages of brigands and the natural infertility of the soil, the few inhabitants were poor to the verge of starvation. Yenan (Yan'an) seems to be the centre of the most desolate area, by far the poorest region I have traversed in China outside the actual deserts.[7]

Some fifteen years and one major drought later, the scene facing Mao and his colleagues could not have improved. Indeed, one of the central themes of Mao's report is the need to build up the population and to open up the large areas of land that had fallen into disuse.

Clearly, considerable effort was needed to ameliorate the poverty of the area, particularly as the disadvantages of nature had been compounded by political and social disruption during the years preceding Mao's arrival. After the middle of the nineteenth century, the northwest was the scene of prolonged and savage fighting in which the large Moslem Hui minority struggled for independence from the Qing regime. Some fifty years later Teichman noted that many places had not yet recovered from the effects of these uprisings.[8] Despite the Qing rulers' success in quashing the rebellion, the underlying conflict remained and it came to the surface in local disturbances in later years. After 1935 the Communist Party had to make special efforts to combat this long-standing racial and religious friction between Moslems and Chinese.[9]

The 1911 Revolution had brought further disruption to the area. Shaanxi and especially the rich Wei He River valley in the south of the province was subject to frequent bouts of fighting as the warlord cliques manoeuvred to gain control of the area.[10] Initially local armies led by the Gelaohui (Elder Brother secret society) seized power. Subsequently, control of the province was disputed by local Shaanxi forces, the Anhui warlords, and the Zhili warlords, with power passing between them as the fortunes of their armies varied. Eventually the 'Christian General', Feng Yuxiang, took over in 1926 as an ally of the Guomindang. Thereafter, Shaanxi was controlled by generals nominally loyal to the Guomindang, the southern half of the province remaining in their hands when the communists occupied the northern part after 1935. Throughout this period minor warlords held large areas of territory and were continually forming and breaking alliances with their more senior colleagues. The northern half of Shaanxi, for example, was the base of Jing Yuexiu from 1911 until 1935, his survival reflecting the ease with which minor warlords shifted their loyalties from one overlord to another and the way in which they acted as important props to the structure as a whole.

As a result of the fighting between the warlords, there was a general growth in lawlessness and banditry in the area. Unable to control the bandits, the warlords came to tolerate them and to use them as a pool from which to recruit soldiers. Men circulated between banditry in the loess hills and periods of service in the warlord armies to the south. For many peasants, bandit groups such as those organized by secret societies became a means of survival and they often took on a semi-political character. Teichman encountered them and underlined the political nature of some of their actions,

The north of Shensi [Shaanxi] . . . was at the time of our visit in the hands of organized troops of brigands of a semi-political character, robbers one day, rebels the next, and perhaps successful revolutionaries the next.[11]

His words have a prophetic ring seen in the light of Liu Zhidan's attempts during the 1920s to build up communist strength in Shaanxi by enlisting the support of the Gelaohui.[12] Shortly after reaching the area, Mao also made efforts to harness the potential of the Gelaohui organization.[13]

Economically, the situation that faced Mao and his colleagues in 1935 reflected the adverse natural and social conditions.[14] Despite the fact that the northern part of Shaanxi was skirted by several long-established trade routes leading from China towards Central Asia, the Border Region was effectively insulated in its backwardness. The new railways at Xi'an (completed 1916) and Baotoun (1923) had not as yet generated any large industrial development, and their potential impact on the economy of the northwest was still not realized. What is more, the dislocation of transport and the disruption of commerce caused by the continual fighting had led to a general decline in normal economic life. Former undertakings such as cotton-growing and spinning and weaving had disappeared, and others such as salt extraction had greatly declined. Available resources were thus not being used.

The warlords had brought corrupt administration and bad government. Their chief energies were devoted to raising sufficient funds to support large armies, foreign loans and purchases of arms, as well as to building up their personal wealth. Taxes were levied at whim and sometimes collected many years in advance.[15] Monopoly control of key commodities provided a major source of funds, especially such items as salt and opium.[16] The pressure on the peasants to grow the latter had contributed substantially to the effects of the Great Northwest Famine.

The agriculture of the area, like that of the rest of China, consisted mainly of smallholder or tenant farmers working a small farm which was often fragmented into several plots of land in separate locations. According to Buck's survey, the average farm size in the Border Region area was 4.17 acres for wholly-owned farms, 4.30 acres for partially-owned farms (of which on average 1.38 acres were rented), and 3.19 acres for entirely-rented farms.[17] In terms of the tenancy rate, Buck found that 68 per cent of farmers in the area owned their land, 23 per cent were part-owners, and 9 per cent were tenants. This compared with his national average of 54, 29 and 17 per cent respectively.[18] On the surface, these figures suggest a more even distribution of land ownership than that Mao quoted to Edgar Snow in 1936. Mao said that landlords and rich peasants made up 10 per cent of the rural population and owned 70 per cent of all agricultural land, middle peasants were 25 per cent of the rural population

7

and owned 15 per cent and the remaining 65 per cent of the rural population consisted of poor peasants and labourers with only 10 to 15 per cent.[19] However, Buck was not concerned to define social classes and he did not measure land ownership in terms of categories such as Mao's. Furthermore, Mao's definitions also took into account the extent to which each class used hired labour and was involved in money-lending. In an attempt to relate Buck's figures to Mao's categories, Schran has put forward the following national estimates for the period 1929–33: landlords and rich peasants made up 12 per cent of peasant households and owned 46 per cent of the land; middle peasants were 29 per cent of households and poor peasants 59 per cent, together owning 54 per cent of the land.[20] Clearly, all these figures must be treated with considerable caution. Nevertheless, they do confirm that over half the peasant population of China lived in poverty and insecurity. While fewer of them in the Border Region area were tenants, nevertheless landlords used their ownership of land as a base on which to build their interests in money-lending, pawnbroking and commerce.

Land rent was collected in three main ways, crop-sharing where the landlord claimed a share of the annual crop and the amount obtained varied with the harvest, cash rent where the tenant paid a fixed cash rent for the year, and cash-crop rent where the tenant paid a fixed amount of crop or its cash equivalent. According to Buck, the dominant form of collection in much of the Border Region area was the cash-crop system which was used on 56 per cent of farms having rented land. Cash rent was next accounting for 30 per cent of farms.[21] In this situation few tenant farmers could hope for any relief in bad years. Whatever the harvest, the rent was fixed. While landlords could not collect their rent during a period of famine, they could still demand back payment later and even charge interest on the delay.[22] The amount of land rent charged varied by area and by type of land. In some places it might be as low as 20 per cent of the crop and in others as high as 80 per cent. According to Chen Boda, the bulk of rents in China ranged from 50 to 60 per cent.[23] Chen also quotes evidence to show that the proportion charged in rent was steadily rising during most of the first half of the twentieth century.[24] Furthermore, while the amount of rent charged in terms of grain was higher on good land than on poor land, tenants farming poor land were paying a higher rate of rent as a proportion of yield.[25] In general the poorest land was farmed by the poorest peasants.

With high rents and heavy taxation, the margin over subsistence was very small for most peasants and also difficult to maintain. Few could accumulate much in the way of savings and there was little reserve in the rural community to draw upon during lean years or, for example, when death or marriage led to additional expenses. According to Buck, only 15 per cent of all farms in the Border Region area had savings of any kind, and around one-third were in debt, 80 per cent of loans being raised for non-productive purposes. The average rate of interest was around 38 per cent per year.[26] Although some peasants were able to turn to relatives or friends for loans, the bulk of rural credit came from the landlord class which, because of its accumulation of land rent, involvement in commerce and ownership of pawnshops, was the only group with the necessary resources. For many peasants the taking of a loan was the first step in a process that led through the mortgage of their land and the forfeiture thereof to complete tenancy, and there is evidence to suggest that this situation was worsening.[27]

In sum, the poorest sections of the peasant population were economically dominated by the landlord class. Furthermore, as a result of civil war, misrule and lawlessness, the rural economy as a whole was in decline, resources were under-used, living standards were falling, and a growing number of peasants were losing any kind of economic security.

In the Jiangxi Soviet, the Communist Party's response to a similar situation had centred on land redistribution through confiscation of landlord and rich peasant holdings, on attempts to reduce rents and interest rates, and on the rehabilitation of the rural economy using existing resources in the context of a few key experiments in cooperative and collective organization. The aims had been as much political in terms of mobilizing peasant support as they had been economic. Furthermore the extent and nature of land redistribution had been the subject of considerable debate within the Party, contributing to the divisions between the various 'right' and 'left' lines.[28] While the Jiangxi policies remained the inspiration for economic work after Mao reached Shaanxi in 1935, they were considerably modified in the light of the new situation in which the Party found itself. The extent of the confiscation programme and its effects on the landlord and rich peasant classes were considerably curtailed, and the drive to reduce rents and interest rates lost much of its vigour for the next few years. In part this reflected the political need to build a united front with various social classes; in part, as Mao makes abundantly clear in his report, the modifications were the result of the greater emphasis given to increasing agricultural production rather than to changing rural society.

THE GROWTH OF THE BORDER REGION 1936–40

The Long March, though desperate at the time, transformed the disaster of the loss of Jiangxi into the triumph that Yan'an became. Ensconced at last in the relative safety of the northwest, the Party could set about ensuring the security of its base area, strengthening its army, and building up its local administration. Over the period 1936 to 1938, these developments took place in the context of two interrelated and pressing political problems. One was the remaining challenge to Mao's authority from opponents within the central leadership. The other was the definition of the Party's stand in the evolution of the second united front with the Guomindang, the basis of which was the patriotic call to resist Japan.[29] Although Mao had gained control of the Party centre at Zunyi in January 1935, his position was not yet beyond question. There was still considerable debate over the direction the Party should take. The physical separation of key leaders into several base areas often with a minimum of contact with each other had led to a lack of organizational and political cohesion. From the 'left' came pressures to resist attempts to move towards accommodation with the Guomindang and to persist in a thoroughgoing agrarian revolution as a means of mobilizing peasant support. Supporters of this approach contemplated continuing the civil war as part of the war against Japan. From the 'right' came calls to form a patriotic united front as quickly as possible and to moderate any Party policies which prevented this. Mao's own position stood in contrast to both

10

these extremes. Initially, his instincts may have inclined towards the 'left' point of view. He was certainly convinced that land reform and political mobilization were closely linked.[30] However, he had also developed a subtle analysis of the changing pressures in Chinese society and was alert to ways of using these to strengthen the Party's position.[31] In the evolution of the united front, while making some concessions he always insisted on maintaining the Party's independence, on keeping as much initiative as possible, and on not losing sight of longer-term goals, principles which were distinct from the 'right' position of subordinating everything to the united front.

After the Xi'an Incident in December 1936 when the establishment of the united front became a reality, the debate within the Party centred on how far it should change its policies and to what extent it should accept Guomindang leadership, especially in respect of its army. Moderation of the land policy and the change from a Soviet-style government to a 'democratic' one nominally subordinate to the Guomindang's central government were inevitable. However, the 'right', inspired by the Comintern and led by Wang Ming after his arrival in Yan'an from Moscow in December 1937, was prepared to go much further than Mao in accepting Guomindang demands for governmental integration and for limitations on communist military independence. While Mao always stressed using the united front to strengthen the Party's position, Wang tended to see the united front as a long-term goal in itself which would shape China's future after the war. As Benton shows, untangling the standpoint of Mao, Wang and other leaders in this debate is made difficult by the contrasts between their public and private statements. This is particularly so for the period of Wang's ascendancy from December 1937 to October 1938 during which time Mao, in public at least, had to adopt many of the stands taken by Wang and his supporters. Nevertheless, at the Sixth Plenum of the Central Committee held in Yan'an from October to November 1938, Mao was able to denounce Wang's slogan of 'everything through the united front' and asserted his own formula of 'independence and initiative'. While the version of his major speech, On the New Stage, which was published at the time contained many fulsome references to the united front and the Guomindang, his secret concluding comments to the Plenum made clear that his standpoint was very different from Wang's.[32] Mao's victory over Wang meant that his position as leader could no longer be seriously challenged. Although his opponents still had influence within the Party, the decline in relations with the Guomindang during 1939 soon justified his stand.

Despite these political problems, the Border Region was rapidly consolidated, and its area expanded steadily after the united front was established. By 1941, it had stabilized at 29 counties [xian] consisting of 266 districts [qu] and 1,549 townships [xiang], with a population of around 1,500,000. Administratively, the counties were divided among five sub-regions as follows:

(1) Yan'an and the directly administered counties: Yan'an city, Yan'an, Fuxian, Ganquan, Gulin, Yanchang, Yanchuan, Anding (renamed Zichang in 1942 in memory of Xie Zichang), Ansai, Zhidan (previously Bao'an, renamed in memory of Liu Zhidan in 1936), Jingbian and Shenfu.

(2) Suide sub-region: Suide, Qingjian, Wubao, Mizhi and Jiaxian.

(3) Guanzhong sub-region: Xinzheng, Xinning, Chishui and Chunyao.

(4) Sanbian sub-region: Dingbian and Yanchi.

(5) Longdong sub-region: Qingyang, Heshui, Zhenyuan, Quzi, Huanxian and Huachi.[33]

A similar pattern of steady expansion also characterized the growth of the Party and Red Army over this period. In the country as a whole, Party membership rose from perhaps 20,000 in 1936 to around 800,000 in 1940, and the Red Army, renamed the Eighth Route Army in August 1937 to signify its nominal inclusion in the command structure of the Guomindang forces, grew from about 40,000 soldiers to nearly 500,000.[34] In addition to the regulars and guerillas in the army, the base areas organized militia and self-defence forces. These acted as reserve forces for the main army and as its source of trained recruits. They also provided local security, information and logistical support. By 1941 over 224,000 peasants were involved in these organizations in the Shaanxi-Gansu-Ningxia Border Region.

They supported the main defence forces in the region which then consisted of 15,000 public security troops and 18,000 soldiers from the Eighth Route Army.[35] However since the regular troops rotated between spells of guard duty in the Border Region and assignments to guerilla base areas behind enemy lines, this latter figure was subject to continual fluctuation.

The structure of the Border Region government was at first a continuation of the Jiangxi Soviet system with a Central Soviet Government and a local Northwest Office. However, a full governmental hierarchy was never established, and policies were initially implemented through the military authorities in each district or through revolutionary committees formed by the military, local activists and Party members. Various mass organizations such as the peasant associations and women's associations were also established to help realize Party policies. During 1937 in line with the united front principles, the 'soviet' system gave way to the 'new democratic' system in which the Border Region Government developed along lines parallel to provincial governments in Guomindang areas. New electoral laws proclaimed in May 1937 were based on universal suffrage and the right of all political parties to nominate candidates. These laws envisaged a hierarchy of elected councils at township, district, county and regional levels, each supervising the work of an executive body. In essence this embodied the spirit of the New Democracy which Mao eventually summed up in his essay of that name of January 1940.[36] The goal was an alliance of various diverse classes all defined as revolutionary in the context of a colonial or semi-colonial country fighting against imperialism and the vestiges of feudalism. Although in other writings of the period Mao stressed the importance of the proletariat as leaders of the revolution in the long term,[37] for the moment the petty bourgeoisie, capitalists and even progressive landlords could play a leading role. The governmental structure was decreed in the new electoral laws and the economy was to be a mixed one incorporating some socialistic elements but retaining an important private sector. In sum, the New Democracy was the Party's minimum programme and, though it might last for a long time, it laid the groundwork for the maximum programme which envisaged the transition to socialism. Although the Communist Party held the initiative and defined the limits, it was prepared to cooperate with others and share some of its power. This principle was formerly incorporated into the electoral laws in March 1940 with the adoption of the 'three-thirds' system which aimed at an ideal distribution of government positions of one-third Party, one–third 'non-Party leftist progressives', and one-third 'middle-of-the-roaders'.[38] The gain for the Communist Party in the New Democracy was the broadest base of support possible. Nevertheless, the system also embodied the dilemmas and tensions of the united front since it implied a constant refinement of judgement, balancing between 'left' resistance to any compromise however trivial and 'right' willingness to compromise fundamental principles.

During the spring of 1937 a campaign was launched to publicize and implement the new election laws. However, the outbreak of war in July and the urgency given to military mobilization meant that the process was suspended. The regional council was not finally elected until the end of 1938 and it first met in January 1939 under the presidency of Gao Gang. This council served until November 1941 when a new one embodying the 'three-thirds' system was elected. Nevertheless, in September 1937 long before the regional council was formed, the Shaanxi-Gansu-Ningxia Border Region Government was established and it proceeded to operate continuously until 1945. Under the chairman, a post held by Lin Boqu throughout, there were eight departments, the Secretariat, Civil Affairs Department, Finance Department, Education Department, Reconstruction Department, Public Security Headquarters, Public Security Commission and Audit Commission. Each of these had its subordinate sections and, in addition, there were a number of specialist agencies concerned with such things as taxation, welfare and education. Beneath the regional government, executive committees were set up at sub-regional, county, district and township levels. The most important of these were the county and township governments. The sub-region and district chiefly served to coordinate the work of lower levels. Township government consisted of a head, who often combined government and Party offices, supported by one full-time secretary, a chief of security and a number of part-time assistants. They supervised the work of the heads of the two lowest levels of the hierarchy, the administrative village area and the natural village. The role of the township heads was very important, but as is shown in Mao's report, they could not always be relied upon to carry out government policies.[39] It was therefore necessary for county and district cadres to maintain as close supervision as possible. Counties were divided into three classes depending on the size of their population, and the number of government cadres under the county head ranged from twenty-five to thirty-five. These cadres were usually divided into five sections paralleling the Secretariat and departments of the regional government. By 1941 there were 7,900 full-time government officials of whom about 1,000 worked in the central government, 4,021 between regional and township level and 2,879 in the townships.[40] In addition there were full-time cadres working in the self-defence forces and the mass organizations. The structure had grown into a complex hierarchy and was tending to increase its bureaucratic procedures.

THE CRISIS OF 1941

The period of unprecedented security and growth that followed the establishment of the second united front came to an abrupt end during 1940. Over the following twelve months the situation changed from one of expansion and stability to one of contraction and desperate shortages. Once again the Party found itself cut off from outside support and was thrown back on its own resources. The key to this new situation was the decline of the alliance with the Guomindang. Once practical cooperation between the two parties became impossible, the economic and political weaknesses that underlay the growth of the previous years came to the fore and setbacks in two areas, the military and the economic, precipitated the crisis.

Ironically, the military difficulties were the product of the successes of the Eighth Route Army against the Japanese. From August to December 1940 it launched a series of attacks on the occupation forces in five provinces in north China during the 'Hundred Regiments' campaign.[41] Roads, railways and communications throughout the area were repeatedly cut. Coal-mining and other production under Japanese control was disrupted and enemy positions were attacked. In all the Japanese suffered considerable losses and they retaliated with the adoption of the brutal 'three-all' strategy, kill all, burn all and destroy all. The aim was to deny the Eighth Route Army large areas of territory, to cut off its supplies and to terrorize the population into withdrawing support. By the end of 1941 the size of the army in the north had fallen from a peak of 400,000 to somewhere in the region of 300,000 and at the same time the population under communist leadership had dropped from 44 million to 25 million.[42] Although the Shaanxi-Gansu-Ningxia Border Region itself was not directly attacked, pressures on it increased and morale was severely shaken. All this served to highlight more sharply the beleaguered state in which the economy of the Border Region now found itself.

Until 1939, the Border Region economy had been relatively stable and the government's sources of finance fairly secure. The Party had not found it necessary to be greatly concerned with economic problems and attention centred on the War of Resistance. Many cadres felt that economic work was somehow unworthy and unimportant.[43] The land revolution of 1936 which lasted until January 1937 when it was called off as a condition for the formation of the united front, was essentially political in its impact, mobilizing peasant support, creating greater social equality and sharing out resources so that the poorer sections of the rural community gained some economic security. These effects were accentuated by a sharp drop in grain tax and by the removal of the many miscellaneous taxes imposed by the warlords. Most of the poor and middle peasants ceased to pay tax at all at this time. However, despite the social changes the revolution brought about and despite its considerable effects on the economies of individual peasant families, it did not increase agricultural output as a whole. In fact Mao blamed 'left' excesses of the land revolution for inhibiting the development of production and said that progress only came after these were stopped.[44] Nevertheless, while it was being carried out the land revolution did have a bearing on the Border Region budget. In the middle of 1936, Lin Boqu told Edgar Snow that monthly expenditure was 320,000 *yuan*, of which 40 to 50 per cent came from confiscations from landlords and rich peasants, 15 to 20 per cent from voluntary contributions and the rest from the government's own economic construction, Red Army lands and bank loans.[45]

Snow was impressed by the financial achievements he saw but it was clear that confiscations could not last for ever and that new sources of economic stimulus were going to be needed before long. In less than a year this was realized through the establishment of the united front. The Border Region gained access to the national economy for trade and the purchase of essential supplies. At the same time it began to receive a monthly subsidy from the Guomindang of around 100,000 *yuan* for government expenses and 500,000 *yuan* towards the running of the army. With this basic financial guarantee, economic development remained of secondary importance. The government could continue to keep agricultural taxation very low and only collected it from the rich. Up to 80 per cent of peasant families paid none at all.[46] The Guomindang subsidy lasted until the end of 1940 during which year it totalled 10.4 million *yuan*,[47] and it ceased after the New Fourth Army Incident of January 1941.[48] This marked the end of effective cooperation within the united front.

Even before the subsidy was cut off the Party had begun to feel economic pressures.[49] Inflation cut the value of the money from the Guomindang until by 1940 it had less than one-seventh of its original value.[50] More importantly, in 1939 when Guomindang forces occupied some parts of the Border Region for a short time, an economic blockade was reimposed. This led to a shortage of goods and a rise in prices which, together with the growing costs of the expanding army and bureaucracy, forced a rapid increase in the amount of tax revenue required. After the New Fourth Army Incident the blockade was tightened so that by the tax period 1940–1 even the poor peasants were brought within the tax threshold and the government saw the need to develop a better system of land registration and assessment in order to improve collection and remove inequities.[51] The sudden change in the situation is reflected by the grain taxation records for 1937 to 1944.

Table A Grain tax in the Border Region, 1937–44

| | Unit: *dan* (= 400 lb) of official grain equivalent | | |
Year	Total grain production[a]	Tax target[b]	Actual collection[c]
1937	1,100,000	10,000	13,859
1938	1,300,000	10,000	15,972
1939	1,370,000	50,000	52,250
1940	1,430,000	90,000	97,354
1941	1,630,000	200,000	200,000
1942	1,680,000	160,000	165,000
1943	1,840,000[d]	180,000	180,000
1944	2,000,000[d]	160,000	160,000

Sources:
(a) *Kangri Zhanzheng Shiqi Jiefangqu Gaikuang* (1953), pp.15–16.
(b) Below, pp. 60–1 and pp. 233–5.
(c) Original estimates quoted in Schran (1976), p. 188.
(d) Lin Boqu's report on the work of the Border Region Government to the Third Border Council, 4 April 1946 in *Shaan-Gan-Ning Bianqu Canyihui Wenxian Huiji* (Beijing, 1958), p. 284.

The blockade and removal of the subsidy also led to the introduction of a number of other fund-raising methods in 1941, including a hay tax to provide fodder for government animals, taxes on wool and cattle, lotteries, levies to support the self-defence army and the sale of government bonds. Most of these miscellaneous taxes remained in force through 1943. The other major sources of revenue were taxes on commerce, imports, exports and salt.

This growth in government demands on the economy after 1939 forced the Party to pay more attention to questions of economic policy. It started to experiment with ways of reducing costs and developing self-sufficiency, and by 1941 this had become one of its major concerns. The situation was exacerbated by the rapid inflation that occurred over the same period.[52] Apart from the inflationary pressures produced in the Guomindang economy, factors causing inflation in the Border Region included the economic disruption brought about by the blockade and the deficit financing that accompanied the issue of the Border Region's own currency in 1941. The fact that many goods had to be smuggled in and out of the Border Region depressed prices of Border Region exports and increased those of imports. This 'balance of payments' problem also reduced the value of the Border Region *yuan* below that of the national currency.[53] Thus the Party's initial reaction after 1939 of increasing taxation and deficit financing, while working in the short term, could not provide a long-term solution to the Border Region's problems. On the contrary, the rapid growth of taxation led to a dampening of peasant enthusiasm to increase production[54] and, even as late as 1942, Mao had to warn senior cadres that juggling with finances was no answer. Furthermore, methods which brought hardship to the poorer sections of the community contradicted the Party's fundamental principles. Instead, the Party increasingly turned to efforts to stimulate the rural economy using existing resources and technology, greater self-reliance by government organs and the army, and selective innovations in collective and cooperative organization where sound economic results could be achieved. Scattered and uncoordinated efforts in these directions over the period 1939–41 coalesced during 1942 to form the basis of Mao's report and the production campaign of 1943.

THE PARTY'S RESPONSE

Mao and the central leadership's response to the crisis took three main forms, political, administrative and economic. The political was the most fundamental since it involved binding the varied elements that had joined the Party during its years of growth into a coherent whole and then providing all Party members with the motivation, inspiration and methodology to match up to the situation. This meant tightening the more relaxed ideological standards that had characterized Party life under the united front by giving Party members a more unified education in Marxist ideology, a clearer definition of principles and goals, and a firmer sense of discipline. Mao also insisted that this political education should place Marxism firmly within a Chinese context, relating the theory to the practice of the Chinese revolution and rejecting subordination to foreign dogmas. In view of Mao's role in the development of the Chinese Communist Party, the process implied a reinterpretation of Party history in order to stress Mao's line and his struggles against his opponents. Any earlier inconsistencies that had occurred in the evolution of his thinking had to be ironed out in order to present an integrated philosophy. Accounts had to be settled with any remaining dissenters, and those who had taken the wrong line previously had to re-examine their mistakes. Mao believed that once this ideological rectification and unification had taken place, Party members would be able to take the initiative against the problems they faced.

The key to this final stage lay in the 'mass line' which was now seen as the core of the Party's political methodology. Summed up as 'from the masses, to the masses', this assumed that new ideas and methods are created by the masses and the Party's role was to find and refine these creations, to place them in the correct Marxist perspective, and to return them to the masses for implementation. This meant building close relations with the people, listening to them, consulting with them and persuading them to follow the correct line. Coercion and 'commandism' which built a wall between superiors and subordinates was seen as counter-productive since the aim was to promote the conscious participation and understanding of the led. However, the mass line did not imply abdicating the responsibility for leadership. The Party was still the vanguard and organizationally it remained tightly centralized. Coercion and suppression could be used against enemies, those who would not abandon their mistaken viewpoints and those whose influence was significant enough to make their challenges to the Party's line a serious threat. Furthermore, since the mass line was underpinned by political rectification during which questions of principle were thrashed out, its focus was policy implementation. It allowed for considerable flexibility within the confines of a defined and all-embracing ideological framework. Overall it was a practical working style which coincided closely with Marxist-Leninist principles concerning the role of the Party and its relationship to the masses. More immediately, the mass line enabled lower-level Party workers imbued with the spirit of obedience to the common ideology to take initiatives in the diverse situations they faced in wartime without the time-consuming need to refer to a hierarchical command system. In other words, it was a political methodology which dovetailed into the guerilla tactics of the army. As might be expected, an extensive campaign with such fundamental implications was not the sudden product of the crises. It grew from ideas and methods which had been in the background for a number of years. Furthermore, its goals could not be achieved overnight if they could be achieved at all. The rectification campaign lasted from 1942 to 1944 in its first intense form and, equally importantly, set the pattern for a continuous process of Party education and reform.[55]

The other aspects of the Party's response to the crisis were deeply influenced by the rectification campaign. The drive for 'crack troops and simpler administration' which applied to government and army organization, was characterized by a shift away from the formalistic and bureaucratic procedures which had grown up in the preceding years towards greater decentralization and more informality. It began in December 1941 as a move to reduce the number of administrative personnel in the face of the growing economic difficulties and it was intensified during 1942. In the bureaucracy the first aim was to reduce the number of full-time cadres from 7,900 to 6,300. In fact this goal was never achieved and by January 1943 the total had risen to 8,200. However, many of these administrators now spent part of their time working in productive undertakings which accounted for a growing percentage of their running costs. The shift to decentralization gave greater prominence to the lower levels of government which was accompanied by the transfer of senior personnel downwards to work in the countryside. At the same time the application of the mass line and the preference for informal procedures led to an end to attempts to replicate the standard structures of Guomindang administration.[56] Nevertheless, the essential structure of the Border Region Government remained the same.

In the army, the decline in troop numbers was transformed into a campaign to intensify the training of crack units, to direct surplus personnel into production, and to recruit more guerilla soldiers than regulars. Thus costs could be reduced, economic growth stimulated, and the morale and quality of the troops could also be raised. In addition political work within the army was strengthened and more emphasis was placed on integrating army, Party and government work.[57]

The guidelines for the economic policies which formed the third aspect of this interlocked set of responses were laid down in Mao's *Economic and Financial Problems*. Essentially they involved selecting those experiments in economic organization since 1939 which met the three criteria of improving the well-being of the masses, increasing production, and serving the Party's cause and then promoting them on a wide scale. At the same time, the role of the government and Party was transformed from one of simply collecting funds from the people to one of active participation in stimulating the growth of the private economy. As pointed out above, policies based on utilizing currently unused or under-used resources and on cooperative organizations, had evolved from the period of the Jiangxi Soviet. The major new economic innovation which aimed initially at overcoming critical shortages in government supplies and subsequently at economic self-sufficiency by government employees was the expansion of self-supporting production by army and government personnel. Mao criticized 'grandiose, empty and unrealistic plans' for large-scale investment in heavy industry and stressed 'down-to-earth and effective economic development' which grew from the existing economic base. The mass line was reflected by greater concern for the people's economic welfare and by the stress on mass participation in economic management. On the one hand cadres were encouraged to consider the needs of the private economy, to actively investigate the situation, and to provide what assistance they could. On the other hand they were told not to carry their help to a level where they interfered too much; they had to 'overcome the desire to monopolize everything, implement the policy of people in control and officials as helpers'.[58] As a result, the Party became deeply involved in the problems of stimulating growth in a mixed economy and in defining the relationship between the public and private sectors. Since the principles of the united front still applied, the goal was not a fundamental transformation of the structure of the economy but rehabilitation, growth, and limited reform.

In sum, the Party's response to the crisis of 1941 was a mixture of ideological revitalization, administrative reform and economic self-sufficiency. The first gave a new sense of purpose and discipline, replacing the prominence previously given to the united front and long-term cooperation with the Guomindang. The second reflected attempts to put the mass line into practice. The third was as much concerned with survival as with revolution, but on its success depended whether or not the Party would be able to mobilize support in the war against Japan and in the struggle against the Guomindang. As Mao put it:

If our Party and government do not pay attention to mobilizing the people and helping them to develop agriculture, industry, and commerce, their life cannot be improved, and the needs of the War of Resistance cannot be met. As a result there will be trouble between the troops and the people. And if we cannot settle the minds of the troops and the people, it is pointless to consider anything else. Therefore the most important task is for the Party and the government to concentrate great efforts on building up the people's economy.[59]

MAO AND THE BORDER REGION ECONOMY

As has been stated, Mao's analysis of the Border Region economy had two main points of focus: the development of the private sector and the growth of self-supporting undertakings run by army and government personnel to supplement the operating and living costs of their units. Since there was virtually no private industry, the private sector consisted of agriculture, handicrafts and commerce. Mao defined its primary role as providing for the people's livelihood. Its function as a source of support for the war and for reconstruction – which it realized through the taxes paid to the government and trade with the public sector – though important, was secondary to the task of providing that livelihood. Mao argued that the only way to raise the living standards of the people was through the growth of the private sector; and it was only by demonstrating its ability to achieve this practical goal that the Party could generate support for its cause. On this he was unequivocal:

The primary aspect of our work is not to ask things of the people but to give things to the people. What can we give the people? Under present conditions in the Shaan-Gan-Ning Border Region, we can organize,

23

lead and help the people to develop production and increase their material wealth. And on this basis we can step-by-step raise their political awareness and cultural level.[60]

The expansion of self-supporting undertakings contributed to this aim by alleviating government demands on the people and improving the living and working conditions of the soldiers and officials. Furthermore, since there was a critical shortage of labour in the Border Region, using the surplus labour of the troops and officials enabled exploitation of under-used resources such as land and salt and the reintroduction of handicraft industries that had fallen into decline, such as textiles. Provided the undertakings were properly organized they could be very profitable. While they originally grew up inclined towards autarchy in terms of simply supplying the needs of the unit operating them, after 1942 Mao saw them as profit-making units involved in commerce and production for society at large. In this, they dovetailed into the other part of the public sector, which consisted of the enterprises run by the government to meet the needs of the Party and government as a whole. On the one hand, self-supporting production relieved the government of the need to invest in particular forms of production. On the other, successful undertakings could eventually be transferred to government control and become State enterprises.[61] Finally, self-supporting production stimulated the private sector either by example as in the case of opening up new agricultural land or by providing a new market as happened when 359 Brigade set up a textile mill and encouraged yarn-spinning as a peasant household subsidiary. Thus the economic value of the efforts of the soldiers and officials was greatly magnified by their entrepreneurial and pathfinding role.

Overall Mao specifically warned against developing undertakings which might harm the private sector:

The economic activities of the army, Party and government should harmonize with the economic activities of the people. Anything which damages the people's interests or causes them dissatisfaction is not allowed.[62]

He did not yet see the public sector as strong enough to play the major role in the economy and in raising living-standards. This might be the eventual goal but it was 'fantasy' in the immediate context. Mao argued that this approach to the development of the 'national' economy was a novel one:

The reason that this is a new model is that it is neither the old Bismarck-ian model of the national economy nor the new Soviet model of the national economy but it is the national economy of the New Democracy or the Three People's Principles.[63]

The model was thus conceived of as a constituent part of the New Democracy and as helping to build the basis on which the next stage of the Party's programme would depend. It was not State-inspired capitalism nor Soviet-model planned industrial-ization based on accumulation from agriculture. Instead it was a form of mixed economy in which the gradual growth of coopera-tive, self-sufficient, and State activities prepared the way for the transition to the maximum programme, the building of a socialist economy.

Agriculture

Agriculture formed the basis of the private sector but the long period of decline had reduced it to far below its full potential in all dimensions. The rural population had shrunk and land had fallen into disuse. By 1937 the cultivated area was a reported 8,431,006 mu (roughly 1,380,000 acres, about one-fifth of the 40 million mu of cultivable land), the number of sheep was be-tween 400,000 and 500,000 and there were around 100,000 oxen and donkeys.[64] Cotton-growing had virtually ceased. The first essential for halting this decline was the establishment of stable and efficient government. Once order was restored, increased input of labour using existing technology to exploit the avail-able land could be sufficient to raise output. Any attempt to restore the agricultural economy through other means would have meant heavy investment in modern inputs, and the economic blockade and lack of capital meant that that was not possible. For the moment the key lay in providing peasants with incentives to expand production, in experimenting with ways of overcoming shortages of labour, and in ensuring that the best traditional technology and methods were widely used.

In terms of production, the goals Mao set for agriculture were to increase grain output, to raise more animals, to plant more fodder, and to grow more cotton. The policies he advocated to achieve these goals were: the reduction of rent and interest rates, the extension of the cultivated area, the introduction of cotton-growing into new areas, improved use of labour, an increase in the availability of agricultural credit, expanded use of best-available techniques plus whatever technical reform was possible, the introduction of progressive taxation and, finally, more direct involvement of cadres in economic work, especially in investigation and development of local resources. In effect these policies fell into four main groups: better use of labour, provision of incentives, technical education, and better planning. Spanning all of them was the active involvement of the Party and government, coordinating, investing, mobilizing, and generally acting as entrepreneur.

As Mao pointed out, the shortage of labour was the key problem, 'under our present backward technical conditions, labour is the decisive factor in economic undertakings'.[65] He put forward two methods for dealing with this problem, increasing the size of the labour force and making better use of what was available. The former was to be achieved through immigration, the mobilization of women to work outside the home, and the mobilization of loafers to start work. The second method depended on spreading the use of mutual-aid farming more widely and on better organization by Party and government. That Mao was prepared to allow rich peasants to take on immigrants as tenants or hired labourers is indicative of the overwhelming emphasis he placed on increasing production. He admitted that it involved exploitation but argued that this was offset by the fact that it provided immigrants with a livelihood and enabled them to accumulate the necessary materials to start farming independently. Furthermore, the extent of exploitation was limited by the Party's presence and by the laws of the Border Region. Having accepted a mixed economy, Mao was willing to make the best use of all its positive aspects. Moreover, exploitation was balanced by the concern of the Party and government in providing free land, settling-in grants, credit, and tax relief. The mobilization of women was chiefly a question of persuasion and propaganda using the techniques of the mass line through the mass organizations. The change was as much social as economic. Loafers were a different matter. Many had a history of opium-smoking and trouble-making and were resented by the hardworking peasants who were glad to see them transformed into productive workers. Mao endorsed the variety of social pressures and enforced labour training used to reform them.

Mutual-aid farming was potentially the most important of the reforms Mao put forward. Although he discussed it chiefly in the context of its effect on the employment of labour, it also held out the possibility of more far-reaching social change. The types of organization Mao supported were based on traditional methods of cooperation developed by the peasants of Shaanxi to overcome their shortage of resources. Attempts to introduce methods of cooperation used in the Jiangxi Soviet were resisted.[66] The traditional forms fell into two broad categories. The first consisted of ways of making up deficiencies in labour or animal power so that essential work was done at the required time. This involved, for example, a small number of families working in rotation on each other's land, or one family providing a fixed amount of labour power in return for a day's use of an ox, or even, on rare occasions, the complete pooling of land, animals, and implements for a year's farming, as might happen when brothers shared a small inheritance.[67] Often there were rules so that each family's input was equalized. Those with weak labour power, for example, would do an extra day's work for the others or make a supplementary payment. These cooperative arrangements were known by a variety of names but fell together loosely under the general heading of *exchange-labour teams*. The second category was a form of *contract-labour hiring*. Groups of landless peasants got together under a leader and offered themselves as teams for hire. They often operated with complex rules and strict labour discipline. The head did not labour but received extra payment for his role in organization and in obtaining work. In some cases peasants with land joined and their land was worked before the team was hired out. The chief characteristics of these two forms of mutual aid were that they were small-scale, shortlived, mainly dependent on family and social connections, and subordinate to the basic structure of the peasant economy which was that of the independent small-holder.

At the same time as they adopted the exchange-labour and contract-labour models, Mao and the Party attempted to change them slightly in order to bring them more into line with the Party's policies. They encouraged the teams to develop stronger leadership and firmer organization so that they continued beyond one season or one year. Poor peasants were exhorted to play a bigger role. Cooperation was expanded to embrace people who were unrelated or who were new to the area, the support of the government replacing to some extent the personal trust between relations and acquaintances which underpinned the traditional arrangements. The scope of the work each team did was extended to cover a whole range of tasks rather than one specific one such as hoeing or harvesting. The teams were also praised as part of the struggle against Japan through their role in increasing output. Exploitation in the form of payments for leaders who did not work and superstitions such as not changing places in the work line in case it caused rain (and hence a loss of work for the team) were discouraged. For the moment Mao and the Party stressed that the wider use of these forms of cooperation could help raise productivity, save wasted resources, spread good farming skills, and generally realize latent productivity. However, on a longer time-scale they were 'the first step in the gradual collectivization of the fragmented, small-peasant, individual economy'.[68]

Related to these two forms of mutual aid was the system of substitute cultivation. This was an arrangement whereby the peasants in a village formed a team to do work for families who had members in the army and in the government and thus lacked sufficient labour power to farm efficiently. Teams like these were organized by township heads and directly supported the war effort. Mao pointed out that the system had to some extent become a burden on the peasants since it was a form of duty imposed by the government. To combat this he proposed that priority should be given to substitute cultivation for families of soldiers, where the patriotic basis of the work was more obvious. Whenever possible government officials should be given leave to work at home during the busiest seasons. He also suggested that this work could be done by exchange-labour teams where they had been successfully organized.

The responsibility for promoting and organizing these methods rested with the Party and government. Mao continuously stressed this point and also underlined various supplementary ways in which official action could help. These ranged from simple things like not holding political meetings when the peasants' time would have been spent in the fields, to the more complex, like mobilizing large numbers of peasants for a specific task such as irrigation work or sowing areas with grass for animal fodder. The examples Mao quotes are practical suggestions for official action. However, they also illustrate the new way in which he wanted cadres to think about economic work. He wanted them to get out of their offices and out of their bureaucratic modes of thought. He wanted them to grapple with practical problems and understand the environment of the people they led. Mao's constant reiteration of this theme reflected both earlier failures and his insistence that Party and government cadres should treat economic work as seriously as they would political and military work.

Many of our comrades still do not know how to investigate objective circumstances minutely, nor do they know how to put forward concrete proposals to provide the conditions for increasing production in different regions and at different times. Slogans put forward in the past for deep ploughing, opening new lands, water conservancy, and increasing production by 400,000 *dan* or 200,000 *dan*, in reality contained much subjectivism. Many peasants were not interested or influenced by them. From this we may conclude that in future we must carry out deep, factual investigation, and solve problems in terms of concrete times, places, and conditions.[69]

A further example of what Mao meant was his discussion of the development of cotton-growing. This required government incentives in the form of credit and rewards, and government help in the form of education and the provision of seeds. It also required careful consideration of vertical and horizontal effects. Vertically, an increase in cotton output implied investment in cotton-ginning machines and in cotton-processing. Horizontally, the cotton seed that was a by-product could be pressed for its edible oil. This not only meant that oil-pressing equipment was needed, but also that the peasants of the Border Region who were unused to eating cotton-seed oil had to be persuaded of its value. Mao's discussion of these various ramifications was illustrative of the new issues the Party and government faced once they became deeply involved in economic work.

The use of incentives to increase production entered most areas of policy. Unlike later years when the mixed economy had begun to disappear, Mao still saw material incentives even at an individual level as being as important as moral ones: 'All empty words are useless, we must give the people visible material wealth'.[70] Indirect incentives were widespread. Immigrants were given tax exemption as an encouragement to come and, as already noted, Mao thought of rent and interest-rate reduction and tax reform as ways of stimulating enthusiasm for production, as much as vehicles for social change. More direct material incentives Mao supported were such things as reductions in grain tax for one year for peasants who bought livestock from outside the Border Region, rewards for peasants who developed good methods of growing cotton, and rewards for labour heroes like the rich peasant, Wu Manyou, who displayed unflagging enthusiasm and all-round skills. Indeed, the fact that peasants could move up the economic ladder to become rich peasants was seen as a stimulus to production. Another incentive the Party and government could use was the issue of credit. Until 1942, the light tax burden had eased peasant demands for credit but thereafter the Border Region Bank was called upon to provide funds. Mao argued that credit should be used as an instrument of government policy to direct investment towards particular goals. He specified the opening of unused land, the planting of cotton, and increasing the stock of draught animals. His overall approach to the role of these various forms of material incentives was most forcefully expressed in his comments on factory labour:

Finally the factory should reward the workers and employees with the greatest achievements and criticize or punish workers and employees who commit errors. Without a suitable system of rewards and punishments, we cannot ensure the improvement of labour discipline and labour enthusiasm.[71]

It is clear from this that Mao's insistence on the importance of ideological education and mass-line politics was combined with a sharp awareness of the role of incentives in the mixed economy he was analysing. The situation was not one in which people would respond to ideals alone. Moral incentives in the form of the labour hero system and social praise were always present but they had to be reinforced by material improvement.

Mao defined the role of technical education in increasing agricultural output entirely within the existing technological base. He emphasized such things as improved land management, extension of the irrigated area, increased hoeing and weeding, deep ploughing, seed selection, and improved methods of animal-breeding and animal care. All of these required intensive use of labour power and none depended on large inputs of capital. They were also areas in which the best of traditional Chinese farming methods could improve upon the practices of the Border Region which was backward even within the context of pre-modern agriculture. In addition, Mao underlined the need for education in cotton-growing since cotton was the major commodity the Border Region lacked and urgent expansion was needed to reduce the Region's import bill. The methods Mao put forward for spreading improvements in technology ranged from agricultural exhibitions and government mobilization to publicizing the example of labour heroes and using school textbooks which taught improved methods. However, Mao did not urge widespread and immediate mobilization to introduce improved techniques everywhere. He was careful to stress that much depended on the actual situation in a locality. In counties where cultivable land was freely available, it was better to encourage the extension of the cultivated area than to promote deep ploughing since the returns would be greater. Effective policy-making depended on concrete investigation and local flexibility rather than across-the-board bureaucratic decision.

Commerce

By contrast with agriculture, where Party policies had a significant effect, the structure of private commerce was left relatively untouched. On the one hand Mao admitted that the Party still

lacked sufficient knowledge to deal with it comprehensively.[72]
On the other hand, the Border Region market, including the
commercial undertakings of the troops and officials, depended
to a large extent on the support and connections of private
merchants.[73] This was particularly true of trade with outside
areas, since long-established contacts between merchants were
important to efforts to overcome the effects of the Guomindang
blockade. The Party and government placed orders with Border
Region merchants who then dealt with their opposite numbers
in Guomindang areas. The Border Region merchants eventually
delivered the goods to the Party and government and were
allowed 'very liberal profits' so that they could cover their
risks.[74] The Party's goal was not to change the system but to
ensure that it ran smoothly. Attempts to control the private
market were realized through the indirect efforts of the
government-run Trading Company and the Chambers of Commerce. The former was able to influence prices either by price
setting as in the case of salt where the government's role was
central, or by price competition where the company entered the
market like any other merchant. The company also helped combat hoarding and speculation by ensuring that producers and
consumers had an alternative to private merchants. The Chambers of Commerce, which were organized on a 'three-thirds'
principle of equal representation by large, medium, and small
merchants, were self-regulatory bodies intended to ensure
adherence to a code of fair conduct. They also helped raise the
quality of business management by providing classes in book-
keeping and literacy. Reportedly these policies and the low level
of commercial taxation did have a salutary impact. Stein's
informants claimed that by 1943 commercial profits were
up to ten times what they had been in 1936, and over the same
period the number of shops in Yan'an city market rose from 60
to 300.

There was, however, one area of commerce in which a major
innovation occurred and that was in the growth of consumer
cooperatives. Like the Trading Company, these were in direct
competition with merchants. The form of organization that Mao
recommended was ownership and control by peasant shareholders who exercised their rights through regular shareholders'

meetings, and close cooperation between the full-time cooperative managers (some of whom were drawn from the ranks of local officials) and local government. The principal task of the management was to look after the interests of shareholders and customers but at the same time it was expected to find ways of implementing government policies. Cooperatives were thus 'the bridge between the economic activity of the government and the economic activity of the people'.[75] Mao also argued that because of their flexibility in developing as integrated consumer and producer cooperatives, they were a convenient way of accumulating capital and of directly linking commerce with a growth in production. The model Mao put forward was the Southern District Cooperative near Yan'an. The successful methods it adopted helped change the conception within the Party of the potential cooperatives represented. At first cooperatives were established as government agencies with the initial share capital coming from the government and a further portion assessed from the peasants. They were thus public undertakings run in the interests of the government. In 1939 it was decided to 'popularize cooperatives' by relating them more closely to the needs of the peasants. However, most cooperatives continued to operate more-or-less like government agencies. They assessed share capital from peasants as if it was a form of taxation and they asked for substitute cultivation on behalf of managers. The problem intensified in 1940 when many army units and official organizations began investing in cooperatives as part of their drive for self-sufficiency. It was not until January 1942 when the Southern district model was put forward that efforts were really made to break away from the government-centred orientation. The Southern District Cooperative became the model precisely because it took this step earlier than other cooperatives and tried to ensure that shareholders got a good return on their investment. As a result it attracted considerable peasant support and expanded rapidly. Economically it combined material improvement for its shareholders with capital accumulation and the expansion of production. Socially, it acted as a nucleus for change in the existing structure. Thus, as in all other policies for the private sector, Mao made tangible material improvement the basis of innovation.

Self-supporting production

The self-supporting production of troops and officials was perhaps the most important and most successful innovation of the Yan'an period. Mao contrasted the limited production of vegetables and pigs by officials in Jiangxi with the deep involvement in industry, agriculture, and commerce which developed in Yan'an. However, like its predecessor, the Yan'an experiment began with the same goal of making up for shortages and improving the living conditions of the troops. It was only when the Party became aware of the potential represented by the disciplined labour of the troops that it began to consider the possibility of achieving self-sufficiency and of supplying some of the needs of the war. The system was then extended to all official organizations and schools. Thereafter self-supporting production became a major feature of the Border Region economy both in terms of its contribution to the government's budget and in terms of its agricultural and industrial importance.

At first efforts were concentrated in agriculture, with some troops opening up new land and producing grain and vegetables. Mao compared this system to the 'camp-field' system of military colonization introduced in the Han dynasty some 2,000 years earlier. In 1939 ambitious plans were made to spread the movement to all troop units and official organizations. However, lack of experience and resources meant that in many cases units overreached themselves and the returns did not match up to expectations. Moreover, important official business was sometimes neglected. In 1940, therefore, a period of retrenchment began in which unprofitable undertakings were closed down or merged, the staff engaged in full-time farming was limited to a smaller number of specialists who could be reinforced with general help at busy times, and experiments in taking peasants as tenants or partners were introduced. At the same time, the Guomindang blockade began to bite more strongly and its effects were intensified by the ending of the subsidy. Many units turned to commerce to supply their immediate needs. They opened up stores and cooperatives, and organized transport teams and small groups of travelling salesmen. For a while, these enterprises became their key source of income and there was considerable competition with much duplication of effort. In addition, with encouragement from the Party, some units began to set up small workshops and factories mainly based on handicraft production. Substantial growth took place in this direction during 1941 and 1942, much of it once again rather haphazard and uncoordinated. By the time of his report in December 1942, Mao was in a position to sum up the errors of the previous four years and to concentrate on the lessons that had been learned.

The model that Mao took for self-supporting production was the 359 Brigade which was transferred to garrison duties in the Border Region in 1940. Its large farm at Nanniwan, south of Yan'an, became the inspiration of the whole production movement. The first point that Mao stressed was that reliance on commerce had been a temporary expedient and could not be seen as a secure foundation in the long term. Commerce did not create value and was only a medium of exchange. Investment should concentrate on agriculture first, industry, handicrafts and transport second, and commerce third. This approach to the relative merits of the three sectors reflected Mao's belief that increased production was the key to survival. Agriculture provided the basic commodities required in the Border Region. Industry, meaning light industry, handicrafts and the salt industry could produce some of the daily requirements and weapons that were desperately needed, even using the makeshift handicraft technology that was available. The export of salt was vital to the Border Region's external trade. Commerce could supply useful supplementary income but could do nothing to build up the economic foundations.

The second point Mao made was summed up under the slogan 'centralized leadership and dispersed operation'. This view of economic organization, which had implications beyond self-supporting production, stressed that dispersed operation was the only way to function when resources and labour power were widely spread and when products were consumed over a large area. It was thus fundamental to agriculture, the processing of agricultural products, and light industry. It also had the advantage of capitalizing on local initiatives and enthusiasm. By contrast, centralized leadership was required to ensure coordination and efficient planning, and to avoid a waste of resources. Furthermore, once local initiative had succeeded in building up an enterprise, rationalization through centralized leadership could help make it more profitable. Within this context, Mao argued that certain key undertakings supplying the needs of large units should be centralized from the beginning. The method he proposed for reconciling the two contradictory tendencies was to establish a central planning agency which could coordinate the production of the Party, government and army systems by drawing up overall indicators for such things as the use of raw materials, production totals, and the distribution of products. Once the plan was decided it should be handed over to the separate systems for implementation. Within each system there should also be an agency to coordinate the implementation of the plan within its area of control. The central planning agency was a planning body but did not have actual control of the way the plan was implemented at lower levels. Mao was thus attempting a compromise between fully centralized organization which brought with it inflexibility and lack of initiative at lower levels and complete decentralization which resulted in poor coordination and wastage. Certain key undertakings had to be centralized, but partial decentralization by system and by area (and not by sector), thus facilitating economic integration within geographical units, introduced flexibility in operation and in developing latent resources. Mao saw this decentralization as especially important during the initial development of an undertaking. In some cases greater centralization might come later as the undertaking expanded and its economic importance grew.[76] This formulation for centralized control and decentralized operation became a key feature of Mao's approach to China's economic development after he rejected the Soviet model in the mid-1950s.

Mao's other points were less concerned with the nature of self-supporting economic development than with the ways of running undertakings. He argued that all enterprises should use proper economic accounting, and profitability should be the main guide. Units should not rely on their status as budgetary organizations with income from government revenue as a means of propping up uneconomic undertakings. Organization should be simple, with the emphasis given to productive employment rather than management. Labour discipline and enthusiasm should be promoted through a strict system of rewards and penalties and through the adoption of piecework wages wherever possible. The main goal should be to increase supplies rather than to obtain a cash income. Finally Mao saw active leadership and 'popularization', in the form of lower-level participation in running enterprises and concern for the well-being of the masses, as essential components of success.

Table B   *Index of the standard of living of soldiers in the Border Region 1939–43*

1939	100
1940	88
1941	84.1
1942	96.3
1943	125.5

The implementation of these policies did have a significant impact on the Border Region economy. Mao stated that in 1942 the supplies produced within the public sector exceeded the amount paid by the people as taxes.[77] By 1944, self-supporting agriculture accounted for just under 40 per cent of the government's grain needs.[78] The effect on the standard of living within the army was equally important. Taking 1939 as the base, Foreman was given the index in Table B for the supply of rations and clothing to soldiers for the years 1939 to 1943.[79] Thus the problems of immediate survival were overcome and a basis for improvement was laid. Furthermore, by 1944 the pattern of development had resulted in 78 per cent of 'modern' factories in the Border Region belonging to the government, 20 per cent to cooperatives, and only 2 per cent to private capital.[80] While Stein was told that the Party would have preferred private capital to play a bigger role in industrial ownership, the concept of government control of the 'commanding heights' in a mixed economy was already firmly established.

The distribution of industrial ownership is not regarded as satisfactory by the Yenan authorities. For their New Democracy aims at giving private and cooperative capital the exclusive right, and the task, of engaging in enterprises other than railroads, mining, armament, and other heavy industries which are to be wholly or partly owned by the government because of their key importance in the shaping of the national economy.[81]

Theoretical Framework

Overall, the economic philosophy Mao expressed in his report was shaped by the context of the New Democracy. He was concerned with a mixed economy and with the welfare of the masses of ordinary peasants who made up the private sector. The Party would only win their support if it could prove its practical ability in economic management. Given the enforced isolation of the Border Region, development had to be based on agriculture and light industry. Everything else depended on linkages with these two. Furthermore, self-reliance and primitive accumulation had to compensate for the lack of capital resources. There was no alternative to organizational reform, intensive use of labour to exploit available land and resources, and improved use of traditional techniques. Mao promoted innovations along these lines so long as they did not undermine the stability of the existing economic structure and thus weaken peasant support. The most radical experiment was the introduction of self-supporting production in the public sector. This brought immediate financial returns, created some key public enterprises, and provided a model of decentralized economic growth. Its importance in Mao's analysis is reflected by the fact that he devoted three sections of his report to it. In all of the policies put forward, Mao argued that success depended on positive action by the Party and government, and on the stimulation of mass enthusiasm. Innovations should build on existing practices but not go beyond what was acceptable to the peasants.

As a whole, Mao's analysis of economic work in the Border Region is not expressed in any clear, Marxist theoretical framework. Nevertheless, it is rooted in his perception of the current political situation and his previous investigations into the class structure in the Chinese countryside. At the time, his political perspective was that of the New Democratic stage of the

38

revolution and not the construction of socialism. The latter was a goal that was unattainable in the Yan'an context and anyway required some intermediate steps. While many of his proposals – such as the cooperatives, centralized leadership and dispersed operation, and the balance between economic sectors – contained the seeds of change and would grow in importance after 1949, in Yan'an they were cast in the New Democratic mould. As Mao said later:

As for building socialism, everyone is new to it. We are all novices. In the past we only carried out the democratic revolution and that was bourgeois in nature. We did not destroy the system of individual ownership and capitalist ownership, but destroyed the system of ownership by the feudal and comprador classes.[82]

In practice, Mao's gain from his experiences in running the Yan'an economy came through his ability to retrieve and refine some aspects of it and to apply those aspects in the different political and economic situation that faced China in the mid-1950s.

THE YAN'AN MODEL IN MAO'S ECONOMIC THOUGHT

The model of economic development just described formed the starting point for Mao's approach to economic problems on the eve of the establishment of the People's Republic. In 1945 he saw the setting up of the political system of New Democracy as a precondition for the development of the productive forces, and the goal of the New Democracy was to transform China from an agricultural into an industrial country.[83] Even in March 1949 when the Party's assumption of power was, contrary to the expectations of 1945, not far off, and when the attractions of the Soviet model and 'leaning to one side' lay before him, Mao still conceived of gradual evolution through a new-democratic stage of mixed development in which the State-owned economy, now enlarged by the industries of the cities, played a key role:

The confiscation of this bureaucrat-capital and its transfer to the People's Republic led by the proletariat will enable the People's Republic to control the economic lifelines of the country and will enable the state-owned economy to become the leading sector of the entire national economy.

. . .

China's private capitalist industry, which occupies second place in her modern industry, is a force which must not be ignored . . . For this reason and because China's economy is still backward, there will be need, for a fairly long period after the victory of the revolution, to make use of the positive qualities of urban and rural private capitalism as far as possible, in the interest of developing the national economy. In this period, all capitalist elements in the cities and countryside which are not harmful but beneficial to the national economy should be allowed to exist and expand.

. . .

Scattered, individual agriculture and handicrafts, which make up 90 per cent of the total value of output of the national economy, can and must be led prudently, step by step and yet actively to develop towards modernization and collectivization; the view that they may be left to take their own course is wrong. It is necessary to organize producers', consumers' and credit co-operatives . . . Such co-operatives are collective economic organizations of labouring masses, based on private ownership and under the direction of the state power led by the proletariat . . . The state-owned economy is socialist in character and the co-operative economy is semi-socialist; these plus private capitalism, plus the individual economy, plus the state-capitalist economy in which the state and private capitalists work jointly, will be the chief sectors of the economy of the People's Republic and will constitute the new-democratic economic structure.[84]

Such an analysis suggests that Mao was concerned to mould the lessons of Soviet experience to the realities of China, just as he had always insisted that Marxist theory should be interpreted and applied in the light of the practice of the Chinese revolution.

The available speeches and documents by Mao of the early years of the People's Republic contain few direct comments on economic affairs. Much of his time was undoubtedly consumed by the organizational problems of consolidating Party power. He was also very active in foreign affairs, developing relations with the Soviet Union and dealing with the Korean War crisis. Perhaps, as he himself said, he still had to 'learn to do economic work from all who know how, no matter who they are'.[85] Nevertheless, it is also clear that Mao's position on many of the issues involved in the New Democracy model changed and changed quickly, and by 1953 his concern with rural problems was already pointing towards the development strategy he would expound from 1955 onwards. These trends in Mao's thinking were particularly apparent in the areas of the application and relevance of the Soviet model, his definition of the current stage of development, and his approach to the question of the relationship between the productive forces and the relations of production.

The extent of Mao's commitment to the Soviet model of economic development as transmitted to China after 1949 remains a moot point. It is often noted that Mao made many positive comments on learning from Soviet experience and that his aim of achieving rapid industrialization inclined him towards the centrally controlled, heavy-industry oriented strategy that characterized the first five-year plan.[86] He later said that the first five-year plan was 'essentially correct'.[87] Nevertheless, Mao's willingness to adopt the Soviet model must be seen in the perspective of his earlier rejection of Stalin's advice and Comintern 'interference', his difficulties in negotiating with Stalin in 1950, and his growing criticism of Soviet methods and Stalin after 1953.[88] Furthermore, his involvement in an agricultural collectivization programme which differed markedly from Soviet practice soon led him to raise important questions about the balance of investment between industry and agriculture, the implications of that balance for overall development, and its ultimate effects on the political alliance between workers and peasants on which the Party depended. In addition, the formal, centralized bureaucracy and professional decision-making implicit in the Soviet model contrasted sharply with the principles of decentralization and mass-line operation which had distinguished Mao's approach to political and economic leadership before 1949. Thus it seems likely that, between 1953 when he called for a 'great upsurge in learning from the Soviet Union'[89] and 1955 when he began to elaborate his alternative strategy, Mao's acceptance of the Soviet model was tempered by his awareness of the differences between the Soviet Union and China and of the fact that not all Soviet experience was positive. Indeed, those aspects of the Soviet model which Mao most readily accepted, such as the need for rapid growth in the State-owned heavy industrial sector, State control of the market, and the transformation of the system of ownership in the countryside, were already implied in his analysis of the new-democratic economy. However, one important development in Mao's approach which was associated with the period of learning from the Soviet Union was an acceleration in his view of how soon the private economy might be transformed. By 1953, the 'fairly long period' of 1949 had given way to a greater emphasis on the early transformation of the economy.[90]

The second factor leading to Mao's shift away from the new-democratic model was a change in his analysis of the current stage of the Chinese revolution. In many respects his definition of the New Democracy reflected his anticipation of a relatively long period in which a united front between various classes in society would be necessary. Although the Guomindang itself was gone, he still saw a need for the Party to unite with the national bourgeoisie in the cities and the rich peasants in the countryside. By 1952 – when Land Reform had destroyed the power of the rural landlords and the Five Anti Movement against bribery, tax evasion, theft of State property, cheating on government contracts, and stealing State economic secrets had undermined the independence of the capitalists – Mao had come to consider the contradiction between the working class and the national bourgeoisie as the principal contradiction in Chinese society.[91] In such a context policies aimed at sustaining the national bourgeoisie and its rural counterpart, the rich peasants and well-to-do middle peasants, would be conservative rather than progressive. They would help prolong the existence of classes whose support the Party no longer needed, and also conflict with the aims of other reforms being introduced. It is not surprising, therefore, that Mao saw fit to emphasize the difference between those who sought to consolidate the New Democracy and his own preference for pushing ahead to explore methods of socialist transformation.[92] Just as during the second united front with the Guomindang, the major problem remained that of defining the correct balance between 'left' excesses, which might lead to a loss of broad support for the Party, and 'right' conservatism, which might abandon the Party's commitment to social revolution. In Mao's view those inclined towards a 'rightist' position were holding the country back and not recognizing the new potential for change. This problem of where to draw the line, of isolating the few opponents of reform and uniting the majority in support of it, was one that Mao continually confronted in his policy initiatives over the ensuing years. It contributed to his thinking on the way to deal with contradictions within society and within the Party. It also helped shape the initiatives he took so that each push up to and sometimes beyond the limits of what was possible, as during agricultural collectivization, the Great Leap Forward and the Cultural Revolution, was followed by a period of consolidation in which the pace and extent of reform were curtailed and a new consensus was sought. Thus Mao's move away from the new-democratic model was not simply the result of experience in implementing Soviet practices but was also the outcome of his changed perception of the alignment of forces within Chinese society.

The third factor which contributed to the development of Mao's economic policies was his thinking on the relationship between the relations of production and the productive forces and between the superstructure and the economic base. Although in Yan'an Mao had proposed organizational reform such as the establishment of cooperatives and exchange-labour teams as a means of expanding production, such innovations were not at the time seen as a shift from 'capitalist' relations of production to socialist relations. Similarly the changes in organization and ownership associated with the new-democratic model were intended to facilitate the growth of a modern, industrial country on the basis of which the transition to socialism could be made. Thus, changes in the relations of production might lead to growth in the productive forces but it was changes in the economic base as a whole that would enable the eventual transformation of society. For many Chinese leaders similar assumptions about the need for building up the economic base as a precondition for further advance in the superstructure underpinned the Soviet model of the first five-year plan. Nevertheless, Mao's experience with the Yan'an experiments and his military philosophy which saw the role of morale, ideology and commitment as more decisive than the actual weapons used,[93] indicate that he was not mechanical in his conception of the relationship between material and social conditions. That is,

43

he did not assume that the economic base automatically determined the superstructure but that the latter could also affect the former. Indeed, he later claimed that the Yan'an cooperatives did contain the 'sprouts of socialism',[94] and he criticized Stalin for not considering the role of the superstructure in helping to change the economic base.[95] During the early 1950s Mao was already stressing such points when he linked changes in the system of ownership with the development of the productive forces and 'socialist industrialization' with the 'cooperative transformation of agriculture'.[96] Subsequently, the practical and theoretical issues involved became the centre of debate within China on the question of whether agricultural mechanization should precede or follow collectivization, and of debate between China and the Soviet Union over the nature of the people's communes and their implications for the building of communism.[97] If Mao was correct, China could move more quickly towards a socialist society than either the new-democratic or Soviet model allowed. And practical economic policies could reflect that goal. If he was wrong, he was guilty of attempting the impossible and might hinder the development of the country. The divisions between Mao and his Party colleagues on this issue and its practical implications contributed substantially to the struggles of the Cultural Revolution.

In sum, Mao's analysis of the stage of development in China after 1949, his concern with the relative importance of the economic base and the superstructure in the transition to socialism, and his experience of the Soviet model in the early 1950s, resulted in the evolution of economic policies that increasingly diverged from Soviet practice. And as part of that process he turned to the experience of Yan'an and stressed its applicability to the economic problems China faced.[98]

Mao began to outline his new approach in the summer of 1955 with his report *On the Cooperative Transformation of Agriculture*.[99] This was followed by a succession of directives and speeches on agricultural problems and culminated in his speech *On the Ten Major Relationships* of April 1956.[100] The fact that Mao initially concentrated on agricultural policy indicates the roots of his rejection of the Soviet model. The latter affirmed the role of heavy industry, urban development, and the proletariat in social and economic revolution. It concentrated power in the hands of urban specialists and neglected investment in agriculture. It denied that the peasants had an important role to play or that the countryside, where most Chinese lived, could be transformed alongside the city. It also implied that an agricultural China must depend on the advanced industrial experience of the Soviet Union for a long period of development. Mao now questioned the relevance of this approach. He wanted the heavy industry which the Soviet model promised but did not believe that it could be obtained by 'draining the pond to catch the fish', that is by distorting the relationship between industry and agriculture and between town and countryside so that the latter provided the capital but got none of the returns. Not only would the slow rate of agricultural growth slow down the pace of industrialization but the bulk of China's population, the peasants, would neither benefit from the new industries nor be any further along the path towards socialism. By contrast, Mao was optimistic of the potential for revolutionary change in the countryside and believed that such change was significant for both economic development and revolutionary strategy. He felt that many Party members lagged behind in their conception of what could be done. Although the full realization of socialism in the countryside might be a gradual process lasting at least fifteen years, he believed that the Party had to give positive leadership from the beginning if it was going to succeed. Delay gave hope and strength to the capitalist elements that the rich-peasant economy constantly engendered. However, Mao did more than affirm his faith in the possibilities for change in the countryside. He also called for greater attention to the linkages between industry and agriculture.

In the first place, as everyone knows, China's current level of production of commodity grain and raw materials for industry is low, whereas the state's need for them is growing year by year, and this presents a sharp contradiction. If we cannot basically solve the problem of agricultural co-operation within roughly three five-year plans, that is to say, if our agriculture cannot make a leap from small-scale farming with animal-drawn farm implements to large-scale mechanized farming, then we shall fail to resolve the contradiction between the ever-increasing need for commodity grain and industrial raw materials and the present generally low output of staple crops, and we shall run into formidable difficulties in our socialist industrialization and be unable to complete it. In the second place, some of our comrades have not given any thought to the connection between the following two facts, namely, that heavy industry, the most important branch of socialist industrialization, produces for agricultural use tractors and other farm machinery, chemical fertilizers, modern means of transport, oil, electric power, etc., and that all these things can be used, or used extensively, only on the basis of an agriculture where large-scale co-operative farming prevails. We are now carrying out a revolution not only in the social system, the change from private to public ownership, but also in technology, the change from handicraft to large-scale modern machine production, and the two revolutions are interconnected. In agriculture, with conditions as they are in our country, co-operation must precede the use of big machinery. Therefore we must on no account regard industry and agriculture, socialist industrialization and the socialist transformation of agriculture as disconnected or isolated things, and on no account must we emphasize the one and play down the other.[101]

Mao went on to expand this analysis of sectoral balance in *On the Ten Major Relationships*.[102] Successful development depended on correctly understanding the interdependence between industry and agriculture. Light industry was an important mediator between heavy industry and agriculture. By producing consumer goods it helped to raise peasant living standards and this, after all, was one of the goals of development and one of the proofs that socialism was better than the traditional economy. It also accumulated funds for investment in heavy industry through its trade with the agricultural sector. Thus the correct way to develop heavy industry was by also stimulating light industry and agriculture. Although technological change through increased inputs from modern industry was essential in the long run, initially agriculture should make effective use of whatever level of technology was available. Mao also argued that the bulk of the funds for investment in agriculture had to be accumulated within that sector, and that such accumulation could only be achieved through cooperative transformation. One of the key arguments of the essays in *Socialist Upsurge in China's Countryside* for which he wrote editor's notes, was that changes in ownership and organization provided both the means and the motivation to increase income and accumulate funds.[103] Mao's political concern for building socialism in the countryside and

cementing the worker-peasant alliance was thus closely integrated with his economic analysis.

As well as sectoral balance, Mao was also concerned with
regional balance.[104] While it was essential to develop industry in
the backward regions inland, it was also important to make full
use of the infrastructure in the relatively developed coastal strip.
While it was necessary to build national unity and central discipline, it was equally necessary to allow local authorities some
independence and initiative. Mao argued that in the first five-
year plan, coastal industry, particularly light industry, had been
relatively neglected, and there had been too much centralization. Neglect of coastal industry meant slower accumulation of
funds with which to develop the interior. Excessive centralization had two bad effects. First, it restricted the possibilities for
developing resources in the localities. Second, since central
control was expressed through a variety of agencies and their
local branches, there were often considerable problems of coordination and many competing demands were made on local
authorities. Mao saw greater consultation and the handing over
of some responsibilities to lower levels as ways of combating
these problems. He wanted a form of regional decentralization
rather than decentralization by economic sectors or economic
units.

Mao's emphasis on a mixture of technologies in agriculture
with reliance on traditional methods wherever effective, was
also reflected in his insistence that industrial policy should
include the development of large, medium and small factories
using a mixture of labour, capital and technology appropriate to
the local conditions.[105] Reliance on large plants using modern
technology required human and capital resources in short supply. If all resources were to be tapped, it was necessary to be
more flexible in the means used.

Two other factors also permeated Mao's approach. One was a
concern with the well-being of people and improvements in
their livelihood. The peasants should not be 'squeezed' as they
had been in the Soviet Union.[106] Furthermore socialism should
raise their standard of living, not decrease it, nor simply maintain it. Mao insisted that each stage of cooperative transformation should and would result in an improvement in the peasants'

material conditions. The second factor was emphasis on self-reliance. This was at first a policy for development within agricultural cooperatives or within localities, but later it came to apply to the country as a whole. This latter development reflected Mao's growing distrust of the Soviet Union and any form of foreign interference in China as much as a conviction that autarchy was essential to economic development. What was at issue was China's political and economic independence rather than the usefulness of foreign trade and technology. In fact Mao took pains to stress that much could be gained from abroad,[107] and it was only some years later that he argued that countries should 'not depend upon others as a matter of principle'.[108]

The evolution of Mao's thinking on these questions over the years 1955 to 1958 took place against a background of rural experiments which met with varying success and growing dispute with the Soviet Union. Eventually his optimism over the potential in the economy, his belief in the impact of superstructural change on the economic base, his drive for national independence, and his alternative economic policies, combined in the Great Leap Forward of 1958. The events of that movement led Mao to develop still further his views on many of the issues discussed above.[109] However, these later developments fall outside the scope of this Introduction. What is at issue is to what extent did Mao turn to his Yan'an experience in grappling with the economic problems of the 1950s? Enough has been said in the foregoing discussion to illustrate that some very fundamental links can be drawn. First, there is the overriding concern with agriculture and rural development. Although there was no urban industry in Yan'an and Mao was not confronted with problems of sectoral balance at that time, his stress on agriculture reflected his awareness of its importance in the lives of the bulk of the people in China, the need to improve their livelihood, and the roots of support for the Party. Urban industry provided a vital new force to which agriculture could look for new inputs after 1949 but rural problems remained of fundamental importance. Furthermore many of the practical rural policies Mao put forward were either similar to Yan'an experiments or consciously developed from them. Second, there is the

48

stress on integrating economic and political goals both in terms of the importance of political ideology as a motivating factor in the economy and in terms of shaping economic policy to further political ends. In Yan'an, the united front had provided the framework, and innovations such as cooperatives, mutual aid, and self-supporting production pointed towards the next stage of social development. In the 1950s, the goal was socialist transformation, and the changes in the system of ownership and organization were also intended to facilitate economic growth. Third, there is a consistent approach to the quality and nature of leadership. The mass line, mobilization, cadre involvement in practical application of policy, and the ability of cadres to take local initiatives in line with general policy were as necessary to implementing Mao's policies in 1955 as in 1942. Without them, he could not have contemplated reviving such policies as 'centralized leadership and dispersed operation' and self-reliance, in which he consciously drew on the Yan'an model. Furthermore, in rejecting Soviet-style professionalized leadership, Mao was as concerned with the nature of the society being created as with the growth of production. Finally, there is the shared theme of self-reliance. The self-supporting production of Yan'an had been a major success, and Mao believed that similar grass-roots efforts using existing techniques alongside changes in the relations of production would still be rewarded, particularly in agriculture and local industry. As at the time of Yan'an, this policy reflected both the limitations on new inputs and the assertion that organizational change could help realize resources latent or unworkable in the traditional economic structure.

These links between Mao's approach in Yan'an and in the 1950s illustrate a strong continuity in economic philosophy and in many areas of practice. It is true that important differences between the two periods, both in the situation faced and in Mao's perception of goals, cannot be ignored. The 1950s presented new problems of industrial organization and growth. There was also a new dimension offered by foreign trade. In Yan'an economic policy was framed entirely within traditional technology. In the 1950s, as Mao pointed out, all sectors of the Chinese economy were embarking on a technological revolution. In Yan'an there was a mixed economy with State intervention in favour of the private sector. After 1949, Mao was intent on the problems of socialist transition and transforming the private economy. Nevertheless, as the frequent references to Yan'an in his writings after 1949 indicate, Mao was aware of the formative influence that period had had on his response to these new issues. In 1942 he had said,

... we have gained experience in running economic enterprises. This is a priceless treasure that cannot be reckoned in figures.[110]

He consistently reminded his colleagues that this experience should be laid alongside that of the Soviet Union in their efforts to transform China after 1949.

Notes

1 The history of the Border Region has been studied extensively and from a variety of viewpoints. Two works covering the main features of the period and devoting a great deal of attention to these key years are Mark Selden's *The Yenan Way in Revolutionary China* (Harvard University Press, 1971), and Kyoko Tanaka's *Mass Mobilization: the Chinese Communist Party and the Peasants* (unpublished Ph.D. thesis, Australian National University, July 1972). The economy of the Border Region is examined in Peter Schran's *Guerrilla Economy: the Development of the Shensi-Kansu-Ninghsia Border Region, 1937–1945* (State University of New York, 1976). A Chinese source concentrating on the years 1941–3, and particularly on the role of Mao Zedong, is Tian Jiaying *Mao Zedong Tongzhi Lun Kangri Shiqi de Zhengfeng Yundong he Shengchan Yundong* (Beijing 1953). A general account of the Border Region can be found in *Kangri Zhanzheng Shiqi Jiefangqu Gaikuang* (Renmin Chubanshe, Beijing 1953). There are also a number of eyewitness accounts written by foreign visitors to the Border Region during the war years. These include Edgar Snow's *Red Star over China* (first published by Gollancz October 1937, and since reprinted many times), Harrison Foreman's *Report from Red China* (Book Find Club, New York, 1945) and Gunther Stein's *The Challenge of Red China* (Pilot Press, London, 1945).
2 For a discussion of this conference, see Selden (1971), pp. 200–7, and Tanaka (1972), pp. 268–71.
3 *Mao Zedong Xuanji*, Volume 3 (Beijing, 1953), p. 894 and *Selected Works*, Volume 3, p. 112.
4 The geographical features of the loess region are described in T. R. Tregear, *A Geography of China* (University of London Press, 1965), pp. 211–14. A first-hand traveller's account with many illustrations is E. Teichman's *Travels of a Consular Officer in North-West China* (Cambridge University Press, 1921).
5 Selden (1971), p. 6; Snow (1937), p.219.
6 For a graphic and chilling account of this earthquake, see U. Close and E. McCormick, 'Where the Mountains Walked', *The National Geographic Magazine*, Volume 41, No. 5, May 1922, pp. 445–64.

7 Teichman (1921), pp. 62–3.
8 *Ibid.*, pp. 112–13.
9 Snow (1937), pp. 319–32.
10 See J. Sheridan, *Chinese Warlord: The Career of Feng Yu-hsiang* (Stanford University Press, 1966), pp. 101–7 and pp. 206–9, and Teichman (1921), pp. 9–12. A fuller account of the Chinese Warlords can be found in Jerome Chen, 'Defining Chinese Warlords and their Factions', *Bulletin of the School of Oriental and African Studies*, Volume 31, Part 3 (1968), pp.563–600.
11 Teichman (1921), p. 60.
12 The early history of communist work in the area before the arrival of the Red Army in 1935 is traced in Selden, 'The Guerilla Movement in Northwest China: The Origins of the Shensi-Kansu-Ninghsia Border Region', Part I, *The China Quarterly*, No. 28, October–December 1966, pp. 63–81 and Part II, No. 29, January–March 1967, pp. 61–81.
13 See Mao's appeal to the Gelaohui in *Mō Takutō Shū*, Volume 5, pp. 59–61. An analysis of Mao's views towards peasant secret societies and a translation of this appeal can be found in S. Schram, 'Mao Tse-tung and Secret Societies', *The China Quarterly*, No. 27, July–September 1966, pp. 1–13.
14 A detailed analysis of the state of the Border Region economy before 1936 is in Schran (1976), Chapter 1. It is only necessary to make a few general comments here.
15 Sheridan (1966), pp. 22–8.
16 Snow (1937), pp. 323–4.
17 J. L. Buck, *Land Utilization in China* (University of Nanking, 1937), p. 197. The survey covered the years 1929–33. As is usually the case, all these figures must be treated with caution. The figures I quote relate to Buck's winter wheat–millet area in which much of the Border Region lay. However, some parts of the region were in his spring wheat area where average farm sizes were much larger. Schran (1976), Chapter 1, attempts to deal with some of these statistical problems.
18 *Ibid.*, p. 196.
19 Snow (1937), p. 92.
20 P. Schran, *The Development of Chinese Agriculture, 1950–1959* (University of Illinois Press, 1969), pp. 16–17.
21 Buck (1937), p. 198.
22 J. Myrdal, *Report from a Chinese Village* (Signet Books, 1966), p. 180.
23 Chen Boda, *A Study of Land Rent in Pre-Liberation China* (Foreign Languages Press, Beijing, 1966), p. 38.
24 *Ibid.*, pp. 60–66.
25 *Ibid.*, pp. 39–48.
26 Buck (1937), pp. 462–7.
27 Selden (1966), pp. 74–6.
28 The development of the Party's land policy in Jiangxi is traced in T. L. Hsiao, *The Land Revolution in China, 1930–1934* (University of Washington Press, 1969).
29. These developments are analysed in detail in Gregor Benton, 'The Second "Wang Ming Line" ', *The China Quarterly*, No. 61, March 1975, pp. 61–94, and in the criticism of that article by Shum Kui Kwang and Benton's rebuttal, 'The Second "Wang Ming Line" ' – Comment, *The China Quarterly*, No. 69, March 1977, pp. 136–54.
30 Schram, *Mao Tse-tung* (Penguin, 1967), pp. 166–8.

31 *Ibid.*, p. 194.
32 See: Benton (1975), especially pp. 91–2. Mao's speech, *On the New Stage*, can be found in *Mō Takutō Shū*, Volume 6, pp. 163–263. Only the last section, edited to remove some of his positive comments about the Guomindang, has been published since 1949. (*Selected Works*, Volume 2, pp. 195–210.) Mao's concluding comments were not published until 1948 (*Mao Zedong Xuanji*, Volume 2, pp. 525–8; *Selected Works*, Volume 2, pp. 213–17).
33 *Kangri Zhanzheng Shiqi Jiefangqu Gaikuang*, p. 7. Figures from Guomindang sources sometimes conflict with those from communist sources but this in part reflects the reorganization carried out by the communists with some of the original counties being subdivided and districts being transferred from one county to another. In his report below Mao frequently refers to the Suide sub-region as the special military area. It was not fully incorporated into the Border Region structure until 1941. Further details can be found in *Shaan-Gan-Ning Bianqu Zhengfu Gongzuo Baogao 1939–1941* (*Shaan-Gan-Ning Bianqu Zhengfu Weiyuanhui*, July 1941, Yan'an).
34 J. Harrison, *The Long March to Power* (Macmillan, 1972), p. 271. The military figures include those of the New Fourth Army in south China.
35 Selden (1971), p. 143.
36 *Mō Takutō Shū*, Volume 7, pp. 147–206. A partial translation with notes on the differences between Mao's original version and the modified post-1949 version (*Selected Works*, Volume 2, pp. 339–84) can be found in Carrère and Schram, *Marxism and Asia* (Allen Lane, 1969), pp. 251–8.
37 See 'The Chinese Revolution of the Chinese Communist Party' December 1939 (*Mō Takutō Shū*, Volume 7, pp. 97–135, especially pp. 125–7; a modified translation is in *Selected Works*, Volume 2, pp. 305–30).
38 The ideal was not always achieved, and there was also some confusion over the precise definition of the three-thirds. Some understood it as balances of Party representation and others as balances of social groupings. See Selden (1971), pp. 161–71.
39 Below pp. 141–4.
40 Selden (1971), p. 152.
41 This campaign is outlined in Chalmers Johnson, *Peasant Nationalism and Communist Power* (Stanford University Press, 1962), pp. 56–9. During the Cultural Revolution, this campaign was described as a strategic mistake and Peng Dehuai was blamed for the problems it created. See, for example, Ding Wang (ed.), *Peng Dehuai Wenti Zhuanji* (Zhong-gong Wenhua Da Geming Ziliao Huibian, Volume 3, Mingbao Yuekan Chubanshe, Hong Kong, 1969), p. 385.
42 Johnson (1962), p. 58.
43 Below, pp. 197–8.
44 Below, p. 70.
45 Snow (1937), pp. 237–8 and p. 271. At that time Lin was finance commissioner of the Central Soviet Government and chairman of its Northwest Office. The Soviet *yuan* exchanged at a rate of 1.21 to the Guomindang *yuan*. The Border Region figures compare with the Guomindang's national budget forecast for 1937–8 of 1.4 billion *yuan* which was, in practice, far exceeded.
46 Below, p. 233 and p. 242.
47 Selden (1971), p. 180.
48 See Harrison (1972), pp. 305–7 for an account of this incident.

49 Schran (1976), Chapter 7, has extensive information on the income and expenditure of the Border Region Government.

50 *Ibid.*, p. 183.

51 Below, pp. 233–43. Despite the efforts made, this reform was only fully implemented in a small number of counties during 1943 and 1944, Tanaka (1972), pp. 243–65.

52 The financial situation in China was very complex during the war period and the various factors relating to the rapid inflation in communist and Guomindang areas are examined in A. Young, *China's Wartime Finance and Inflation 1937–1945* (Harvard University Press, 1965).

53 Statistical information on the rate of inflation can be found in Schran (1976), especially Table 4.5, p. 94 and Table 7.3, p. 184, and *yuan* exchange rates for 1941–4 are listed in Table 7.1, p. 178.

54 Below, p. 75.

55 The campaign has been widely studied. Boyd Compton, *Mao's China: Party Reform Documents 1942–1944* (University of Washington Press, 1952) gives a basic account together with the translations of the major documents studied. Selden (1971), pp. 188–207 and Chapter 6 *passim*, and Tanaka (1972), *passim* examine its impact on the Party and the Border Region.

56 Tanaka (1972), pp. 160–78.

57 See the 'Central Committee Resolution on the Unification of Leadership in the Anti-Japanese War Bases', September 1942, in Compton (1952), pp. 161–75.

58 Below, p. 116.

59 Below, pp. 65–6.

60 Below, p. 232.

61 Below, p. 156.

62 Below, p. 200.

63 Below, pp. 151–2.

64 *Kangri Zhanzheng Shiqi Jiefangqu Gaikuang* pp. 14–15 and below, pp. 66–7.

65 Below, p. 165.

66 Two sources with considerable detail on traditional peasant methods of cooperation are *Shaan-Gan-Ning Bianqu de Laodong Huzhu* (Jinan Shudian, 1946) and *Shaan-Gan-Ning Bianqu Zuzhi Laodong Huzhu de Jingyan* (Huabei Shudian, 1944). *Shaan-Gan-Ning Bianqu de Laodong Huzhu*, Chapter 2, points out that efforts to introduce Jiangxi models were abandoned in 1940.

67 *Shaan-Gan-Ning Bianqu de Laodong Huzhu* (1946), Chapter 1, lists ten main kinds: exchange of labour; exchange of labour and animal power; joint raising and use of draught animals; pooling of animals to form a yoked pair for heavy ploughing; exchange of ploughing teams; pooling of animal teams for transport and threshing; complete pooling of land, animals and labour; farming another's land while he worked for hire and sharing out his money income; farming another's land while he organized everyone's animals as a transport team; and closely united cooperation between related families.

68 *Shaan-Gan-Ning Bianqu Zuzhi Laodong Huzhu de Jingyan* (Huabei Shudian, 1944), Part 1.

69 Below, pp. 74–5.

70 Below, p. 232.

71 Below, p. 163.

72 Below, p. 227.
73 Below, pp. 125–6 and pp. 184–8.
74 Stein (1945), pp. 143–55.
75 Below, p. 118.
76 Below, p. 150.
77 Below, p. 148. This may have been an optimistic account for 1942 or it may have reflected the fact that the grain tax was sometimes excluded from the revenue accounts, see Stein (1945), p. 165. Schran's figures suggest that public production may have contributed slightly less than total income from agricultural taxation but that 'it even began to rival the latter as the primary source of revenue', Schran (1976), pp. 196–7.
78 *Selected Works*, Volume 3, p. 242.
79 Foreman (1945), p. 74. See also Schran (1976), pp. 205–15.
80 Stein (1945), p. 142.
81 *Ibid*. This approach was, of course, not new to China. Qing dynasty investment in economic modernization had stressed the role of government supervision, and the Guomindang had control of many key economic undertakings, hence Mao's criticism of 'bureaucrat-capitalism'.
82 Speech to the Supreme State Conference, 13 October 1957, in *Mao Zedong Sixiang Wansui*, August 1969 (hereafter *Wansui* (1969), reprint by the Institute of International Relations, Taipei), p. 128.
83 'On Coalition Government', 24 April 1945, *Selected Works*, Volume 3, p. 303.
84 'Report to the Second Plenary Session of the Seventh Central Committee of the Communist Party of China', 5 March 1949, *Selected Works*, Volume 4, pp. 367–9.
85 'On the People's Democratic Dictatorship', June 1949, *Selected Works*, Volume 4, p. 423.
86 For example, C. Howe and K. R. Walker, 'The Economist' in D. Wilson (ed.), *Mao Tse-tung in the Scales of History* (Cambridge University Press, 1977), pp. 185–86.
87 'Speech at the Second Plenary Session of the Eighth Central Committee', 15 November 1956, *Selected Works*, Volume 5, p. 333.
88 J. Gittings, *The World and China, 1922–1972* (Eyre Methuen, 1974), pp. 236–46 and S. Schram, *The Political Thought of Mao Tse-tung* (Penguin, 1969), pp. 415–18.
89 Quoted in Gittings (1974), p. 244.
90 'Refute Right Deviationist Views that Depart from the General Line', 15 June 1953, *Selected Works*, Volume 5, pp. 93–4 and 'The Only Road for the Transformation of Capitalist Industry and Commerce', 7 September 1953, *Selected Works*, Volume 5, pp. 112–14.
91 6 June 1952, *Selected Works*, Volume 5, p. 77.
92 'Refute Right Deviationist Views that Depart from the General Line', 15 June 1953, *Selected Works*, Volume 5, pp. 93–4.
93 'On Protracted War', May 1938, *Selected Works*, Volume 2, p. 143 has a classic formulation of Mao's view.
94 'Talks at the Chengtu Conference', March 1958, *Wansui* (1969), p. 175. Translated in S. Schram, *Mao Tse-tung Unrehearsed* (Penguin, 1974), p. 117.
95 'Speech on the book "Economic Problems of Socialism" ', November 1958 or 1959, *Wansui* (1969), p. 248, translated in *Miscellany of Mao Tse-tung Thought* (Joint Publications Research Service – hereafter JPRS – 61269–1

pp. 129–32, and 'Critique of Stalin's "Economic Problems of Socialism in the Soviet Union" ', 1959(?), *Mao Zedong Sixiang Wansui*, Red Guard publication 1967 (hereafter *Wansui* (1967)) p. 156, translated in JPRS 61269–1, pp. 191–200.

96 'Two Talks on Mutual Aid and Co-operation in Agriculture', October and November 1953, *Selected Works*, Volume 5, p. 134 and 'On the Co-operative Transformation of Agriculture', 31 July 1955, *Selected Works*, Volume 5, p. 196.

97 For a discussion of the former see J. Gray, 'The Two Roads: Alternative Strategies of Social Change and Economic Growth in China', in S. Schram (ed)., *Authority, Participation and Cultural Change in China* (Cambridge University Press, 1973), pp. 139–44, and of the latter, D. S. Zagoria, *The Sino-Soviet Conflict 1956–61* (Atheneum, 1967).

98 See, for example, 'Talk Opposing Right-Deviation and Conservatism', 6 December 1955, JPRS 61269–1, pp. 27–9.

99 *Selected Works*, Volume 5, pp. 184–207.

100 The editors of *Selected Works*, Volume 5, have concentrated their selection of documents for the period July 1955 to April 1956 exclusively on economic questions. The official version of 'On the Ten Major Relationships' is in *Selected Works*, Volume 5, pp. 284–307. An earlier version is in Schram (1974), pp. 61–83. An evaluation of the differences between the two versions by Schram can be found in *The China Quarterly*, No. 69, March 1977, pp. 126–35.

101 'On the Co-operative Transformation of Agriculture', 31 July 1955, *Selected Works*, Volume 5, pp. 196–7.

102 *Selected Works*, Volume 5, pp. 285–6.

103 *Selected Works*, Volume 5, pp. 235–53.

104 See 'On the Ten Major Relationships', *Selected Works*, Volume 5, pp. 284–307.

105 See his comments on these issues in 1959, JPRS–61269–1, p. 194 and p. 209.

106 'On the Ten Major Relationships', *Selected Works*, Volume 5, p. 291.

107 *Ibid.*, p. 303.

108 'Reading Notes on the Soviet Union's "Political Economics" ' 1960 or 1961–2, JPRS 61269–1, p. 296.

109 See the discussion in Howe and Walker, in Wilson (1977), pp. 174–222.

110 Below, p. 221.

ECONOMIC AND FINANCIAL PROBLEMS

by Mao Zedong

December 1942

1

A BASIC SUMMARY OF PAST WORK

The general policy guiding our economic and financial work is to develop the economy and ensure supplies. But many of our comrades place stress on public finance and do not understand the importance of the economy; engrossed in matters of revenue and expenditure as such, they cannot find solutions to any problem, hard as they try. The reason is that an outmoded and conservative standpoint is doing mischief in their minds. They do not know that while a good or a bad financial policy affects the economy, it is the economy that determines finances. Without a securely-based economy it is impossible to solve financial difficulties, and without a growing economy it is impossible to attain financial sufficiency. Our financial problem is that of supplying funds for the living and operating expenses of tens of thousands of troops and working personnel, in other words, the problem of supplying funds for waging the war. These funds come from taxes paid by the people and from production carried on by the tens of thousands of troops and working personnel themselves. We shall simply be resigning ourselves to extinction unless we develop both the private and public sectors of the economy. Financial difficulties can be overcome only by down-to-earth and effective economic development. To neglect economic development and the opening up of sources of finance, and instead to hope for the solution of financial difficulties by curtailing indispensable expenditures, is a conservative notion which cannot solve any problems.

In the last five years we have passed through several stages. Our worst difficulties occurred in 1940 and 1941, during the friction of the two anti-communist drives. For a time we were almost without clothing, cooking-oil, paper and vegetables, footwear for the soldiers and winter bedding for the working personnel. The Guomindang tried to strangle us by cutting off the funds due to us and imposing an economic blockade; we were indeed in dire straits. But we pulled through. Not only did the people of the Border Region provide us with grain but, in particular, we resolutely built up the public sector of our economy with our own hands. The government established many self-supporting industries. The troops engaged in an extensive production campaign and expanded agriculture, industry and commerce to supply their own needs. The tens of thousands of personnel in the various organizations and schools also developed similar economic activities for their own support.[1] It is by such means that we have been overcoming our difficulties. Do not these indisputable historical facts prove the truth that supplies can be ensured only through economic development? While we still face many difficulties, the foundation of the public sector of our economy has already been laid. In another year, by the end of 1943, this foundation will be even firmer.

Developing the economy is the correct line, but development does not mean reckless or ill-founded expansion. Some comrades who disregard the specific conditions here and now are setting up an empty clamour for development; for example, they are demanding the establishment of heavy industry and putting forward plans for huge salt and armament industries, all of which are unrealistic and unacceptable. The Party's line is the correct line for development; it opposes outmoded and conservative standpoints on the one hand and grandiose, empty and unrealistic plans on the other. This is the Party's struggle on two fronts in financial and economic work.

While we must develop the public sector of our economy, we should not forget the importance of help from the people. They have given us grain, 90,000 *dan* in 1940, 200,000 in 1941 and

---

[1] Both the Chinese text of *Mao Zedong Xuanji*, Volume 3 (Beijing, 1953), p. 894 and the English text in *Selected Works*, Volume 3, p. 112 (Foreign Languages Press, Beijing, 1965), insert the following sentence here: 'This self-supporting economy, which has been developed by the troops and the various organizations and schools, is a special product of the special conditions of today. It would be unreasonable and incomprehensible in other historical conditions, but it is perfectly reasonable and necessary at present'.

160,000 in 1942,[2] thus ensuring food for our troops and working personnel. Up to the end of 1941, the grain output of the public sector of our agriculture was meagre and we relied on the people for grain. We must urge the army to produce more grain, but for a time we shall still have to rely mainly on the people. The Border Region has only 1,400,000 inhabitants, a small population for so large an area, and the provision of such large quantities of grain is not easy. Besides, the people transport salt for us or pay a substitute salt levy, and in 1941 they purchased government bonds, worth 5 million *yuan*, all of which is no small burden. To meet the needs of the War of Resistance and national reconstruction, the people must shoulder such burdens, the necessity of which they very well realize. When the government is in very great difficulties, it is necessary to ask the people to bear a heavier burden, and they understand that too. But while taking from the people we must at the same time help them to replenish and expand their economy. That is to say, appropriate steps and methods must be adopted to help the people develop their agriculture, animal husbandry, handicrafts, salt industry and commerce, so that they gain at the same time as they lose[3] and only thus can we sustain a long war against Japan.

Disregarding the needs of the war, some comrades insist that the government should adopt a policy of 'benevolence'. This is a mistake. For unless we win the war against Japan, such 'benevolence' will mean nothing to the people and will benefit only the Japanese imperialists. Conversely, although the people have to carry rather heavy burdens for the time being, things will get better for them as the difficulties confronting the government and the troops are overcome, the War of Resistance is sustained and the enemy is defeated; and this is where the true benevolence of the revolutionary government lies.

Another mistake is 'draining the pond to catch the fish', that is, making endless demands on the people, disregarding their hardships and considering only the needs of the government

---

[2] The following note is given in *Selected Works*, Volume 3, p. 113. 'These figures are the totals paid in agricultural tax (public grain) by the peasants of the Shaanxi-Gansu-Ningxia Border Region from 1940 to 1942'. For further details on grain-tax figures see Selden (1971), pp. 181–7.

[3] *Mao Zedong Xuanji* and *Selected Works*, Volume 3, p. 113 here have the insertion: 'and, moreover, gain more than they give;'.

and the army. That is a Guomindang mode of thinking which we must never adopt. Although we have temporarily added to the people's burden, we have immediately set to work building the public sector of our economy. In the years 1941 and 1942 the army, the official organizations and the schools met most of their needs by their own efforts. This is a wonderful achievement without precedent in Chinese history, and it contributes to the material basis of our invincibility. The greater our self-supporting economic activities, the more we shall be able to lighten the people's tax burdens. In the first stage, from 1937 to 1939, we took very little from them; during this stage they were able to build up considerable strength. In the second stage, from 1940 to 1942, the burden on the people was increased. The third stage will begin in 1943. In the next two years, 1943 and 1944, if the public sector of our economy continues to grow and if all or most of our troops are in a position to engage in farming[4] then by the end of 1944 the people's burden will again be lightened, and they will again be able to build up strength. This is a possibility which we should prepare to turn into actuality.

We must refute all one-sided views and advance the correct slogan of our Party 'Develop the economy and ensure supplies'. With regard to the relation between public and private interests, our slogans are 'Give consideration to both public and private interests', and 'Give consideration to both troops and civilians'. We consider only such slogans to be correct. We can guarantee our financial needs only by expanding both the public and private sectors of our economy in a realistic and practical way. Even in difficult times we must take care to set a limit to taxation so that the burdens, though heavy, will not hurt the people. And as soon as we can, we should lighten the burdens so that the people can build up strength.

The Guomindang diehards regard construction in the Border Region as a hopeless undertaking and the difficulties here as insurmountable; they are expecting the Border Region to collapse any day. It is not worth arguing with such people; they will never see the day of our 'collapse' and we shall unquestionably

---

[4] Mao here used the phrase *tun tian*, 'camp-field system', which has historically been used in China to describe troops farming land to provide for their own needs as military colonists.

grow more and more prosperous. They do not understand that under the leadership of the Communist Party and the Border Region revolutionary government the masses always give their support to the Party and government. And the Party and the government will always find ways to get over economic and financial difficulties, however serious. In fact we have already pulled through some of our recent difficulties and will soon overcome others. We encountered difficulties many times greater in the past and surmounted them all. With intense fighting going on every day, our base areas in northern and central China are now facing much greater difficulties than the Shaanxi-Gansu-Ningxia Border Region, but we have already held out for five-and-a-half years in these areas and can certainly continue to do so till victory. For us there is no ground for pessimism; we can conquer any difficulty.

After the present conference of senior cadres we shall put into effect the policy of 'better troops and simpler administration'.[5] It must be carried out strictly, thoroughly and universally, and not perfunctorily, superficially or partially. In carrying it out, we must attain the five objectives of simplification, unification, efficiency, economy and opposition to bureaucracy. These five objectives have a very important bearing on our economic and financial work. Simplification will reduce non-productive expenditures and increase our income from production; it will not only have a direct and healthy effect on our finances, but will lighten the people's burdens and benefit them economically. In our economic and financial set-up, we must overcome such evils as disunity, assertion of independence and lack of coordination, and must establish a working system which is unified and responsive to direction and which permits the full application of our policies and regulations. With the establishment of such a unified system working efficiency will rise. All our organizations, and particularly those engaged in economic and financial work, must pay attention to thrift. By practising thrift we can cut out a great deal of unnecessary and wasteful expenditure, which amounts possibly to tens of millions of yuan. Finally, people engaged in economic and financial work must overcome surviv-

---

[5] For 'better troops and simpler administration' see 'A Most Important Policy', *Selected Works*, Volume 3, pp. 99–102.

ing bureaucratic practices, some of which, such as corruption and graft, over-elaborate organization, meaningless 'standardization' and red-tape, are very serious. If we fully attain these five objectives in the Party, the government and the army, our policy of 'better troops and simpler administration' will achieve its purpose, our difficulties will surely be overcome, and we shall silence the gibes about our approaching 'collapse'.

Below, we shall discuss separately various objectives of financial and economic work, concretely summarize experience in past work, and put forward the general policies for work that should be carried out in 1943.

2
ON THE DEVELOPMENT OF AGRICULTURE

The general strategy for economic and financial work in the Border Region is to develop the economy and ensure supplies. This being the case, the first and most important questions are 'How has our economic work been done in the past?', 'What are the successes?', 'What are the shortcomings?', and 'What should be our strategy henceforth?'.

The economy of the Border Region is divided into the two large sectors, the public and the private. The private sector of our economy consists of all agriculture, industry, and commerce undertaken by private individuals. The public sector of our economy consists of the agriculture, industry, and commerce undertaken by the government, troops, official organizations and schools. The functions and relationship of these two sectors are such that the private sector provides the livelihood of the 1,400,000 people of the Border Region. At the same time, through taxation, it assists the government and troops, and supports the sacred cause of the War of Resistance and the reconstruction of the country. The public sector provides the bulk of the living and operating expenses of several tens of thousands of Party members, government workers and soldiers, thus reducing the amount taken from the people and building up their resources so that these can be obtained in future urgent need. The principles used here are 'Give consideration to both public and private interests' and 'Give consideration to both troops and civilians'.

If our Party and government do not pay attention to mobilizing the people and helping them to develop agriculture, industry, and commerce, their life cannot be improved, and the needs of the War of Resistance cannot be met. As a result there will be trouble between the troops and the people. And if we cannot settle the minds of the troops and the people, it is pointless to consider anything else. Therefore the most important task is for the Party and the government to concentrate great efforts on building up the people's economy.

However, relying on the taxes handed over by the people alone cannot meet the needs of the War of Resistance and the reconstruction of the country. This is particularly true of the Border Region where the area is large and the population sparse, and where there has long been a large contradiction between the taxes paid by the people and the expenditure of the government. Therefore, we must also concentrate great efforts on managing the public sector of the economy. This is an extremely great responsibility borne by our government, troops, official organizations and schools. In the past few years we have had great successes in this work. In 1943 we must achieve even greater successes so as directly to meet the needs of the War of Resistance and the reconstruction of the country. The more the public sector of the economy grows, the more the burden carried by the people can be reduced. This is another way of building up the resources of the people. And the instrument which unites and reconciles the private and public sectors is the currency.

The private sector comprises agriculture, animal husbandry, handicrafts, cooperative undertakings, the salt industry, and commerce. Here I shall first deal with agriculture.

The agriculture of the Border Region was depressed during the period of the land revolution.[1] At that time there was much uncultivated land in Yan'an, Ansai, Bao'an,[2] Ganquan, Huachi and the three eastern counties,[3] etc. On the border between Huachi and Bao'an, there was an area called Erjiachuan which was more than 200 *li* long yet only twenty or thirty households lived there. As early as the Tongzhi period (1862–74) there was no one living in Wuyasi and Zhangjiacha in Bao'an county.

[1] Mao is here referring to the land redistribution of 1934–7 which by 1942 was considered to have entailed left-wing excesses under the influence of the Wang Ming line. See the discussion in Selden (1971), pp. 64–5.
[2] Renamed Zhidan county in 1937 in memory of Liu Zhidan.
[3] Meaning Yanchuan, Yanchang and Gulin.

Fucunchuan in Ganquan county, and Jinpenwan and Mashichuan in Yan'an county had for the most part ceased to be cultivated. Cotton-planting had ceased throughout the Border Region. The decline in animal husbandry was very great. Only 400,000 – 500,000 head of sheep remained and 100,000 oxen and donkeys. Textiles, the transport of salt, and other subsidiary undertakings had all been disrupted in the same way. In particular the textile industry had almost completely disappeared. By 1938, only 70,000 packs of eating salt were exported.[4] All this shows how depressed the agriculture of the Border Region was at that time. Agriculture was only speedily restored and developed after the Central Red Army came to the Border Region and civil war ceased, after the local bandits were cleaned up and the peasants were given security, after the 'left' economic policy was corrected and a mild taxation policy was adopted, and after the Party and government's call for the development of agriculture had greatly raised the enthusiasm of the peasants for production.

Table 1.1 gives the statistics for livestock, cotton-planting, and opening up of uncultivated lands in the past four years.

Table 1.1   *Agricultural activity 1939–42*

Year	Area of new land opened (mu)	Area of cotton planted (mu)	Livestock		
			Oxen	Donkeys	Sheep
1939	1,002,774	3,767	150,892	124,935	1,171,366
1940	698,989	15,177	193,238	135,054	1,723,037
1941	390,087	39,087	202,914	137,001	1,724,203
1942	281,413	94,405	–	–	–
Total	2,373,263	–	–	–	–

Explanation:
(1) The statistics for the livestock of Jiaxian and Mizhi counties have not been included: the 1939 figures for livestock include the 1940 total for seven of the counties.
(2) The figure for the area of new land cultivated is for the amount of new land opened each year. The figures for cotton planted and for livestock are the annual totals for the whole of the Border Region.

[4] That is, exported out of the Border Region.

These statistics show that year by year the cultivated land of the Border Region has expanded, the acreage of cotton planted has grown, and the amount of livestock has increased. Moreover, the real totals are more than those shown in the statistical table. As a result much of the formerly uncultivated land has become productive. For example, there are now more than a hundred households in Erjiachuan and all the land of the area has been cultivated. Wuyasi and Zhangjiacha are now both fully inhabited. In the past, all eleven districts in Yan'an county had unused land. At present only Jinpen and Liulin districts, half the Central district and one township in Yaodian district have uncultivated land. In 1939, there were only about 300,000 mu of ploughed land in Yan'an. In 1942, there were 699,538 mu. There used to be a lot of uncultivated land in the counties of Ansai, Anding, Yanchuan, and Yanchang. Now there is very little. Before 1940 the Border Region bought grain from Luochuan county and east of the Yellow River. Now, not only is it unnecessary to buy grain from outside, there is even some surplus grain which is exported to the region of Yulin. Some people have moved here from other areas, livestock has increased, but we do not feel a shortage of grain. In the light of all these facts there is no longer any doubt that the Border Region can be self-supporting in grain.

Cotton-growing has not only again reached its pre-revolutionary peak, but has also developed. For example, the districts of Yongping, Yongsheng and Yuju in Yanchuan county did not previously grow cotton. Now they have all started growing it. The same is true of Yan'an. The profit from cotton is greater than the profit from grain. The return from 1 mu of cotton is on average 700 yuan or more, whereas if grain were planted the return would only be 200 yuan. The ratio is thus 3:1. In 1939, the area planted to cotton was only just over 3,700 mu. In 1942 it was more than 94,000 mu, and the quantity produced reached 1,400,000 jin. This was a great achievement. However, the amount needed by the Border Region is 3 million jin. This is our future task.

The increase in livestock has also been very rapid. For example, in 1937 there were only about 8,000 sheep in Yan'an. Now there are more than 60,000. In 1937 there were only 70,000 sheep in Huachi, now there are more than 120,000. Before the land revolution, there were only five flocks of sheep in Zhang-jiahe of Third township, Dongyang district, Yanchuan county. (There was no grazing land and there could only be thirty to fifty head in each flock.) Now there are thirteen flocks. Oxen and donkeys have increased by almost two-thirds since the time of the civil war. As a result in 1940 and 1941 we were able to export 500,000 packs of salt. If it were not for the increase in oxen and donkeys, this salt would have been very difficult to move out.

However, the development of agriculture has not been even. Those areas with relatively all-round development and rather more successes include the counties under direct administration[5] and the Longdong sub-region, in particular Yan'an, Ansai, Ganquan, Huachi, Quzi and the three eastern counties. This is because they have a lot of land, few people, and the climate is quite good. These counties also have the biggest share in the subsidiary work of salt transport and at the same time, the largest amount of public expenditure. The area that has not developed is the special military area [jingbeiqu],[6] because it has a large population and the land is limited. There is no possibility of enlarging the ploughed area. They have had some success there in the gradual restoration of household spinning and weaving work. Moreover, there has been some emigration to the Yan'an area, which has eased the distribution of population and land.

The speed of development has also varied. Development was faster before 1940, particularly in the years 1939 and 1940. In these two years 1,700,000 mu of new land were opened up. In 1940, the number of sheep increased by nearly 600,000, and oxen and donkeys by over 50,000. But in 1941 and 1942 only about 600,000 mu of land were opened up. This is only one-third of the previous two years. There were fewer sheep in 1941 over 1940, and the number of oxen and donkeys only increased by 10,000 (in reality there was a reduction). However, in these two years cotton-growing and textiles both developed.

The above outlines the development of agriculture in the

[5] That is, the eleven counties administered directly from Yan'an.
[6] That is, the Sui-Mi sub-region. This area only came under the full control of the Border Region Government during 1940.

Border Region. Now I want to say a few words about how this development took place.

Before the civil war ended, agriculture was in decline. Afterwards it developed. How did this development come about? Apart from the arrival of the Central Red Army, the cleaning up of the local bandits, and the realization of peace so that the peasants could live and work securely, there were the following six reasons.

(1) The 'left' mistakes in economic policy were corrected and the policies to build up the resources of the people were implemented. Although the peasants had obtained a share of land, they were afraid to develop production because of the 'left' economic policy. In addition, because agriculture was disrupted both before and after the revolution, the base was very weak and hindered growth. The Central Committee corrected the 'left' policy and thus put an end to the peasants' tendency to fear developing production. The peasants were then willing to buy more implements, and the rich peasants dared to take on tenants [an huozi] and long-term labourers [gu changgong]. The milder policies restored confidence and helped the extension of production. At the same time the high price for grain and the great profit in subsidiary undertakings stimulated the peasants' zeal to produce, and made agriculture develop rapidly. This laid the basis for the levy of 200,000 dan of grain tax and 26 million jin of hay tax in 1941.

(2) Calls were made for the development of production. The Production Mobilization Conference for cadres held by the Central Committee (1939), the Second Party Congress of the Border Region (1939), the first meeting of the Border Region Council (1941), and the first agricultural exhibition, all called for the development of production. These calls played a major role in promoting growth. They first aroused the cadres, and then through them penetrated deeply to the masses, mobilizing men, women, old, young, and even loafers [er liuzi] to take part in production. They increased the labour force, and finally destroyed the peasants' fear of developing production. Thus the amount of new land opened up in 1939 was more than 1 million mu, and real imports of livestock were also greatest in that year.

(3) The immigration policy. A major reason for the enlargement

of cultivated land by 2,350,000 mu in the past four years has been that those regions with large amounts of land have absorbed large numbers of immigrants, and increased their population. For example, in 1937 Yan'an (including Yan'an city) only had a population of 34,000. Now its population is roughly 70,000. Because of this, cultivated land in this county has increased from around 300,000 mu to roughly 700,000 mu. In 1936 Ansai only had a population of about 20,000. Now it has a population of more than 40,000. Ganquan originally had about 8,000 people. Now it has more than 14,000. In 1939 Yanchang only had a population of 25,000. Now it has more than 32,000. Yanchuan had the least amount of uncultivated land, but between 1938 and the present its population has increased by over 10,000. Huachi only had a population of 35,000 in 1938. Now it has a population of more than 40,000. Other places such as Bao'an, Anding, Jingbian, and the counties of the Longdong and Guanzhong sub-regions have also increased their population. These immigrants came mostly from Hengshan, Yulin, Shenmu, and Fugu,[7] and secondly from the special military area. They all came voluntarily and were not organized by the government. They were willing to come because there was land and they were treated well. The various counties organized the existing householders to give help with grain, tools, and cave houses, etc. At the same time the rich peasants took on tenants, which also helped the immigrants. The increase in immigrants not only enlarged the area cultivated, but also increased livestock, and stimulated commerce. Therefore the immigrants were one of the factors in the development of agriculture.

(4) The policy of incentives. Immigrants do not pay grain tax for three years, and their other obligations are reduced. If some of the peasants planting cotton do not make as much profit as those planting grain, the government pays compensation. If livestock is purchased from outside the Border Region, there is a reduction in grain tax by a fixed amount in the first year. In addition, there were the rewards to labour heroes given at the two agricultural exhibitions, which also brought about great results. For example, Wu Manyou and Mao Kehu of Yan'an and Du Fafu of

---

[7] All counties in the north of Shaanxi province, near the Great Wall.

Ganquan were rewarded at the first agricultural exhibition. Now they have become very good, rich peasants. They all pay more than 5 *dan* of grain tax (in the Border Region 1 *dan* is 300 *jin*). Moreover, they have encouraged other peasant householders in the villages to develop production. All these things have promoted the development of agriculture, in particular of grain and cotton.

(5) The reduction in the wastage of labour power, and the better adjustment in the use of labour power. Because we were busy fighting during the civil-war period, we did not pay attention to production and the land was neglected. After peace was established, there were frequent exercises and guard duties by the self-defence army [*ziweijun*] and many kinds of meetings. Therefore, each month each able-bodied man missed at least three working-days. Later this kind of wastage was reduced. Furthermore, before 1941 not much grain tax was collected, there was little tax grain transport duty, and the amount of work missed was comparatively limited. In recent years in rural areas, contract-labour teams [*zhagong*] (short-term work for others done collectively under a boss) and exchange-labour teams [*biangong*] (mutual aid among the masses, and also done collectively) have developed and made better adjustment in the use of labour power.[8] We have mobilized loafers to take part in production. The number of women joining-in production has also increased. All these things have helped the development of Border Region agriculture.

(6) The policy of agricultural credit. Formerly there was no agricultural credit but this was offset by the mild taxation policy. Now that grain tax has increased and particularly as 80 per cent of peasant households must pay it, those households (roughly one-third) lacking oxen, agricultural tools, and food grain must be helped with credit. Moreover, a supply of credit is very necessary for certain kinds of agriculture that must be developed (like cotton-planting), for agricultural subsidiaries (like spinning and weaving), and for certain regions which need more development. Although only 4 million *yuan* credit was

[8] See the Introduction above, pp. 27–9; Selden (1971), pp. 242–9; and 'Get Organized', *Selected Works*, Volume 3, pp. 153–61 for a further discussion of these teams.

given in 1942, of which merely 1,500,000 *yuan* was for oxen, over 2,600 oxen and nearly 5,000 agricultural implements were bought and cotton-planting also expanded. It cannot be denied that this was a great help. But because finances are limited and we can only lend according to the government's financial strength, we still cannot provide enough credit to match the needs of the peasant households. However, a little is always better than nothing, and it does give some help.

The above are several of the major factors in the development of agriculture; below I shall discuss several major lessons to be drawn from our work.

(1) Act according to the conditions of the area and the season. Agricultural regions and seasons are different, and methods of development are also different. For example, there is no uncultivated land in the special military area (apart from a small amount in Qingjian). The cultivated land area cannot be enlarged. Sheep-herding is limited by the pasture land available. There is also a lack of pack-animals for the transport of salt. The policy of rent reduction has not yet been thoroughly implemented. Because of these things, grain production has not increased in those areas, and with the exception of spinning and weaving, subsidiary undertakings have not developed. Although improved techniques such as more frequent hoeing of weeds, greater use of manure, and more deep ploughing were introduced there long ago, we should still carry out more investigation of the situation, and at the right time do our utmost to increase production. However, if we were to employ these improved techniques in areas where land is plentiful, population sparse, and working methods primitive, they would not be very effective because they all need an increase in labour power. From the point of view of the peasants of the latter kind of area, deep ploughing is not as good as planting more land. Applying more manure is not as good as opening up more uncultivated land. Planting more land is especially good in areas with low rainfall. Therefore, in these areas the call to improve agricultural methods is in general ineffective at the present time. To really increase production in these regions the most important thing for the moment is to rely on opening up unused land. If in the six years from 1937 to 1942 the increase in ploughed land was

roughly 3 million *mu*, then the amount harvested in 1942 was at least 500,000 *dan* more than in 1936, which is equivalent to 250,000 *dan* of hulled grain (each *dan* is 300 *jin*).[9] If we estimate the grain production of the Border Region in 1942 to be 1,500,000 *dan* of hulled grain, then over six years the increase in grain production through the increase of ploughed land is approximately one-sixth of the total. Some of this increase in cultivated land is new land opened up by immigrants, and some is expansion of land farmed by the original households. All this shows us that in directing agriculture, we must adopt different methods in different regions. In one region we should make deep ploughing the key, and in another enlarging the area ploughed. We must also make distinctions with respect to timing. At a time when there is unused land that can be cultivated, we should mainly encourage the opening up of new land. When uncultivated land has been exhausted, then we must turn to encouraging deep ploughing. We must not only make these distinctions between large regions, we must also make them within a county, a district and sometimes even within a township. For example, if certain villages in a township have rather a lot of unused land, we should encourage the opening up of unused land there. If in other villages there is little or no unused land, we should encourage deep ploughing. While there is still uncultivated land in a township, we should encourage the opening up of land. When all the lands have been opened up, we should encourage deep ploughing. Although we have had some successes in the past few years in our work, much has been too empty and generalized. Many of our comrades still do not know how to investigate objective circumstances minutely, nor do they know how to put forward concrete proposals to provide the conditions for increasing production in different regions and at different times. Slogans put forward in the past for deep ploughing, opening new lands, water conservancy, and increasing production by 400,000 *dan* or 200,000 *dan*, in reality contained much subjectivism. Many peasants were not interested or influ-

---

[9] Usage throughout the text indicates that Mao is using the terms *culiang*, 'coarse grain', and *xiliang*, 'fine grain', to mean 'grain' and 'hulled grain' respectively rather than to distinguish between different types of grain as might have been the case. *Xiliang* is often used as an official equivalent.

enced by them. From this we may conclude that in future we must carry out deep, factual investigation, and solve problems in terms of concrete times, places, and conditions.

(2) As yet the peasants in a large number of areas still pay heavy rents and heavy interest rates, and the policy of reducing these has not been thoroughly implemented. On the one hand peasants must bear the burden of paying rent and interest to the landlords, and on the other they must pay grain tax and money tax to the government. They get too little for themselves, which dampens their enthusiasm to produce. Thus there is no possibility of increasing production. From this we may conclude that we must conscientiously implement the decrees to reduce rent and interest rates.

(3) As a result of the increase in grain tax, and the newly levied hay tax, sheep tax, and salt-transport requirement, the peasants' enthusiasm for production has diminished. In the two years 1941 and 1942 the peasants paid a large amount of grain tax, hay tax and salt tax, and during these years they expanded the area of ploughed land by only 600,000 mu, merely 60 per cent of the increase in 1939. Livestock did not increase in 1941, and sheep even declined (of course epidemics had some effect). Immigration also dropped. In 1942 only 4,843 households came. Moreover, 3,527 old households moved out, the reason mainly being that they feared further burdens. Another reason was that the amount of grain tax collected increased progressively according to the amount harvested and not according to the area of land worked. This method, although rational in terms of sharing the burden equally, hindered the growth of investment in agriculture. It lowered the peasants' enthusiasm to invest in the land because for the same land a good harvest meant paying out a lot and a poor harvest meant paying out little or even nothing. If taxation was based on the area of land worked, this point could be corrected. The enthusiasm of the middle and rich peasants could be raised, and there would be no detriment to the poor peasants. From this we may conclude that there must be limits to the grain tax and hay tax, and at the same time we must improve the methods of taxation so as to promote agricultural production.

(4) Policies should be thoroughly implemented. For example, we stipulated that for three years we would not take grain tax

from new immigrants or from those planting cotton, but in fact we have 'welcomed' grain tax from immigrants, and we have levied one-half of the grain tax for land planted to cotton. We originally stipulated that when livestock was bought from areas outside the Border Region we would reduce grain tax by a definite amount for the first year, but this has also not yet been implemented. In addition regulations for giving rewards for increased production have not been fully carried out. All these things not only affect the authority of the government but also diminish the enthusiasm of the peasants. From this we may conclude that henceforward everything pertaining to the decrees announced by the government must be resolutely implemented.

(5) More equitable adjustment in the use of labour power and other methods helpful to peasants, such as exchange-labour teams, contract-labour teams and so forth, have a strong influence on agricultural growth. However, with the exception of some counties like Yan'an, we have still not done enough to organize and promote them. There are certainly many comrades among the county cadres who are actively striving to put ideas to the people, and who have originated many good methods for mobilizing the masses to develop production. They have created many model examples. However, many other comrades are not like this. They lack the spirit of factual investigation and enthusiastic effort. They lack creativity. They feel that there is no work that they can do for agriculture, or they do not know how to set-to. Therefore they only raise empty slogans like 'spring ploughing' or 'autumn harvest'. They remain passive, and let the peasants do things as they like. The government simply keeps a record of what is done. But in fact there are many things to be done. Many good methods can be thought up. For example, during spring ploughing in 1942 some of the peasants in Yan'an felt very discouraged. Instances of moving out, splitting up the family, and selling livestock in preparation for reducing production occurred. From the point of view of the comrades who lack enthusiasm and creativity, these phenomena would be insoluble and it would be best to accept fate and let such bad things happen. But the comrades from Yan'an were not like this. They were neither passive nor bureau-

cratic. They were able to grasp the key to the problem and adopt active methods. They overcame the difficulties. At that time, the Party and government did much propaganda work, and gave help with grain, cave houses, and agricultural tools. Afterwards not only did production not decline, but cultivated land increased by 80,000 mu. This example proved that there is much work in agriculture that can and should be done by the local Party committees and the local government. Moreover, so long as they grasp the key points and find a method, then when they act they can be effective. From this we may conclude that cadres must be active to overcome difficulties, they must unite with the masses, and according to the needs of the masses create vigorous methods to solve their problems. They definitely cannot be passive and bureaucratic.

In order to give our comrades a clear-cut standpoint on this extremely important question of uniting closely with the masses and conscientiously solving their difficulties, I here specially reproduce for reference the reports of the comrades of Yan'an county on how they handled the problem of opening up unused land, how they handled the problem of refugees, and how they handled the problem of loafers.

What follows is the original report.

HOW WAS YAN'AN COUNTY'S PLAN TO OPEN UP 80,000 MU OF UNUSED LAND IN 1942 COMPLETED?

(1) We relied on the labour power of immigrant refugees to open up uncultivated land.

There were 25,428 refugees in the period 1940 to 1942. On the basis of five of them equalling one labour power, there were 5,086 labour powers. Each labour power can open up 10 mu of new land in one year, giving a total of 50,860 mu. (Ten mu is the average figure for the land opened up by refugees in the past three years. In 1942 the land opened up by each labour power was more than this.)

(2) We relied on the labour power of original households and animals to open up unused land, totalling 29,399 mu.

The original households had 10,616 labour powers. The work could be done with each labour power opening up less than 3 mu.

(3) However, the organization of labour power is a major task. This year we adopted methods of collective labour, such as contract-labour teams and exchange-labour teams. We also organized women and loafers to take part in production.

Altogether we organized 487 contract-labour teams. We also drew 4,939 good labour powers into collective labour (exchange-labour teams). This was almost one-third of the total number of labour powers (according to statistics for this spring, there were 15,702 labour powers in the whole country), which meant that out of every three people one took part in collective labour. The method of contract labour was to form a group of eight to ten good workers from a village and establish a foreman [gongtou]. Then they opened up new land and hoed weeds either for themselves or for others. Sometimes the foreman took part in physical labour, in which case he received pay valued at two labour days per day worked. If he did not take part, he only received pay valued at one labour day per day. Those forming contract-labour teams were either entirely from the local village, or came from outside, or were organized with people from outside the village together with peasants from the village.

The peasants were very pleased that we organized loafers to take part in production. It increased their enthusiasm for work.

More and more women joined in production each year. In particular refugee women took part in opening up uncultivated land, and even more of them in hoeing. There were thirty-nine in Liulin district this year. The refugee women of Third township in Chuankou district did not have any hoes. They went to the mountains and waited until others were tired and resting, then they took up the hoes and began opening-up land. When the others had finished their rest they handed back the hoes and waited again.

(4) We relied on production plans for each peasant household. In 1942, this county laid emphasis on determining production plans for each peasant household based on discussions with that household and with its agreement. The government printed a standard form to record plans including such things as opening up new lands, hoeing weeds, and so forth. When a plan was determined, it was posted up in the home of each family so that afterwards the government could examine the production plan of each household according to the form. When determining peasant household plans we had to pay attention to the following points:

  (i) The production circumstances of the previous year.
 (ii) The conditions for the increase of production in the current year.
(iii) The amount of labour power (human and animal).
 (iv) Obtaining the agreement of the man concerned.
  (v) The need for constant examination and supervision of work.

(5) The effect of agricultural credit was important, in particular the 100,000 yuan credit given to refugees for agricultural tools. When the refugees arrived they did not have a thing. To open up unused land, first a mattock was needed to clear away the scrub and then a hoe to break the

land. After agricultural credit was issued and the problem of tools was solved, the refugees' desire to open up new land was very strong. In six days they were able to open up 3 mu. In 1942 agricultural credit was given rather late. The earlier credit is given the sooner more land can be opened up. (Note: do not violate the agricultural season.)

(6) During spring ploughing, mobilization work had to be reduced as much as possible. The peasants were allowed the time to open up new land and to take part in production.

(7) The government had a tight grasp on the work of opening-up unused land. Only three months were available for this. With a hundred-day plan, each day opening up 800 mu, it was necessary to have a labour force of 1,600. This was one-tenth of the labour force of the whole county. By 19 April we had only opened up 15,000 mu. This was still far short of completing the task, and already two-thirds of the time had gone. Therefore beginning on 20 April, after a rainfall, there was a twenty-day assault. In the twenty days more than 50 per cent of the whole task was completed. Between 10 March and 19 April, 15,000 mu of land was opened up. This was 18.7 per cent of the work. In the twenty day assault, 46,442 mu of land was opened up, which was 58 per cent of the work.

In the assault the best districts were the following:

Luilin district: the ratio of new land opened up during the period of assault to that opened up before was 1,294.4:100.

Yaodian district: the ratio was 1,184.4:100.

Chuankou district: the ratio was 432.1:100.

Altogether the county government held two meetings of district heads to inspect the work, and issued three directives. The cadres of the county government went down to the districts and townships more than three times.

The districts checked up on the work of the townships up to seven or eight times in some cases, and three times at the very least. The townships also checked up many times on the work of the villages.

The tight grasp of the leadership and the strict check-ups played a decisive role in the completion of the task.

HOW TO SOLVE THE PROBLEM OF REFUGEES TAKING PART IN PRODUCTION

(1) [Table 1.2 refers to] statistics on the flow of refugees into Yan'an county in recent years.[10]

Putting it simply, the number of households more than doubled, and the number of people just about doubled.

The refugees who came settled mainly in Chuankou, Liulin, Jinpen, and Yaodian districts. In these districts there was a lot of unused land.

[10] The 1947 edition of the selected works has a number of mistakes in its figures so I have followed the 1949 Hong Kong edition for this table.

Table 1.2   *The flow of refugees into Yan'an county
(Yan'an City excluded), 1938–42*

Year	Households	Number of people
1938	249	1,200
1939	533	1,976
1940	1,137	6,090
1941	5,040	14,207
1942	1,050	6,231
Total	8,009	29,704

Comparison with 1937	Households	Number of people
1937	7,703	32,705
Increase during 5 years	8,009	29,704
Percentage increase	103.9%	90.8%

(2) Statistics on how the government helped the refugees solve problems in production after they had come (Table 1.3).
(3) The methods for solving refugees' difficulties in production were:
(i) There was a lot of land. We proposed that the ownership of publicly-owned uncultivated land should go to those who opened it up. If the owner of privately-owned unused land did not open it up, we let refugees do so. The three-year exemption from tax was an incentive.

Table 1.3   *Allocation of State aid to refugees, 1940–42*

	1940	1941	1942	Total
Allocation of land (in *mu*)	10,220	3,451	6,335	20,006
Grain (in *dan*)	669.9	495	458.48	1,623.38
Seeds (in *dan*)	40.18	8.2	47.37	95.75
Agricultural tools (items)	424	2,133	427	2,984
Oxen	979	82	212	1,273

Notes:
(a) In 1942 13,555 *jin* of sweet potatoes [*yangyu*] were given to the refugees in addition, and on 273 occasions they were helped with oxen.
(b) Agricultural tools were ploughshares, rakes and hoes.

(ii) The problem of a place to live. In the beginning they lived in old cave houses or broken-down cave houses. Many of the others who came afterwards were joining friends, relatives, or people of other social relationships. They lived in the cave houses of those friends or relatives. Having settled down, they dug out their own cave house. In other cases one person came in the first year and dug out the cave house. In the second year the family came and moved into the house.

(iii) We made arrangements among the peasants for grain to eat. We proposed that if 1 dou of grain was borrowed before spring, after autumn 1 dou and 3 sheng should be repaid. This was a profit of 30 per cent. It encouraged the original households to lend grain and the government guaranteed repayment. Another method was to urge the original households to hire help [diao fenzi], to take on share-cropping tenants [an zhuangjia] and to contract short-term labour [lan gong] from among the refugees. Conditions were decided voluntarily by both sides. Allowing the original households to exploit a little was not a problem because when the refugees first came they did not have a thing. Although they were exploited, we could not let them starve.

Statistics for this year (1942) [are shown in Table 1.4].

Table 1.4   *Households reliant upon employees for food grain in 1942*

Hired help [*diao fenzi*]	359 households
Share-cropping tenants [*an zhuangjia*]	466 households
Short-term contract labour [*lan gong*]	184 households
Total	1,009 households

These households relied on their employers for food grain. However, the hired helpers [*diao fenzi*] could only get supplies for themselves. Hired farmhands and short-term contract labourers were able to get food grain for their family members as well. There were 650 households of the latter kind. At a rate of three people per household, this was altogether 1,950 persons. If we add on the 359 hired helpers, the full total was 2,309 people relying on their employers for grain. If they had asked for aid from the government, at a rate of 5 dou per man per year the amount of grain needed would have been 1,154.5 dou. What a large amount this would have been! Therefore on the basis of mutual agreement between employer and employee, the hiring of farmhands, helpers, and short-term contract labourers solved many great problems. It not only solved the problem of food grains. It also enlarged production and increased the supply of grain. Taking each household as one labour power, there were 1,009 labour powers altogether. One labour power could produce 2 *dan* of grain, so in total they could increase grain production by 2,018 *dan*. After consumption this still left a surplus of 863.5 *dan*. By the following year these people were in a position to carry out production by themselves.

(iv) The peasants were urged to help the refugees with seed and land to work. Seed was repaid after autumn, and a rent paid for land with the government as guarantor.

(v) The institution of credit for agricultural implements for refugees was very effective in solving the problem of supplying tools to open up new lands. If arrangements for any problem (food grain, supply of agricultural implements, etc.) were not good, the opening up of unused lands could have been impeded. Therefore it was necessary to solve each problem rapidly and at the correct time. A delay of one day reduces the amount of land opened up.

(vi) As for the problem of burdens on the refugees, we resolutely carried out the decisions of the government of the Border Region on treating them well. For three years we made no demands on them, and instead the government helped them solve all kinds of difficulties. This year the government cadres of the county, districts, and townships saved 10 *dan* of grain for issue to the refugees. While solving the problem of grain for refugees to eat, Third township in Central district made great efforts to reduce their burdens.

(4) Why did the refugees want to come to Yan'an?

(i) We have really solved the difficulties of refugees. The solution of the refugee food-grain problem in 1940 had a particularly wide influence. In Chuankou district alone 300 *dan* of grain was supplied. Therefore many more refugees came in the year 1941.

(ii) Although government calls had a great impact, the effect of the refugees themselves telling their own friends, relations and other social acquaintances of the good treatment they received was even greater. We found that very few refugees who came to us had refugee certificates issued by Suide sub-region. This was because they feared that after having accepted settling-in funds or registration cards from there, they would not be free or they would become public property. They preferred to get money through their own personal relationships.

(5) Opinions concerning future immigrant refugees.

(i) Get more to come by encouraging refugees to use their social connections.

(ii) The government at county and district levels should conscientiously solve problems for them.

(iii) The government of the Border Region should issue some grain and funds to help them, with repayment after autumn.

(iv) Persist in carrying out the decisions to treat refugees favourably.

HOW TO MOBILIZE LOAFERS TO TAKE PART IN PRODUCTION

(1) Statistical summary [given in Table 1.5].

Table 1.5   *Mobilization of loafers, 1937–42*

Year	Original number of loafers	Number joining in production	Number not yet taking part in production
1937	1,629	299	1,330
1938	1,246	578	668
1939	543	120	423
1940	359	175	184
1941	184	126	58
1942	145	40	105

Note:
The chief reason for the increase in loafers in 1942 was that in 1941 Jinpenwan was taken from Gulin county and placed under the administration of this county. According to statistics, that district had forty-three idlers.

Explanation:
(i) In Panlong district, a certain spirit medium beat his 'three mountains' knife[11] into a hoe. He told the masses he would not swindle people again and would work hard in future.
(ii) At Lijiaqu in Third township of Chuankou district, Hui San and Gao Wu were each given the task of opening up 6 mu of uncultivated land this spring. They completed this and even exceeded it by 2 mu. At Tianjiagelao in Fourth township, Yang Yingcheng was given the job of opening up 6 mu. He opened up 9 mu.
(iii) In Liulin district this year, seven men were reformed and joined in production. In Wuyang district twelve men were investigated. After a struggle, nine of them took part in production. In Fengfu district there were eight men. At Ganguyi in Yaodian district eight men were organized in two groups to go to Zhangjiakou to open up new land.
(iv) At Nanyigou of Third township in Fengfu district, Bai Fenyu was a shaman before 1936. By 1941 he had an ox and hired a man. He had 200 sheep and had become the village head. He paid 10.2 *dan* grain tax, 200 *jin* salt tax, and 500 *jin* hay tax. This year he has got another ox and hired a helper. He has expanded production and his prospects are very good.
(v) Because the government mobilized them to take part in production, the loafers of Panlong district said: 'If things go wrong this year gov-

[11] The 'three mountains' refer to three mythical islands where magic spirits are presumed to live.

ernment men will be even more strict with us'. For example, Li Dejin from Lijiabian in Fourth township used to smoke opium. This year he has opened up 6 mu of new land and also stopped smoking. In the whole district there were twenty-seven loafers. They have written guarantees that they will do well in production, and as a result twenty of them are very good.

(vi) At Liujiaping in Mudan district there is a man (name unknown) with extremely bright prospects now that the government has mobilized him to join-in production. Later he sought out one of the government personnel and treated him very well saying: 'The government was right to get us to take part in production'. Cao Yucheng from the same district used to be a loafer. He did not farm and he did not cut firewood. Winter and summer, wearing a ragged old cotton-padded jacket he would curl up on the cold *kang*.[12] Each day he would smoke one-fifth of an ounce [*er qian*] of opium. His wife and children cried from cold and hunger. After the revolution and educated by the government, he has become the production director of Fourth township. Everybody praises his method of work. He is a labour hero. Moreover he keeps a close watch on loafers. He forces them to make production plans. Every five days he goes up into the hills to supervise them. Under his direction Liu Guai and Yan Fenghe have each planted 24 mu of land this year.

(2) Our methods of mobilization are:

(i) Doing propaganda, educational, and persuasive work to get them to take part in production. Having got some grain their prospects improve.

(ii) The government gives them definite production tasks, such as opening up uncultivated land (see examples above). They are inspected at regular intervals. Moreover special people in the villages are designated to supervise their production.

(iii) Urging the masses to struggle against them, and to force them to join production. This year in the two villages, Jinpenhe and Yunshansi in Third township, Panlong district, production competitions were organized. In this situation, Chang Degong, a loafer in Jinpenhe, was forced by the villagers to go up into the hills to open up new land. He has opened up 3 mu. At the moment he is preparing to plant 15 mu.

(iv) Organizing the loafers in collective labour. The loafers are concentrated in the district town and organized into teams to open up new land. After they get rid of the opium-smoking habit, they can go home. The land opened up and farmed is given to whoever does the work.

(v) The government solved some of the loafers' production difficulties.

(3) Results.

The masses were very pleased that the government made the loafers take part in production. The masses opposed them very much because

---

[12] The brick-bed of north China, heated by a fire beneath it.

they did no work at all, paid no grain tax, and caused trouble every time there was mobilization work. As for the loafers themselves, after they obtained some real results from production, they realized that the government was acting for their betterment. The above examples clarify this point. As for those who were extremely stubborn and refused to change, some even running away when the government tried to mobilize them, on their return they joined in a little light productive labour. In this county no loafers have become bandits.

We have not referred to this report of the leading comrades of the Party and government of Yan'an county without purpose. The spirit of the comrades of Yan'an county is entirely the spirit of Bolsheviks. Their attitude is enthusiastic, and there is not the slightest passivity in their thoughts and in their actions. They are not at all afraid of difficulties, and are able vigorously and firmly to overcome them all. Look how responsible they are towards their work: 'In 1942 agricultural credit was given rather late. The earlier credit is given the sooner more land can be opened up!' 'It was necessary to solve each problem rapidly and at the correct time. A delay of one day reduces the amount of land opened up!' 'Determine the production plans of each peasant household.' 'The tight grasp of the leadership and the strict check-ups played a decisive role in the completion of the task.' How vastly different and how much better is this spirit than that of those timid people who draw back full of sighs when they meet difficulties, and of those who are not conscientious in their work and try to get by and neglect things! Imbued with such spirit, there is not one thing that the comrades of Yan'an did not handle realistically and practically. They have a full understanding of the feelings, needs, and concrete circumstances of all the people of Yan'an county. They are completely united with the masses. They carry out extremely good investigation and research, and thus they have learned the Marxist art of leading the masses. They are entirely without subjectivism, sectarianism, and the Party 'eight-legged essay'. How does this compare with those subjectivists who do not solve problems according to the demands of the masses but according to their own subjective imagination? And with those bureaucrats who do no investigation and research work at all and, though they work for many years, have no idea of what is going on beneath them? Is there not a world of difference between them? We hope all the comrades of the Border Region will have this spirit of the comrades of Yan'an, this attitude towards their work, this one-ness with the masses, this willingness to carry out investigation work, and thus also learn the Marxist art of leading the masses to overcome difficulties so as to make our work successful what-ever is undertaken. Quite a few of the comrades of the various counties of the Border Region are like or more or less like the comrades of Yan'an. We hope that the model experience of these comrades can quickly spread to all counties, districts, and town-ships.

The above is a summary of agricultural work in the Border Region in the past. What follows are the tasks for the year 1943.

The major demand on agriculture is to increase the produc-tion of grain and cotton (subsidiary undertakings will be discus-sed elsewhere). In the light of the present need for grain and cotton, and also in order to strive for some grain and cotton for export, it is still necessary for us to mobilize the peasant masses to increase the production of hulled grain by 200,000 *dan* and to increase the production of cotton by 1,600,000 *jin*. Is there any hope that this can be achieved? In the six years between 1937 and 1942, it is estimated that roughly 3 million *mu* of unculti-vated land was opened up and the production of grain increased by 500,000 *dan*. Well then, is it possible in the next few years once again on the basis of opening up new land and other methods to increase the production of grain by 400,000 *dan* equivalent to 200,000 *dan* of hulled grain? In the years between 1939 and 1942 the land planted to cotton exceeded 90,000 mu and the raw cotton produced reached 1,100,000 *jin*. Well then, in the next few years is it possible to increase the land planted to cotton by more than 100,000 *mu*, and the cotton produced by more than 1,600,000 *jin*?

We consider that all this is entirely possible.

If the peasants are able to increase the production of hulled grain by 200,000 *dan*, then even if they hand over 200,000 *dan* of grain tax as in 1941, they will still only have to give the govern-ment the amount of increase. They themselves will be able to keep an amount equal to the entire previous harvest. As for cotton, even if in future we levy some in tax, the peasants will still be able to keep the largest part of the harvest, and the problem of cotton cloth supply for the Border Region can be solved.

What are the policies which will effectively attain the above targets and not remain just empty words? According to our past experience the following eight policies must be implemented: (1) the reduction of rent and the reduction of interest rates; (2) an increase in the opening up of uncultivated land; (3) an increase in the planting of cotton; (4) not violating the agricultural seasons; (5) better adjustment in the use of labour power; (6) an increase in agricultural credit; (7) improvement in technical skill; (8) implementing progressive taxation. In what follows I shall deal with each of these eight points separately.

Our first agricultural policy is the reduction of rent and the reduction of interest rates. Approximately one-half of the 1,400,000 people of the Border Region have received a share of land. The remainder have not yet done so, such as those in the Suide-Mizhi special military area, Longdong sub-region, Fuxian county and many places in Sanbian sub-region and so forth. In these regions we should carry out the reduction of rent and interest rates in accordance with government decrees. This is an extremely important policy for increasing the peasants' enthusiasm for production. After rent and interest rates have been reduced, the peasants' burdens from the landlords are less and the amount they can keep themselves is increased. Thus their enthusiasm for production is greatly raised and they can produce more. The Northwest Bureau [Xibei Ju] has already made concrete arrangements with the Border Region Government over this policy and I will not speak more of it here.[13]

Our second agricultural policy is to increase the amount of uncultivated land opened up. Peasants in areas where there is a lot of uncultivated land consider that deep ploughing is not as good as opening up new land. We should therefore organize the peasants in the counties, districts, and townships where such land exists to develop it as a means of increasing the production

---

[13] The Northwest Bureau was a leading Party organ in the Border Region. It was headed by Gao Gang, one of the original leaders in the area before the Long March. Selden (1971), p. 205 argues that it was one of the bodies used by the Party to curb growing government bureaucracy.

of grain. Besides land freshly cultivated by the original households, we must mainly rely on encouraging immigrants to come
and develop unused land. At present the conditions are right for
getting immigrants. The various counties should do a large
amount of organizational work. According to circumstances
they should determine specific tasks for the new and old households separately. Like Yan'an county they should make specific
sowing and planting plans for each household. Such plans
should include both the opening up of new land and the planting of cultivated land. For 1943 the planned increase in production of grain for the entire Border Region has been fixed as
80,000 dan of hulled grain. This should be achieved through the
people and the troops opening new lands and improving
agricultural methods.

*Our third agricultural policy is to increase the planting of
cotton.* The entire Border Region needs 3 million jin of cotton. If
on average each mu of land can yield a net total of 20 jin of raw
cotton, we only need 150,000 mu of land for cotton. If each mu
can only yield a net total of 15 jin or even less, we shall need
200,000 mu. We should prepare our cotton land according to the
latter estimates. But because households planting cotton for the
first time lack experience and faith, even if we expand the area
planted to cotton, the harvest will not live up to expectations.
Therefore it is not possible to attain the full target for cotton
production in a single year and we should increase cotton land
by 56,000 mu in 1943. Together with the previous 94,000 mu,
the total will be 150,000 mu making it possible to increase
production to 2,250,000 jin. There is no problem over land and
seed for planting this area of cotton, but there is a great shortage
of cotton-ginning equipment. If each ginning machine can gin
60 jin of cotton per day on average, we need 300 machines in
order to be able to gin 3 million jin of cotton in half a year. In
1943 there will be 2,250,000 jin of cotton to be ginned. For this
we need more than 200 machines. However, at present there are
only a hundred or so broken and old machines of which only
fifty can be used every day. If we attempt to gin 2 million jin of
cotton on fifty machines we will need two whole years. Therefore solving the problem of ginning the cotton is a vitally necessary part of the policy of expanding the planting of cotton. A

further point is that up to the present the peasants of the Border Region have still not learned to press cotton-seed oil. With 2 million *jin* of cotton we will also get 4 million *jin* of cotton seed. Each 100 *jin* can produce 12 *jin* of cotton-seed oil. If we can solve the problem of pressing the oil, then the return to the peasants growing cotton will increase. Their enthusiasm for growing cotton will also rise. In relation to the above needs, in 1943 the government should do the following work to expand the planting of cotton. (1) Allocate the planting of cotton to peasant households with suitable land so as to make a total of 150,000 *mu*. Help the households planting cotton with seed, manure and techniques. Those who have difficulties with draught animals and implements should be given credit. (2) Construct cotton-ginning machines and spare parts, and supply them to the peasants planting cotton. Help them to repair old machines. At the same time organize them to buy cotton-ginning machines from outside areas, helping with credit. In these ways solve the problem of ginning the cotton. (3) Do research into methods of pressing cotton-seed oil so that the peasants planting cotton will be able to extract 480,000 *jin* of oil from the 4 million *jin* of seed (each *jin* is worth 15 *yuan*, a total value of 7,200,000 *yuan*). (4) Organize joint public and private cotton cooperatives to undertake work such as cotton-ginning, making up into bundles, selling, pressing oil and so forth. (5) Give rewards to peasants good at growing cotton and introduce good methods of planting cotton and ginning so as to increase the enthusiasm of the peasants growing cotton and to raise the amount and quality of the cotton.

Our fourth agricultural policy is not to violate the agricultural seasons. That is, in busy agricultural seasons we should allow the peasants to cease all meetings and mobilization work which is not related to agriculture. Under the present circumstances in the Shaan-Gan-Ning Border Region, in busy agricultural seasons we should stop all meetings and mobilization of the peasant masses outside of their agricultural work, so as to economize on labour and animal power, and let it all be used for agricultural production. Essential meetings and mobilization should be carried out during gaps in the work. The previous mistake of holding too many meetings and too much mobilization must be corrected.

Our fifth agricultural policy is better adjustment in the use of labour power. To this end there are the following methods: incentives to immigrants, mutual-aid labour, mobilization of women, mobilization of loafers, emphasizing support for families with kin serving as soldiers in the War of Resistance, granting leave of absence to take part in production, obtaining help from the troops, and so forth. All of these assist in adjusting the use of labour power.

As regards incentives to immigrants, we must rely on cooperation between the government and the people. The methods to be employed are as follows. (1) the Party and government of the Suide-Mizhi special military area should be responsible for organizing immigrants with a total of 5,000 labour powers to go to the directly administered counties to open up unused land. However, the basic principle must be voluntary participation, and all kinds of propaganda and organizational work should be done. (2) The government should set aside some grain for lending to immigrants who need help. It should also provide credit for agricultural implements and fully carry out preferential treatment by waiving grain tax for three years. (3) The old households should be encouraged to help the new households by lending grain, giving up some cultivated land, lending out cave houses, and so forth. In these loans the peasant doing the lending should be permitted to charge some interest, with the rate freely decided by the two parties. (4) Peasant households with a good basis should be organized to take on the poorest immigrants as tenants [huozhong]. The amount of rent should not be excessively low, so that the old households will be happy to take them on. (5) Immigrants from outside should be encouraged to come by old households who have contact with outside areas. Each county in the frontier areas should have a special person responsible for their reception. He should tell them about regions where there is land to be opened up so that they can go there and settle down. For example recently 600 refugees from Henan came to Longdong sub-region; they should be welcomed in this way.

Mutual-aid labour means that within one village or among several villages the peasant households not only plough and plant their land independently but in busy seasons also carry out mutual aid. For example, on a voluntary basis five, six, seven or eight households can become one group. Those that have labour power can supply labour power. Those that have animal power can supply animal power. Those that have a lot can supply a lot, those that have little can supply a little. In rotation and collectively they can plough, hoe, and harvest for each household in the group, and they can settle accounts in autumn. Work can be repaid by equal amounts of work. Those who supply more can receive supplementary wages from those who supply less, according to the wage rate of the village. This method is called mutual-aid labour. The mutual-aid cooperatives and ploughing teams previously set up throughout the Jiangxi Soviet were all organized according to this method. In villages with a large population, several small teams can join together into a mutual-aid cooperative. The teams have a team head and a deputy head. Cooperatives have a cooperative head and a deputy cooperative head. Adjustment in the use of labour can also take place between cooperatives. These, then, are the labour cooperatives of the peasant masses. They are extremely effective. Not only do they mean that peasant households which lack labour power can plant, hoe and harvest at the correct time, but also those households which do not lack labour power can, through collective labour, get even more profit from their planting, hoeing and harvesting. This method is entirely beneficial and has no drawbacks. We should promote it widely. The system of exchange-labour teams which some areas in the Border Region have already implemented is the same method. Each county should strive to organize mutual-aid cooperatives and greatly expand collective labour by the peasants. Apart from this, there are contract-labour teams. These are also welcomed by the peasants of the Border Region. The method is not one of mutual aid but a kind of hired-labour organization for the busy agricultural seasons. Several people or even more form a group and collectively work for the people who hire them. When they have finished working for one household they go to another. It is another method of adjusting the use of labour power. All areas should help those who come from outside to do contract labour by helping them to find work to do and so forth.

As for mobilizing women to take part in production, although many of the women of the Border Region have bound feet, they are still a large labour force second only to the men. They can take part in various kinds of supplementary agricultural work such as planting vegetables, sowing seeds, hoeing weeds, feeding livestock, taking food to the fields, drawing water, and gathering the harvest, etc. There are also some who can take part in basic labour. They have generally done these things in the past. In future we should spread propaganda and encouragement widely, stimulating their enthusiasm for labour so as to raise agricultural production. Comrades in the leading organs of Party and mass organizations for women have as yet not found the orientation for their work. They feel there is nothing that they can do. In fact their first task should be that of looking into and helping the women of the Border Region to play a wider role in productive labour, so that all those women who can take part in labour go to the production front and together with the men solve the great problem of how to increase production. There are still a large number of women in the Border Region who have not untied their bound feet. This is a great hindrance to labour and production. We should use the two methods of propaganda and compulsion so that within a few years we make them untie their bound feet. Henceforth no one is permitted to bind the feet of young girls, no matter who they are.

As for mobilizing loafers to take part in productive labour, we have already had some remarkable successes over the past few years. After the various counties did this work, the number of loafers greatly decreased. However, in those regions where they still exist we should use both persuasion and compulsion to mobilize all of them to go to the production front during 1943. The experience of Yan'an county in this work is good, Bolshevik experience. Mobilizing loafers to take part in production not only increases the labour force but also reduces the number of bad people doing bad things. It is supported by the people and strengthens social peace.

When emphasizing support for families with members working in the War of Resistance, we have in the past put support for families with civilian personnel in first place and support for families with kin serving as soldiers in the War of Resistance second. This is entirely wrong. Now we should reverse this and put support for families with kin serving as soldiers in the War of Resistance first. The system of substitute cultivation [*daigeng-zhi*] should first be applied conscientiously for those family dependants of soldiers in the army resisting Japan who lack labour power (making no distinction between our own army and friendly armies). Secondly it should be applied to those dependants of workers in the Party and government who truly lack labour power. In those areas where labour cooperatives [exchange-labour teams] have been successfully organized, the solution of this problem can be entrusted to the cooperative.

Granting leave of absence to take part in production means that in the busy agricultural seasons Party and government officials in the Border Region whose families have difficulties are each year permitted to return home on two occasions, each time for several days, so that they can take part in family-based agricultural production. The primary and secondary schools of the Border Region should also stop classes in the busy agricultural seasons, letting the students and local teachers return home to help production. This is another method of adjusting the use of labour.

The armed forces assisting in production means that each busy agricultural season the troops of the Border Region spend several days helping the peasants in the areas around where they are stationed with the ploughing, hoeing and harvesting. Moreover they do not receive any payment (they eat their own food). On the one hand this can help adjust the use of labour power, and on the other hand it can strengthen the relationship between the army and the people. The political work departments of the army should plan this work.

If all the above seven ways [listed on p. 90] of adjusting the use of labour power are well implemented, they will be of great help to agricultural production in the Border Region. Among them the most important is the mutual-aid cooperative, which should be realized generally throughout the whole Border Region.

Our sixth agricultural policy is to increase agricultural credit. In 1942 the government issued credit for draught animals, cotton-planting, water conservancy work and so forth. This was greatly appreciated by the peasants, and helped some of them to overcome their difficulties. One-third of the peasants of the Border Region lack draught animals and agricultural implements. This is an extremely important problem. If we want agriculture to develop, helping this huge number of peasant masses to solve their difficulties is a very important policy. One way of doing this is to increase agricultural credit. In 1942 under the sponsorship of the Border Region Bank, 1,580,000 yuan of credit for draught animals and agricultural implements was issued to 8,025 peasant households in the seven counties, Yan'an, Ganquan, Fuxian, Ansai, Zichang,[14] Gulin and Zhidan. Together with capital of more than 1,030,000 yuan amassed by the peasants themselves, this bought 2,672 draught animals, and 4,980 pieces of agricultural equipment. Over 100,000 mu of new land was opened up and grain production increased by an estimated 26,000-odd dan. In addition, the three counties Yanchang, Yanchuan and Gulin issued 1,530 yuan of credit for planting cotton and for cotton-seedlings. The area planted to cotton grew by over 51,000 mu and could produce an estimated increase of 870,000 jin of cotton. In view of the achievements through agricultural credit in 1942, a further 17 million yuan should be lent in 1943 in addition to re-lending the 3,110,000 yuan. Of this, 14 million yuan should be credit for agricultural implements and draught animals, and 3 million yuan should be for planting cotton. Based on the experience in issuing credit in 1942, methods for credit in 1943 should pay attention to the following points.

(1) Credit should be given in those regions which have a lot of unused land to new and old immigrants and old households of poor peasants who have labour power but lack implements, draught animals and grain, and to peasant households which have planted a lot of land but have no money with which to hire labour for hoeing.

(2) After trials by the Commodities Bureau [Wuzi Ju], we should introduce loans in kind, buying draught animals and suitable implements from outside or assisting peasant households themselves to purchase them. Only in this way can we truly increase the draught animals and agricultural implements in the Border

[14] Anding county was renamed Zichang in 1942 in honour of a fallen hero.

Region. Otherwise the peasants can only buy implements and animals from the rich peasants and landlords of the Border Region with their Border Region currency. This merely has the function of adjusting the ownership of animals and tools within the Border Region and does not increase the total stock of animals and implements.

(3) Agricultural credit for next year has already been increased. We should also alter the policy used this year of concentrating issue of credit in the counties around Yan'an. We should issue a suitable amount to the Sui-Mi, Longdong, Sanbian, and Guanzhong sub-regions. But this should not be done on an egalitarian basis. Instead it should be issued in a planned way to those counties, districts and peasant households where there is a lot of unused land, where the need for funds is greatest, and where there can be profitable production.

(4) The organization for issuing credit must be improved. That is to say, credit must be issued through district and township governments, and cooperatives which have the trust of the masses. Therefore the cadres of the districts and townships must be made to recognize the great significance of agricultural credit in the development of agriculture. They must not look upon it as a disaster-relief system. They may not adopt a policy of egalitarian distribution nor an irresponsible attitude.

(5) The formalities for issuing credit must be simple. Use the local methods for giving credit with which the peasants are already familiar. There is no need for formalities such as the 'letter of request for credit', etc.

(6) Of the total agricultural credit of 20,110,000 *yuan*, set aside 3 million *yuan* specially as credit for cotton and wheat seedlings. The households which borrow this can repay in kind after the cotton and wheat harvest. Although these funds are specified as funds for cotton and wheat seedlings, the peasants should be able to use them freely. Such credit is of mutual benefit to public and private interests. The government gets repayment in kind and the peasants can reduce exploitation through paying high interest rates on loans.

(7) The issue of credit should not violate the agricultural seasons. The Finance Department [*Caiting*] and the Border Region Bank should make rapid plans so as to issue half of the entire

total of credit before the end of the lunar year this year, that is about 10 million *yuan*.

Our seventh agricultural policy is to improve agricultural techniques. Improving techniques means carrying out research into things that are feasible, starting from the existing agricultural techniques and the peasants' production skills in the Border Region. The aim is to help the peasants improve the major processes in the production of grain and cotton and to increase production. Some improvements are very possible. We have already had quite a lot of experience. It is wrong to lack faith and enthusiasm on this point. However, there is no basis for boasting of the possibility of great improvement, or for considering that we can realize modernized, large-scale agricultural techniques in the Border Region.

How should we implement this policy? We consider that the following things should be done.

(1) We should build effective water conservancy projects. Jingbian provides an example. In Yangqiaopan, Changcheng district, Jingbian county there are 25,000 *mu* of land that can be irrigated. They have already irrigated 5,000 *mu*. In 1943 they want to carry out further construction. According to the Jingbian comrades, 1 *mu* of dry land only yields 1 *dou* of hulled grain. However, 1 *mu* of irrigated land can be planted three times per year. The first planting is spring wheat which yields 8 *dou*, equal to 4 *dou* of hulled grain. The second planting is black beans, yielding 4 *dou* equal to 2 *dou* of hulled grain. The final planting is turnips, yielding 2,000 *jin*. Each *jin* is worth 0.3 *yuan* and the total value is 600 *yuan*. On the basis of each *dou* of hulled grain being worth 150 *yuan*, this is the equivalent of 4 *dou* of hulled grain. These three things give a total equivalent of 1 *dan* of hulled grain. This is ten times the yield of dry land. Therefore the peasants of Jingbian often proudly say 'Plant wheat first and then black beans. The black bean forest contains turnips too'. The major problems in constructing irrigated land are those of the distribution of land rights, of mobilizing manpower, of organizational leadership, and of building ditches and dykes. If one of these four is not right then nothing can be achieved. In 1942 the comrades of Jingbian led the peasants to construct six dykes in Tuwan and Yangqiaopan, etc. After the

dykes they built ditches, channelling in the water to irrigate the land. First of all they solved the question of land rights by dividing the new irrigated land between landlords and peasants at ratios of 70 per cent to 30 per cent, 60 per cent to 40 per cent, or half and half. This aroused the enthusiasm of the peasant masses. According to the comrades from Jingbian: 'So long as the problem of land rights is solved, it is easy to call on the peasants. For example, we constructed ten irrigated areas. Over a hundred new households came in addition to the existing 200 peasant households and of these more than thirty came from other districts.' They also say:

'Government funds are very important in the construction of irrigated land. However we must mainly rely on the organization of manpower and on unutilized capital. In Jingbian we built 5,000 mu of irrigated land in 1942. Altogether we used 28,560 labour days, which is an average of 5.7 per mu. The total funds were 858,000 yuan. Of this 210,000 yuan came from public funds and 648,000 yuan from unutilized capital absorbed. Of course a large proportion of these resources was made up by the ordinary folk giving their labour instead of cash.'

As regards organization and leadership, the Jingbian comrades say:

'We adopted the following two methods of leadership when building irrigated land. First we organized water conservancy committees of three to five men from good peasants in the locality. These were responsible for balancing equitably the use of labour, tools, and so forth. However, it was often difficult for them to solve problems of property rights and water-use rights, hindering the implementation of water-conservation work. Therefore it was necessary to have a second method whereby the government delegated cadres to assist in leadership and to solve difficult disputes among the masses. Cadres from the Water Conservancy Bureau [Shuili Ju] and a further three delegated by the county government took partial control of construction at the ten sites.'

The comrades of Jingbian have also decided that in 1943 they will continue by constructing 4,000 mu of irrigated land in Yangqiaopan. However since there were originally only sixty-households there and in 1942 only about forty new households came in, the total of a hundred or so households still leaves a problem of labour power. They have therefore decided to appeal for a hundred households to come in 1943. At present they have already begun to dig out cave houses and to prepare dwellings. 'Settling a hundred immigrant households is a heavy task. Since most of them came from Hengshan and many will be refugees, they will need a lot of credit if we are to succeed. If the immigrants arrive, together with the labour power already in the area there will be no difficulty in constructing 4,000 mu in 1943.' As well as this the comrades of Jingbian have also built a kind of 'water-logged land' [shuimandi]. Water-logged lands are 'large pieces of flat land surrounded on three sides by high mountains and on the fourth side by a deep gully [tian gou]. Some are 2,000 to 3,000 mu and some are 200 to 300 mu. The soil of such land is very good but on top of it is piled sand and gravel which obstructs the seedlings and spoils the quality of the soil'. The method of constructing water-logged land is 'to build a solid dyke along the side of the gully on top of which sand willows [shaliu] and pea-trees [ningtiaozi] (in winter this supplies food for the sheep) are planted. This dyke prevents the water that runs off the mountains during the course of the year from flowing away through the gully. It all lies on the land. The mud is very thick. It is extremely fertile and has a high water-content. It is very good for planting crops. Furthermore, each year the area expands and the mountain gullies become flat land. Thus the productive area is increased'. The yield of this water-logged land is more than double that of dry land. 'Five mu [15] of dry land yields 1 dan of grain but 5 mu of water-logged land can yield 2 or 3 dan.' The comrades of Jingbian only discovered how to build this water-logged land during the mobilization for the spring ploughing in 1942. Therefore it has as yet only been tried out in two places totalling 1,000 mu. They are preparing to construct such lands in a good many places in 1943 and the total area will be over 13,000 mu. They say 'In the entire county from 50,000 to 60,000 mu of water-logged land can be built'. I have given the example of Jingbian in detail to prove that the case for building water conservancy works is far from hopeless. Conditions for doing so exist in several places. In particular the conscientious and practical spirit of the comrades of Jingbian provides an

[15] The term 'shang' is used but Mao supplies the following definition: 'In the Yan'an area of the Border Region each shang is equal to 3 mu, but in the Jingbian area each shang is equal to 5 mu'.

effective model for the various counties. Although the water-conservancy conditions in other counties cannot be the same as those in Jingbian, by relying on the leadership of the Party and government and the efforts of the people some water conservancy can be started in those places where conditions are really right. In 1943 the government should set aside 2 million *yuan* as funds for carrying out water conservancy works in the Yangqiao-pan area of Jingbian, the Huluhe area of Fuxian and so forth.

(2) We should popularize the use of superior-quality seeds. If we have good seeds we can get a bigger harvest even without increasing labour and manure. For example the Guanghua agricultural station has already successfully tried out the 'wolf's tail' seed. It has a high yield, is resistant to insects and birds, and can be planted anywhere. Their sweet-potato yield is also higher than average. We should encourage the peasants to plant them. First each county should select one or two districts and order some peasants to carry out tests. If they find the soil and climate suitable, then such seeds can be popularized so as to increase production.

(3) We should encourage the opening up of new land and the turning over of the earth during autumn, as this can reduce insect pests and promote the aeration of the soil. It can also conserve the water content and increase the harvest of the following year.

(4) After popularizing the organization of mutual-aid cooperatives, we should encourage the peasants to increase the number of times they hoe weeds. The purpose of hoeing weeds is not only to get rid of weeds and to help the seedlings, but also to conserve water and resist drought. If we increase the number of times we undertake hoeing, we can increase the amount of harvest even if we do not use much manure.

(5) In the summer and winter of 1943 the five sub-regions should separately hold exhibitions organized by the Reconstruction Department [*Jianting*] and five special offices [*zhuanshu*]. In the light of the experience of the two previous agricultural exhibitions in the Border Region, we should improve the layout, introduce and promote the achievements of model-peasants, and popularize an agricultural production movement in the labour style and skills of Wu Manyou. In 1943 the agricultural exhibi-

tions of the sub-regions should include the achievements of the troops, the official organizations and schools in agricultural production. This will encourage their agricultural production and will also promote unity between the troops and the people.

(6) In 1943 the *Liberation Daily* and *Border Region Masses Daily* should widely promote the Wu Manyou production movement so that many more Wu Manyous will be created within the five sub-regions.

(7) The primary and secondary schools of the Border Region should run general agricultural knowledge classes and edit textbooks for winter study containing practical information on Border Region agriculture with the aim of improving agriculture and increasing production.

(8) The Reconstruction Department should call a meeting of experts to get down to research on the 'willow-root' water which flows from the hilltops, so as to deal with it in a scientific manner and to prevent people from contracting 'limping sickness' after drinking it.[16] If this problem can be solved then much fertile land in the neighbourhood of the hills can be put under the plough and become good arable land.

Our eighth agricultural policy is to implement progressive agricultural taxation. In the past agricultural taxation was in the form of national salvation grain tax. Although it was levied on progressive principles, the amount levied each year was not standard. The amount levied per family varied from year to year. In 1941 there were cases of taxes being apportioned out [*tanpai*]. Although an assessment method [*pingyizhi*] was instituted in 1942 as being more equitable, there were still inequalities. The most important failing was that the amount of tax was not fixed. This dampened the enthusiasm of the peasants for production. We propose that in 1943 the government should examine and register the land held by the people, and thereby construct a simple progressive agricultural tax. The amount of tax should be decided according to the amount of land, its quality, and so forth. In this way the peasants will be able to calculate the amount of tax themselves according to the amount and quality of the land they farm. Once the peasants can do this, they can work

[16] I am indebted to D. Holm of the Contemporary China Institute for bringing the existence of this disease to my attention. See Foreman (1945), pp. 48–9.

out the ratio between income and expenditure for the family for the entire year. They can then set-to and produce with greater enthusiasm for production. This will guarantee an increase in the production of grain. Moreover, inequalities will not arise when the government levies the tax. After carrying out the preparatory work in 1943, we can implement progressive taxation in 1944. Counties where preparation is completed early, can carry it out on a trial basis in 1943.

Reduction of rent and of interest rates, an increase in opening up new lands, popularizing the planting of cotton, not violating agricultural seasons, better adjustment in the use of labour power, an increase in agricultural credit, improvements of agricultural techniques, and preparation for implementing a progressive tax – these eight items are the effective agricultural policies which we can and must carry out in 1943. With the exception of the progressive tax for which we can make preparations and which can be tried out in a few counties, the other seven items should be implemented immediately. Many of them should commence during the winter of 1942. Otherwise the time will be lost and they will become empty words.

The above is a summary of our work as regards agriculture in the private sector and our strategy for 1943. What follows is a discussion of closely related agricultural subsidiary undertakings such as animal husbandry and handicrafts.

3

ON THE DEVELOPMENT OF ANIMAL HUSBANDRY

The three major subsidiary undertakings of the peasants of the Border Region are animal husbandry, salt transport, and textiles. It is well known that the breeding of cows and donkeys plays a decisive role in agriculture and salt transport. The breeding of sheep is closely related to the supply of bedding and clothing. Last year the peasants of the Border Region harvested more than 1 million *jin* of wool. Including sheep exported the estimated value was more than 20 million *yuan*, which is proof of the importance of sheep. The greatest enemies of livestock are the many diseases and the lack of fodder. If we do not solve these two problems, there can be no development. In the first place the destructive power of disease is very great. For example in the spring of 1941, more than 20,000 sheep died in an epidemic in Jingbian. In 1942 more than 16,000 died of the same cause in Dingbian. In the summer of 1941, more than 500 cows died of cattle plague in Yan'an. In the summer and autumn of 1942, 574 cows died in Zhidan. This shows how disease is the great enemy of the livestock of the Border Region. Secondly, the lack of fodder also greatly hinders the raising of livestock. In the spring of 1941 when 20,000 sheep died in Jingbian, most of the 30,000 lambs also died. Besides the epidemic, an important factor was the lack of fodder. At the same time over 2,000 cows and horses died of hunger there. Another keenly-felt difficulty in recent years is the lack of fodder supplies on salt-transport routes, which greatly hinders the transport of salt.

Our task is to protect livestock and increase breeding. In order to attain these goals we should implement the following policies.

Prevention of disease. The important thing here is for the

county and district governments to call meetings of local vet-
erinarians and old experienced peasants to do research into
simple methods of preventing and curing animal diseases, and
to encourage the use of these methods among peasant families
with livestock. This is a very simple thing to effect. Secondly,
the Reconstruction Department should order its agricultural
station to increase veterinary equipment, to do research into
animal diseases in the Border Region, to produce large amounts
of serum and vaccine, and to propagate and implement effective
methods of prevention and cure.

Popularize the planting of grass for animal pasture. Most of
the animals of the Border Region are put out to pasture. Where
the pasture is not good, disease easily arises. Therefore we
should widely promote the planting of alfalfa [musu], particularly on and near the salt-transport routes. This will benefit both
the transport of salt and the development of animal husbandry.
In 1942 the government originally planned to plant 30,000 mu of
alfalfa, but ultimately only 23,000 mu were planted because
there were not enough seeds. In 1943 the county governments
should transport more seeds from Guanzhong and issue them to
the peasants in areas where planting is planned. They should
also encourage the peasants to buy some themselves. In addition
they should mobilize the peasants to cut large quantities of grass
in the autumn and to store it up for winter use. This will not only
avoid illness induced by animals eating cold grass [sic], but also
stop the peasants from selling animals because of lack of winter
fodder. We should look to the experience of Jingbian in this
respect. Warned by the great loss of livestock in the spring of
1941, the comrades in Jingbian have done much work in the past
two years. They have appealed to the peasants to plant alfalfa,
create fields for pasture, cut autumn grass, plant willow trees,
and dig up grass roots as means of providing fodder. First of all,
they called upon the peasants to plant over 2,000 mu of alfalfa in
1942. Most of the seed was issued by the government, and the
peasants were very enthusiastic. They are once again preparing
to issue some credit for seeds to the peasants in 1943, and they
are specially calling upon the peasants themselves to prepare
seeds. As a way of encouraging them to plant large amounts of
alfalfa, they are giving rewards to those who do very well.

Secondly, they prepared more than 4,000 mu of pasture fields in 1942. The grass on this pasture land is mainly reed grass [luwei]. This flourishes in the ponds and large marshes in the desert land bordering on Mongolia. Each mu yields more than 500 jin. The pasture fields that existed before the revolution were later destroyed, and the cows and sheep wandered around at will. Now they are mobilizing the masses to restore them. It does not take a lot of labour, and cutting the grasses after autumn prepares for winter use. Thirdly, in the mountainous areas of Jingbian there is a lot of reed grass, white grass [baicao], bing grass [bingcao], desert rushes, and so forth. These are of great help for the livestock, if they are harvested in autumn. In 1941 the masses were organized to gather 5 million jin. In 1942 they again mobilized each man to cut 100 jin. As yet they have not worked out the latter total. Fourthly, they encouraged the masses to plant willow-trees, sand-willows, and pea-trees. The leaves and twigs can be fed to camels and sheep, which is another way of providing fodder. At the same time this supplies fuel which pleases the masses. The duty of the government is to supply seeds and encourage planting. Fifthly, in Jingbian the animals eat both the leaves and the roots of the white grass and bing grass. During spring ploughing the strongest men in Jingbian plough the land in the morning, dig-up roots in the afternoon, and feed the livestock in the evening. The women and children spend the whole day digging-up roots. Each person can dig-up more than 100 jin, and this plays an important part in the supply of fodder. However, the government must make good arrangements since, as there are many people digging, there are arguments over land rights. The landless refugees make it even more difficult. According to the Jingbian comrades:

'With these methods we solved many problems for the people. Of course the grass grew well in 1942 because there was a good rainfall. However, animal husbandry also developed because of the above five methods for providing fodder. In 1942 over 60,000 lambs survived throughout the county and there were very few deaths. With the exception of a few areas, there was a great reduction in the loss through disease of fully-grown sheep, and cows, donkeys, horses and so forth. Excluding sheep, the livestock of Jingbian requires 30 million jin of fodder per year. We can get at least 10 million jin with the above five methods.'

Fodder is a life-and-death question for livestock. We hope that the comrades in the various counties will make a plan for fodder in 1943.

Ban the slaughter and export of female animals. The slaughter of all cattle is forbidden and old cattle can only be killed after inspection.

Improve animal breeds. We should investigate experience in cross-breeding, select good breeds of donkeys and sheep, and popularize them among the people. This should be done first of all in Ganquan and Yan'an and then spread to other counties. Besides this the government should purchase *tanyang* sheep[1] from Yanchi. These should be issued for breeding to peasant families with many sheep. Each *tanyang* ram can be mated with twenty ewes. The wool of this sheep is extremely fine and soft, and each sheep yields 2 *jin* per year.

If we can conscientiously implement the above methods, there can be even greater expansion of livestock in the Border Region. I hope the Reconstruction Department and the comrades in the various counties will pay attention to this.

[1] A description of the qualities of this fat-tailed sheep can be found in H. Epstein, *Domestic Animals of China* (Commonwealth Agricultural Bureau, Farnham Royal, Bucks, 1969), p. 40.

4

ON THE DEVELOPMENT OF HANDICRAFTS

Handicrafts in the Border Region exist in two forms. The majority are subsidiary family undertakings and a proportion are independent handicrafts. The largest is the spinning and weaving undertaken by women. However, for many years past a large proportion of local yarn and local cloth has been displaced by foreign yarn and foreign cloth. Only recently, because of our encouragement, has there been some resurgence. Even so the peasants of the Border Region still want to take their surplus products, skins, and salt-transport trade to outside regions in exchange for large amounts of foreign yarn and foreign cloth. Their own spinning and weaving industry is still far from sufficient to supply their own needs. I shall therefore take textiles as the key popular handicraft for discussion here. In addition I shall deal with silk and oil-pressing, ignoring others for the moment.

SPINNING AND WEAVING

The people, the troops, and official personnel need 250,000 bolts of coarse cloth per year (each bolt is 2 feet 4 inches wide and 100 feet long [Chinese measurement]).[1] Of this, the amount required by the troops and official personnel is roughly 50,000 bolts, and that by the people 200,000 bolts. What is the present supply? The seven publicly-run textile mills produce approximately 11,000 bolts per year. The seven large and small textile cooperatives run by the people produce roughly 18,000 bolts per year. There are no statistics for the amount of local cloth pro-

[1] According to Selden (1971), p. 256, this was equivalent to 120 by 3 English feet.

duced by the women at home, but it is estimated to be around 30,000 bolts per year. Public and private annual production totals 100,000 bolts,[2] 150,000 bolts less that the amount needed. That is easy to say, we can already supply 40 per cent of our needs, which is a great achievement. But we are still 60 per cent short, and meeting this is our future task. This task is very great, and we shall need several years to complete it. But it can be done if we rely on, improve and expand the existing textile enterprises run by the government and by the people. If we have the raw cotton, we can in a planned way encourage the women to spin yarn and to weave cloth made half of local yarn and half of foreign yarn. Gradually we can reduce the import of foreign yarn, until eventually we reach the position where we use only our own yarn to weave cloth. In this way we can solve the problem.

As regards weaving, the responsibility rests first with the publicly-run mills. In 1942 publicly-run textile mills were capable of producing 11,000 bolts of cloth. This could supply almost half [sic] of the needs of the troops and official personnel. In a few more years we can be completely self-sufficient. Second, we must encourage women to weave cloth as a popular industry. In the Suide sub-region the women can already produce more than 30,000 bolts per year. However, the widths and lengths are not uniform. The people do not like to buy it. They still prefer imported cloth. If improvements can be made, there are good prospects for increasing the production of cloth. Third, the people's cooperatives can already produce 18,000 bolts per year. This can be further developed. We must rely on the combination of these three forms to provide the cloth required by the Border Region. However in the first place the greatest problem is the supply of yarn. At 12 *jin* of yarn per bolt, we need 3 million

[2] The figures quoted by Mao here are very different to those compiled by Selden (1971), p. 256 from other sources. For 1942 Selden gives sixteen public mills, producing 14,565 bolts, twenty-seven cooperatives producing 4,500 bolts, fifty private mills producing 12,000 bolts and home production at 14,158 bolts, a total of 45,223 bolts. Mao's figures in the following discussion often appear contradictory. This may be due to printing errors or to changes in definitions. In Chapter 5, below, p. 114, Mao refers to twenty-seven textile cooperatives and in Chapter 7, p. 157, to seven mills run by systems directly controlled by the Central Committee.

jin to weave 250,000 bolts of coarse cloth entirely from local yarn. If we use a mixture of half local yarn and half foreign yarn, we will need 1,500,000 jin of local yarn and 150,000 bundles of foreign yarn. At present the cloth woven by publicly-run mills and the people's cooperatives is made from this mixture of half local and half foreign yarn. However, there is still not enough local yarn. We must greatly expand the amount of spinning done by the people, and improve the quality of the yarn. Therefore it is extremely important for the Border Region to gradually expand handicraft spinning and weaving among the people, to increase the quantity, and to improve the quality.

How should we gradually solve these problems? In the light of past experience, we propose the following methods.

(1) First we should reorganize and expand spinning and weaving among the people in the counties of the Suide special military area. The way to do this is, under the direction of the special office of the military area, to unite the efforts of the Commodities Bureau and the Daguang Yarn Factory of 359 Brigade, issuing raw cotton to women and ordering them to produce more local yarn to supply the yarn needs of the publicly-run cloth factories. This method was effectively implemented in 1942. It should be continued and expanded in 1943. Apart from supplying yarn to the publicly-run cloth factories, the people of the special military area may weave cloth themselves. The Commodities Bureau can determine measurements and quality, and guarantee a market. That is, the cloth can be purchased by the Commodities Bureau either for its own use or for selling among the people. Next, the government should invest 1 million yuan in order to increase the quantity of local yarn. Based on the experience of the Southern District Cooperative of Yan'an county which organized spinning by women in 800 households, lending funds to 3,000 households in Yan'an and Ansai will increase the number of spinning-machines in the two counties by 3,000 in 1943. Organizing spinning by women in 1,000 households in Qingyang and Quzi counties will increase the number of spinning-machines by 1,000. These credit funds can be handled by the Commodities Bureau, which can issue raw cotton and spinning-machines. It can purchase the local yarn produced to supply the needs of the publicly-run factories. Next, in order to

increase cloth production the government should invest a further 1 million *yuan* either as loans or as share capital in the existing cloth-weaving cooperatives run by the people as a means of expanding their undertakings.

Here we should consider the plan for Yan'an county. In their *Plan for Production and Construction in 1943*, the comrades in Yan'an say:

In 1943 we shall increase the number of women able to spin and weave by 4,000. Estimating that they will be able to spin 18 *jin* of yarn each in a year (1½ *jin* per month), this gives a total of 72,000 *jin*. In addition, there were already 1,000 women able to spin in 1942. Each year one of these can spin 20 *jin*, giving a total of 20,000 *jin*. The two groups can together spin 92,000 *jin*, which can be woven into 8,363.6 bolts of cloth. However, this is still 4,886.4 bolts short of our needs. We plan to solve this problem within two or three years, and to achieve complete self-sufficiency. The population of this county is 64,000 (excluding the city of Yan'an). Of these, 42,000 are adults. Each adult needs one-quarter of a bolt of coarse cloth per year (a suit of plain clothes requires 11 feet of cloth and half a suit of padded clothes requires 14 feet of cloth, a total of 25 feet: each bolt of coarse cloth is 100 feet long). Their total requirement is therefore 10,500 bolts. The 22,000 young people each need half the quantity of cloth required by an adult. A bolt of cloth is enough for eight and their total requirement is 2,750 bolts. The annual requirement for the whole county is thus 13,250 bolts.

The 92,000 *jin* of yarn spun in 1943 will be woven into 8,363.6 bolts of coarse cloth. This requires 56 looms (each loom can weave 150 bolts of coarse cloth per year). In 1942 there were twelve looms in the villages and factories of this county. Thus we must expand the number in the village by forty-four during 1943 using the cooperative structure. There are three methods for doing this. The first is investment (i) in incentive awards to encourage women to spin, 50,000 *yuan* (ii) in producing 5,000 *jin* of raw cotton at 100 *yuan* per *jin*, 500,000 *yuan*, and (iii) in expenses for spinning- and weaving-equipment, 1,000 spinning-wheels at 100 *yuan* each, 100,000 *yuan*, and 44 looms at 1,000 *yuan* each, 44,000 *yuan*. The total required for the above items is 694,000 *yuan*. Second, looms in the villages should be set up by the peasants organizing themselves into partnerships. The government can help them overcome their difficulties by training skilled workers, or by investing capital for looms and so forth. Third, for every 2 *jin* of raw cotton issued, 1 *jin* of yarn should be collected. The cotton cloth woven in the villages may be used by the peasants themselves. The Gaodan Yarn Spinning Factory should play the leading role in encouraging women to spin, and in training workers.

This plan by the comrades in Yan'an is really worth looking at. If the people of Yan'an, who lack experience of spinning and weaving, are able with the encouragement of the Party and government to become fully self-sufficient in yarn and cloth within two or three years, other counties without experience should also be able to solve the problem within a similar or slightly longer period. We hope that the comrades in the various counties will all make such a plan. As for the various counties where the peasants have experience, such as the special military area, the problem should be solved even more easily. According to the calculations of the comrades in Yan'an, adults make up two-thirds of the population and children one-third. One bolt of cloth is enough for four adults or eight children. Therefore, the yearly cloth requirement for the 1,400,000 population of the Border Region is not 200,000 bolts but 337,500. According to the opinions of the comrades in Yan'an a large quantity like this can be provided within two or three years. In sum, by relying on the masses setting-to and on the leadership of the Party and the government any difficulty can be overcome.

(2) The Reconstruction Department should do research into the people's experiences in spinning in order to improve the quality of local yarn so as to prepare to produce Border Region cloth entirely from local yarn, gradually reducing and ultimately stopping the import of foreign yarn. If the quality of yarn cannot be improved then we cannot suspend dealings in foreign yarn.

(3) Improve the woollen goods made by the publicly-run factories. Using woollen goods in place of some of the cotton clothing and bedding used by the army is a way of reducing the consumption of cotton cloth.

(4) In 1943 official personnel should set a personal example and wear local cloth without exception. At the same time they should encourage the people to use more local cloth and less foreign cloth. According to the situation in the development of local cloth, the Commodities Bureau can gradually limit the import of foreign cloth.

The above methods will help us gradually to solve the great problem of self-sufficiency in cotton cloth. Although it can only be done gradually, it is nevertheless entirely possible. We must resolutely implement all methods for doing so.

COTTON-SEED OIL

In 1942 the peasants of the counties planting cotton harvested around 3 million *jin* of cotton seeds capable of giving 360,000 *jin* of oil, and, with the expansion in cotton-planting, from 5 to 6 million *jin* of seed can be obtained next year which can further increase the quantity of oil. We should prevent all this being wasted. Cotton-seed oil is edible but the peasants of the Border Region are still not accustomed to it. If the government does not promote it, they will not extract the oil. Therefore the government of the Border Region should invest 300,000 *yuan* and, through the governments of the counties where cotton is planted, encourage the peasants to experiment with pressing cotton-seed oil. After the experiments succeed, it can be widely promoted. The oil can be bought by the government. This will not only provide edible oil but also at present oil prices of 30 *yuan* per *jin* give the peasants an income of 10,800,000 *yuan* from 360,000 *jin* of oil.

SILK

In the counties of Suide, Qingjian, Anding, Yanchuan, Gulin and so forth many peasants rear silkworms. It is a relatively large subsidiary undertaking. For example, in Anding alone there were 3,585 peasant households rearing silkworms during 1942. They harvested 23,662 *jin* of silkworm cocoons, at a value of 600,000 *yuan*.

Our sewing and repair industry needs silk thread and our woollen-blanket industry needs silk edging. We can also use silk thread for the woof when weaving cotton cloth as a means of reducing the import of foreign yarn. Therefore, we should develop the silk production of the Border Region. The way to do this is for the government to issue 300,000 *yuan* in credit to the peasant families to expand the rearing of silkworms. Credit should be given especially to those peasant households which have a good record in rearing silkworms. Moreover, the Commodities Bureau should buy the peasants' silk through the local cooperatives and order woven silk articles from the peasants in order to promote the expansion of the silk industry.

The total investment in the above three undertakings, spinning and weaving, oil-pressing, and silk, is 2,600,000 *yuan* (yarn spinning 1 million, cloth-weaving 1 million, oil-pressing 300,000 and silk 300,000). Although these funds are not great, they can stimulate the people to progress a little in solving the urgent needs of the moment. In 1943 when we have even more experience, we should consider increasing the amount of capital. Spinning and weaving are particularly important. Unless the people set-to and the public sector helps, the problem cannot be solved as a whole.

Here I have only taken up spinning and weaving, oil-pressing, and silk. Other items have not been mentioned. The counties can, according to actual circumstances, do research into handicrafts which are related to the people's economy and which need stimulus from the Party and the government, and they can make their own plans.

5

ON THE DEVELOPMENT OF
COOPERATIVES

There were already cooperatives in the Border Region during the civil-war period. Since the War of Resistance began, the Border Region government has continued to promote them, and after five-and-a-half years of hard effort they have gradually expanded.

In the four years from 1937 to 1941 the number of consumer cooperatives increased from 130 to 155 and the number of cooperative members from 57,847 to 140,218. The share capital grew from 55,525 *yuan* to 693,071 *yuan*. The value of sales increased from 261,189 *yuan* to more than 6,008,000 *yuan*. Profits rose from 4,800 *yuan* to over 1,020,000 *yuan*, and the public accumulation fund [*gongjijin*] increased from 3,500 *yuan* to over 173,000 *yuan*.

If we compare the October 1942 Statistics for the nineteen county capitals with those of 1941, the number of cooperative members has increased from 97,297 to 115,899. The share capital has risen abruptly from over 712,900 *yuan* to more than 6 million *yuan*, and the profit has also grown from 858,000 *yuan* to more than 3,398,000 *yuan*.

The largest amount of share capital owned by individual members of consumer cooperatives is around 10,000 *yuan* and the lowest is around 4 or 5 *yuan*.

The distribution of consumer cooperatives at the end of 1941 was as follows: Yan'an, twenty-eight; Ansai, twelve; Yanchang, eight; Gulin, eight; Dingbian, eight; Qingyang, Huachi, Quzi and Yanchuan, seven each; Anding, Fuxian and Wuqi, six each; Ganquan, Jingbian and Heshui, five each; Yan'an city and Mizhi, four each; and Suide, two. There are still no statistics for the other counties.

Turning to producer cooperatives, ten were established in 1939 with the support of the government and the assistance of the northwest office of the Chinese Industrial Cooperative [Gonghe].[1] Thereafter some consumer cooperatives with large amounts of capital also ran producer cooperatives. By October 1942 the number of producer cooperatives had increased from ten to fifty. The number of employees engaged in production had increased from 199 to 563. Share capital had grown from 11,130 yuan to 2,491,600 yuan, and the total value of monthly production from 60,000 yuan to over 2,300,000 yuan.

According to this year's statistics the distribution of producer cooperatives is as follows: Suide, sixteen; Yan'an, seven; Gulin, five; Yanchang, five; Yanchuan, five; Ganquan, three; Ansai, three; Jingbian, two; Qingyang, one; Jiaxian, one; Mizhi, one; Anding, one.

Among the fifty producer cooperatives there are twenty-seven large and small textile cooperatives, thirteen in Suide, four in Yan'an, two in Gulin, and one each in Ganquan, Fuxian, Yanchang, Yanchuan, Ansai, Anding, Jiaxian and Mizhi. Altogether they employ 497 people and their share capital is 1,700,000 yuan. Six have twenty-five or more employees, the rest ranging from three to over ten. If these twenty-seven cooperatives were working at full capacity, they could produce 30,000 bolts of cloth annually (each bolt 100 feet) [Chinese measurement]. At the moment they are only producing around 22,000 bolts, 6,000 woven blankets, 4,152 dozen woollen towels, and 8,400 dozen pairs of woven socks.

There are five dyeing cooperatives, two in Yanchuan, two in Suide, and one in Yanchang. They employ a total of thirteen people, their share capital is 128,000 yuan, and each year they can dye over 7,000 bolts of cloth. There are five producer cooperatives pressing cotton-seed oil. Of these, two are in Gulin, two in Jingbian, and one in Yanchang. They employ a total of nineteen people, their share capital is 245,000 yuan, and each

---

[1] A description of Gonghe can be found in E. Snow, Scorched Earth (Gollancz, 1940), Volume 2, pp. 213–27 and pp. 309–16. Impressions of the work done by the Northwest Office during this period can be found in Rewi Alley, Fruition: The Story of George Alwin Hogg (Caxton Press, Christchurch, New Zealand, 1967).

year they can press 10,000 *jin* of cotton-seed oil. There are nine flour mills, two each in Ansai, Ganquan, Yanchang, Yanchuan and one in Gulin. They employ a total of twenty-four people and their share capital is 262,000 *yuan*. There are four blanket-making cooperatives, two in Yan'an, one in Qingyang, and one in Suide. They employ a total of forty-two people and their share capital is 152,000 *yuan*. Each year they can produce 7,600 blankets. There is one pottery cooperative in Yan'an county. It employs seven men, its share capital is 3,000 *yuan*, and each year it produces six kiln-loads of pottery.

The above statistics show us that both consumer and producer cooperatives have expanded greatly in terms of membership, share capital, profit and undertakings. However, this development has been uneven. In the past five years it has gone through three stages. Moreover, qualitative development only began to advance rapidly during 1942. Before 1939, cooperatives everywhere were based upon share capital from the government with the addition of some share capital assessed from the masses. At this time their nature was basically that of publicly-run enterprises and for the most part they became shops publicly-run by the county and district governments. Cooperative enterprise was not facing the masses, but was chiefly facing the government. It was providing funds for the government and all decisions were taken by the government. This was the first stage. After 1939, the slogan 'Popularize the Cooperatives' was put forward. However, most places still used the old method of assessing share capital from the masses to carry out this so-called 'popularization'. Thus the masses still regarded the cooperatives as a burden, assessed upon them and not as something of their own. Cooperative personnel were still the same official personnel. They ordered the masses to do substitute farmwork on their land on their behalf. The masses could not see the great benefits of the cooperatives for themselves and, on the contrary, considered that the cooperatives increased the labour burden they had to bear. After 1940, the duty of all the local governments to achieve self-sufficiency in production was increased. Thereafter the large shareholders in many cooperatives were not the people but government organs. It was thus even more difficult for the cooperatives to give due consideration to the interests of the masses. This was the second stage. It was only in January 1942 that the Reconstruction Department put forward the strategy of 'overcome the desire to monopolize everything, implement the policy of the people in control and officials as helpers', based on the experience of the Southern District Cooperative of Yan'an county. It was only by implementing this strategy that cooperatives everywhere did away with the method of levying shares by assessment, and gradually built up close relations with the masses and experience in being concerned for the interests of the masses. Thus, in merely ten months the share capital has risen sharply by more than 5 million *yuan*, and undertakings have also expanded. This has played a great role in organizing the economic strength of the people, reducing middleman exploitation, and developing the people's economy. This is the third stage. It is only in this stage that the cooperatives of the Border Region have in general begun to follow the right path.

The above outlines the path of development of most cooperatives. However, there have been exceptions. For example the Southern District Cooperative of Yan'an county got on to the right path somewhat earlier. Through several years of hard experience, this cooperative has become a model cooperative truly supported by the people. During 1942 cooperatives from the counties of Suide, Anding, Ansai, Ganquan, Yanchang, Wuqi, etc. have advanced by studying this model cooperative.

What, then, are the special features of the Southern District Cooperative? It has the following good points.
(1) It has smashed dogmatism and formulism in cooperatives, and it does not cling to old ways and regulations. The Southern District Cooperative began as a consumer cooperative. However, its undertakings have extended into every aspect of the economic life of all the people of Southern district. It does not just manage consumer undertakings but handles supply and distribution, transport, production and credit. It has organized six producer-cooperatives for textiles, oil-pressing, blanket manufacture and so forth, and one transport team with more than a hundred animals. It has become a comprehensive cooperative. It does not concentrate on the percentage of income

that should be devoted to the cooperative's own public accumulation fund and public welfare fund [gongyijin], but strives to share out its profits to the members. It does not place a limit on the share dividend and each member receives a return on his shares regardless of the number held. It does not limit the right of members to dispose of their shares, and each member has the freedom to withdraw his shareholding at any time. Nor does it limit the nature of the membership. People from all social strata can join. (Since Yan'an is an area that has gone through land revolution, allowing people from all classes to join is no hindrance to the leadership of the cooperative by the Communist Party.) They can also belong to the organs of the cooperative. Moreover, it is not necessary to have ready cash to become a shareholder. Before the cooperative won complete confidence among the masses, it permitted them to become shareholders, using government bonds [gongzhaiquan] and savings bonds [chuxupiao]. In this way the share capital was increased. When the cooperative came to have the confidence of the masses and the masses wanted to take out shares but had no money, it allowed them to use any articles of value such as grain, livestock, eggs and firewood to buy shares. Therefore, all the people praise it.

(2) It has smashed formalism in cooperatives, and conscientiously carried out the policy of facing the masses and working for the benefit of the people. It has therefore gradually come to be loved and respected by the masses. For example, every year during spring ploughing, it makes early arrangements to transport shovels from Hancheng and other places, selling them to the peasants at a price lower than the market price. It organizes various productive enterprises, which not only absorb unemployed workers, take on apprentices, and employ the family dependants of working personnel, but also expand profits, guarantee the supply of daily necessities to the people of the area, and increase the income of the people. The Southern District Cooperative has organized more than 800 women to spin yarn. Each month they can spin 1,400 jin. This has increased the monthly income by 70,000 yuan. The managerial policy of the consumer cooperative is to fully ensure the supply of necessary commodities for the people, not only letting them make fewer

trips for their purchases but also charging prices cheaper than those found in shops of large towns.

(3) It uses the policy of benefiting both the public and the private sectors as the bridge between the economic activity of the government and the economic activity of the people. On the one hand it carries out the financial and economic policies of the government and on the other it adjusts the burdens of the people so as to make those burdens more acceptable, raises their income, and increases their enthusiasm. For example, in 1941 when the government was mobilizing for the salt-transport levy, the Southern District Cooperative got the people of the district to hand over a money substitute, and its transport team transported the salt for the government on behalf of the people. Before the government collects the tax grain, the cooperative mobilizes the people to pay it to the cooperative itself in accordance with the amount of tax collected in the previous year. The cooperative guarantees to pay the tax grain for the current year on behalf of the cooperative members and also accepts the tax grain handed over as share capital paid in by people to join the cooperative. Thus on the one hand the cooperative acts on behalf of the government, ensuring the payment of tax grain but using it to make a profit before it is finally paid over. On the other hand the people not only pay their tax grain but also get some share capital. As a result some households with surplus grain have even wished to pay two years' worth of tax grain to the cooperative. No matter what the increase in tax grain the following year, the cooperative undertakes to pay the difference. More than forty households in the district have done this. In this way the burdens of the peasants have been fixed, their income has increased, and their enthusiasm for production has also been raised. Another example was when the government of the county and district wanted the people to pay educational expenses and expenses for the guard posts of the self-defence army. The cooperative again paid these for the people from its profits. In this way the government was saved the trouble of collecting the expenses and the people were not burdened with the payment. The government policies of encouraging immigration and assisting refugees can also be carried out by the cooperative (it can give credit to the refugees and immigrants

and so forth). In all these ways the interests of the government, the cooperatives, and the people, the interests of the individual and the collective are closely united.

(4) It changes the organizational structure of the cooperative according to the wishes of the people. It does not hold congresses of all the cooperative members, but allows the members to elect delegates from each village. It does not use the method of assessment for raising share capital, but rallies groups of activist cooperative members to go and encourage the people to take out shares. It does not limit the share capital of the cooperative members, and it divides the profit according to shares held. However, in solving the cooperative's problems it does not consider the number of shares owned. Each shareholder has equal rights.

The above are the features of the Southern District Cooperative. As a consumer cooperative, its characteristics conform to the basic spirit of consumer cooperatives and grow from the life, culture, economy, and politics of the people of the Border Region. As a producer cooperative, while not a cooperative of the producers themselves but an enterprise where shareholders hire labour, its present structure is a means of absorbing unused rural capital to develop handicrafts and corresponds to existing conditions in the Border Region where handicrafts are not developed and handicraft workers are few.

Since 1936 the Southern District Cooperative has gone through six to seven years of trial and hard struggle. Now it has grown from 160 members to include more than 90 per cent of the households of the Southern district. The number of voluntary members is 1,112. The amount of share capital has risen from 159 yuan to 2 million yuan. It has grown from one cooperative to sixteen cooperatives. The net profit has risen from several tens of yuan to 1,620,000 yuan for the first ten months of 1942. It has developed the agricultural, industrial and commercial enterprises of the people of the district and looked after their economic welfare, becoming the economic heart of the people of Southern district.

In the large but underpopulated Border Region where the economy is almost entirely a small-scale peasant economy, it is necessary to rely upon truly popularized cooperatives to play a pivotal role in implementing the economic policies of the government and in organizing and encouraging the people to develop the economy. Thus the road of the Southern District Cooperative is the road for all the cooperatives of the Border Region. A movement to develop cooperatives in the style of the Southern District Cooperative is a major item of work for expanding the economy of the people of the Border Region.

For this reason, the Party and government should carry out the following work in cooperatives throughout the Border Region in 1943.

(1) The Reconstruction Department should be responsible for studying the experience of the Southern District Cooperative and for compiling a small handbook as educational material for the fourth section [ke] of all county governments and for the personnel of all cooperatives. Furthermore, we should use the opportunity presented by holding meetings in Yan'an to take working cadres from all parts of the Border Region on a tour of the Southern District Cooperative.

(2) All the enterprises run by the Commodities Bureau should help successful consumer and producer cooperatives with supplies and distribution. They should sell commodities to the consumer cooperatives, and supply raw material to, and guarantee the purchase of products from, the producer cooperatives. The government should issue 3 million *yuan* to the Commodities Bureau in 1943 to help in adjusting the cooperatives' supplies and distribution.

(3) In order to stimulate cooperatives, the government must clearly stipulate and conscientiously carry out a reduction in the cooperatives' tax burden.

(4) The Border Region Government and the governments of all the counties should seek out students educated to the upper primary school or higher level for training as accountants or managers so as to ease the difficulties of all cooperatives over these.

(5) The personnel of the cooperatives must implement the policy of 'popularization' and adopt the wages system, doing away with the system of substitute cultivation for cooperative personnel. They must improve cooperative organization and simplify administration. They must make them into proper enterprises

and not official organs. They must reduce the working personnel and reduce expenditure.

In order to ensure that everyone fully understands the history of the development of the Southern District Cooperative, we have specially invited its director, Comrade Liu Jianzhang, to write a report which now follows.

THE HISTORY OF THE YAN'AN SOUTHERN DISTRICT COOPERATIVE

First period

On 2 December 1936, we began to propagandize the people to buy shares. At that time each share was worth 0.30 *yuan* in soviet currency. After twenty days there were 160 members with 533 shares giving a total value of 159.90 *yuan*.

Wang Tianjin was elected director, Liu Jianzhang accountant, and Li Shengzhang buyer.

Dividends were paid quarterly and the gross profit for the first quarter was 199.44 *yuan*.

Expenditures were made up of payments to the three personnel 9 *yuan*, food 45 *yuan*, stationery 3.50 *yuan*, woollen socks and gloves to support the front 13 *yuan*, help for the dependants of troops of the War of Resistance 15 *yuan*, support for the small school 8 *yuan*, and public welfare fund 10 *yuan*. After expenses, the dividend per share was 0.18 *yuan*, and the total dividend 95.94 *yuan*.

On the occasion of this dividend, we held a cooperative members' congress attended by all. At this meeting we reported on the work done by the cooperative, shared out the dividend, and gave the members dinner. The meeting produced great results. The members themselves proposed that since the cooperative was helping the dependants of soldiers in the War of Resistance, assisting the small school, and supporting the front with woollen socks and gloves and so forth all on their behalf, everyone should buy more shares. This was the first period.

Second period

Wang Shengming became treasurer. I planned a large increase in the share capital. Director Wang was not satisfied. He argued that an increase in share capital should be carried out when the situation demanded it. I wanted to take the matter to the county government for discussion and later we went to see Liu Shichang head of the national economy department [*guomin jingjibu*] of the county government. Department head Liu permitted an increase in share capital. Since Wang Tianjin disagreed with everyone, the county government moved him to another post.

In March 1937, Liu Jianzhang was elected director, Wang Shengming accountant, and Li Shengzhang remained as buyer. Once again there were three people. On one hand we managed the business and on the other we increased the share capital. The date for the second payment of dividend was 2 June 1937. The total of new shares issued was 2,697, which together with the previous issue made a total of 3,230 with a value of 969 yuan at the maintained rate of 0.30 yuan per share. The sum of 3,657 yuan was handled in turnover [guoliushui] during the three months and the gross profit was 276 yuan. Expenditures included support for the small school 6 yuan, support for the dependants of soldiers in the War of Resistance 12 yuan, donation to the appeal for support for the front 20 yuan, public welfare fund 10 yuan, three months' food 53 yuan, staff payments 13.50 yuan, and office expenses 3.50 yuan. After expenses the dividend per share was 0.05 yuan, a combined total of 161.50 yuan. As before, a congress of cooperative members was held when the dividend was paid. Two-thirds of the members attended. We reported on the activities of the cooperative. At that time we had bought 30 dan of grain on behalf of the troops and had also acted as an agent in the purchase of all the charcoal and firewood used by the reception centre of the Northwest Military Committee [Xibei Junwei]. All income from this business was in soviet notes, but the ordinary people did not agree. They asked the cooperative to request goods as a pledge when acting as a purchasing agent. On the one hand they should give some goods and on the other we could accept some soviet notes. At this time the cadres of the cooperative worked hard and patiently to bring about agreement between the people and the troops. After this we built up relations between the army and the people. If the soviet notes held by the people could not be used to buy things in other places, the cooperative could buy them. When this was announced, the members gained a greater understanding of the cooperative and stated that 'the cooperative was able to act on their behalf'.

Third period

Beginning in June 1937 we again planned to increase the number of cadres. Sun Shenghua was promoted to be buyer. He worked for one month, every day acting as buying agent for the troops which he found very troublesome. He said he wanted to stop working. Despite repeated attempts at persuasion and education, he was determined not to work for the cooperative and so he left. Li Shengcai became buyer. We planned to open a firewood shop at Goumenshang. The cooperative put up 200 yuan capital and it became an independent unit. Li Shengzhang was director of the shop with his wife as cook and Li Shengcai as assistant. In three months the gross profit was 400 yuan.

The current account for the running of the cooperative and the shop was 7,175.60 yuan and the gross profit 538.70 yuan. Three yuan in soviet currency was equivalent to one yuan in national currency [baipiao], giving a converted value of 175 yuan [yang yuan]. When cooperative members took out shares, 1 yuan in Soviet currency was taken as equivalent to 1 yuan in national currency. We donated 25 yuan for the front and 10 yuan to help the small school. The director for women's affairs of the district was robbed by local bandits and new bedding for her cost 4.50 yuan. The public welfare fund was 12 yuan. Losses on forged notes came to 8.50 yuan, payments to staff 45 yuan, food 90 yuan, and office expenses 7.50 yuan. New shares issued numbered 2,130, making a total of 5,360 with a value of 1,596 yuan. Dividend per share was 0.02 yuan.[2]

During this period, the porters in Ansai county, Bao'an county, and our own district organized a salt-transport cooperative. They pooled their capital and formed a partnership setting up a salt-transport team with a total of twelve donkeys, horses and mules. Together with more than one hundred privately-owned animals, they regularly went to Yanchi to transport salt which was sold through the cooperative. This also encouraged porters from other counties to invest 320 yuan in the shop. During this period the soviet currency used to buy shares was converted entirely into national currency.

We reported to the September cooperative members' meeting. Everyone expressed the opinion that making the soviet notes worth 1 yuan in national currency instead of 0.30 yuan had increased the trust of the members. We proposed an increase in the share capital, made a census of the population and surveyed the conditions of the people's economy. The three townships of the district had 432 households with a population of 1,733. There were 222 ox-drawn implements and 323 oxen, 125 donkeys and 270 sheep. The total value of the people's economy for the whole district was 220,000 yuan including livestock, land, houses and all assets. Excluding grains, the average annual expenditure per head on clothing, agricultural implements, salt, matches, etc. was 40 yuan, making a total of 69,320 yuan. We proposed to the meeting that each person should increase his share capital to 20 yuan so that we could provide daily necessities for the people. The members agreed to increase the share capital and to lengthen the accounting periods from quarterly to half-yearly.

[2] On the basis of the number of shares and the total dividend, the dividend per share should have been stated as 0.03 yuan. The discussion is not clear, due to the mixed use of the terms yuan and yang yuan. The distinction made early in the paragraph is not adhered to in subsequent discussion. Snow (1937), p. 234 states that in mid-1936 the exchange rate was 1.21 yuan in soviet currency for 1 yuan in national currency.

Fourth period

The fourth period ran from September 1937 to February 1938. The original value of 0.30 yuan per share was raised to 0.50 yuan. The total number of shares was 5,360 valued at 2,680 yuan. The current account was 22,875 yuan and the gross profit 1,732.30 yuan. Outgoings were the public accumulation fund 110 yuan, the public welfare fund 68 yuan, woollen socks and gloves to support the front 245 yuan, support for the dependants of troops in the War of Resistance 18 yuan, support for the small school 12 yuan, payments to cooperative personnel and hired labour 310.50 yuan, food 90 yuan, entertainment expenses 38.50 yuan, office expenses 61.50 yuan, incentives for personnel 60 yuan and repairs 285 yuan. After expenses the dividend per share was 0.08 yuan and the total dividend was 428.80 yuan. Although the cooperative members' meeting for the previous period had proposed raising the share capital per person to 20 yuan, this had only been partly realized because of difficulties in the people's economy. This time the meeting planned to establish a credit cooperative with share capital of 1,000 yuan. People could come to this cooperative for short-term loans for marriages and funerals without paying interest. As soon as this slogan was put forward, the members said they would guarantee the raising of all share capital. The aim was to provide assistance. We also planned to open a restaurant in Liulin.

Fifth period

This ran from March to August 1938. First of all we increased the number of cadres, recruiting Wang Yaoming, Mao Keye, Li Shenghai, Huang Baozhong, etc. Within three months we raised 1,060 yuan share capital for the credit cooperative and in addition increased other share capital by 110 yuan. Including previous share capital the total was 3,890 yuan. The current account for the six months was 42,500 yuan and the gross profit was 3,633 yuan. Expenses were woollen socks for troops at the front 185 yuan, relief appeal donations 22 yuan, incentives 80 yuan, repairs 230 yuan, meetings and entertainment 85.60 yuan, office expenses 189 yuan, payments and salaries (twenty-four people) 864 yuan, and food 900 yuan. After expenses the dividend per share was 0.10 yuan and the total dividend 778 yuan. When the dividend was distributed we held a meeting of cooperative members' group leaders. We planned to accumulate 500 yuan to buy ploughshares. Each ploughshare cost 0.25 yuan so we could buy 2,000. We also planned to expand with an oil-pressing shop [youfang], a flour-mill [fenfang], and a public welfare centre [gongyixin] so as to establish commercial relations in Yan'an city. On this occasion none of the group leaders disagreed.

Sixth period

This ran from September 1938 to February 1939. We changed the share value from 0.50 yuan to 1 yuan, and we increased share capital by 4,510 yuan making a new total of 8,200 yuan. The current account for the six months was 49,860 yuan and the gross profit 4,118 yuan. Expenses included support for dependants of troops in the War of Resistance 34 yuan, the public accumulation fund 654 yuan, the public welfare fund 100 yuan, incentives 131 yuan, entertainment 180 yuan, miscellaneous expenses 116 yuan, salaries and payments to personnel (thirty people) 867 yuan and food 1,116 yuan. During this period all plans were realized. We bought 2,000 shovels in Hancheng. Each shovel was worth 0.50 yuan and the market-price was 0.90 yuan. We sold them to cooperative members at 0.60 yuan each, a saving of 0.30 yuan and a total saving of 600 yuan. The oil-pressing shop and flour-mill were established. In this period we still paid a dividend on a half-yearly basis. There was a total of 850 cooperative members.

Seventh period

This ran from March to August 1939. We started planning to do business in partnership with private individuals. In the area there were some people who wanted to go into business but feared that the government would increase taxation on them. So they invested their money together with the cooperative as individual shareholders in a joint venture. First we set up a business in partnership with private individuals in Sanshilipu including a noodle shop and a restaurant. The cooperative put up 200 yuan and the individuals 800 yuan. Through this partnership business we solved many problems for the people. We made a rule allowing the freedom to invest or withdraw share capital from the cooperative. This lasted until the end of the year when the government, reaffirming the principles of cooperatives, pointed out that the cooperative had developed the private economy and this was not allowed. So this business was broken off.

In the same year we expanded share capital by 860 yuan, making a new total of 9,016 yuan. Cooperative members numbered 960.

The current account was 57,600 yuan and the gross profit was 4,778.60 yuan.

After deducting the public accumulation fund, public welfare fund, and other expenses, the net dividend was 0.10 yuan per share and the total dividend 901.60 yuan.

In the course of paying out this dividend, many difficulties arose. On one hand the expansion of share capital was slow and the rise in commodity prices high, making it difficult for the cooperative to operate. On the other hand, the people reckoned there was no increased

125

profit for the individual, and were unwilling to invest in more shares. We tried again and again to propagandize and persuade them but they remained unwilling to invest more. I myself reckoned that unless we formed partnerships with private individuals, the cooperative could not develop, and that we should do business in such partnerships without government approval. I put this forward for discussion at a management meeting and it was agreed that it should be done.

Eighth period

In September 1939 we again went into partnership with individuals to set up the Xinghua Branch Cooperative at Sanshilipu, the Limin Cooperative at Goumenshang, the Minsheng Herbalist at Liulin, and the Lihe Cooperative at Nanzhuanghe. Using the cover of being joint public and private ventures, they attracted over 100,000 yuan of capital from private investors. The people working in the branches got personal shares. We drew up contracts. There was still complete freedom in making investments and withdrawals and the cooperative did not lay down any restrictions. Subsequently when the county government learned about this, it wanted to see the contracts. After seeing them, it approved the formation of partnerships. The original cooperative was changed into the head cooperative of the district, and the various townships set up branch cooperatives. Excluding the branch cooperatives, the head cooperative again increased share capital by 2,629 yuan, making a new total of 11,645 yuan. The current account for the head and branch cooperatives together was 158,350 yuan and the gross profit 18,250 yuan. Expenses were 8,895.13 yuan and the net profit was 9,354.07 yuan. The dividend per share was 0.10 yuan, including the branch cooperatives. Having set up branch cooperatives, the head cooperative was strong enough to establish productive undertakings. In 1940 in partnership with the Guanghua Store, we bought mules and set up a transport team, benefiting from cooperation with private individuals. The original capital of the transport team was 5,000 yuan. By the end of the year, it had expanded to have 160 mules and was regularly transporting salt goods. We also set up a textile mill and a leather-workshop. The West District Cooperative and the Xinmin Cooperative at Dufuchuan collectively set up a trans-shipment warehouse and two felt-workshops at Qilipu. At first shares were taken out on an individual basis so that there could be several cooperative members within one family. Later this became troublesome, so they were combined, taking the household as the unit. Each family became one cooperative member, and there was a total of 853 members.

After the membership had been combined in this way households had 300–500 yuan to 1,000 yuan invested. At the same time, small merchants and porters from other counties had also joined the branch cooperatives with share capital of 10,000 yuan. In particular the porters who came frequently from the counties of Luochuan, Fuxian, Ansai, Bao'an and Sanbian invested in the cooperative. When the dividend was paid in the ninth month [sic], we held a meeting of members' representatives and reported on the reasons for the expansion of the cooperative. After examination we put forward the general aims for future work. First we wanted to increase shares by 30,000 yuan and we asked the representatives to guarantee that this would be done. Secondly, we planned to accept local products and to sell them on behalf of the people, to supply the people with all daily necessities, and to take responsibility for buying goods from other areas. Thirdly, the salt, matches, and ploughshares needed by the people of the district would not be bought from outside but would be supplied by the cooperative. We reckoned that the 7,135 people of the district consumed 2 qian[3] of salt per head per day and 4.5 jin per head per year, making an annual total of 32,107.5 jin. At a price per jin 1 yuan below the market-price, we could save over 32,100 yuan. Each family used five packs of matches per year, a total of 8,675 packs for the whole district. At a price per pack 5 yuan below the market-price, we could save 43,375 yuan. The district used 1,500 ploughshares per year. At 15 yuan below the market price we could save 22,500 yuan. The total saving for these three items could be 98,050 yuan. The district population's annual consumption of cotton cloth for making clothes was 7,000 bolts. Each bolt required $2\frac{1}{2}$ jin of raw cotton, a total requirement of 17,515 jin. The total value was 3,500,000 yuan. If the yarn was spun by the people, they could earn half of it, that is, 1,750,000 yuan. We reported on our plans to the members at this meeting. After approval by the members, we increased the number of machines for spinning and weaving by peasant women.

Ninth period

In August 1941 we increased share capital in the form of shares taken out as government bonds for national salvation (jiuguo gongzhai). The government mobilized the people to buy government bonds for national salvation. The amount of bonds to be taken out by the people was added on to their share capital. The dividend on this share capital was paid towards the government bonds of 33,000 yuan. In this difficult situation for the people, we helped them ease their burdens and raised their faith in our ability to do so.

The new share capital was 33,070 yuan. Combined with the old, this gave a total of 44,715 yuan for the head cooperative. The share capital for the various branch cooperatives was 120,000 yuan, and for the transport team it was 80,000 yuan. The combined total was thus 244,715 yuan and the membership was 1,018. The current account for

[3] 10 qian per liang [ounce], and 16 liang per jin.

the head and branch cooperatives together was 1,161,840.70 *yuan* and the gross profit was 284,317.40 *yuan*. Expenses were 138,849.30 *yuan* and the net profit was 145,469 *yuan*. The dividend per share of 1 *yuan* was 0.70 *yuan*. When issuing the dividend we proposed that each dividend of 0.70 *yuan* could be valued at 1 *yuan* if invested as share capital. This increased members' trust and a lot of the dividend was added on to the share capital. People taking out additional shares could use local products, firewood and grain as money, calculating the value higher than market price. For example, each *jin* of grass was valued 0.20 *yuan* higher than the market price. This was true of all investment in kind and it also increased the people's trust.

Tenth period

In 1942 we set up a sock-weaving factory. When we began propagandizing for share capital, we made each share worth 20 *yuan* and presented the members with a pair of socks. Afterwards, with the increase in the cost of raw cotton, we raised the value of each share to 40 *yuan*. The total share capital was 30,000 *yuan*. We set up the sock-weaving factory and it now has six machines. In Yan'an city we set up the Yunhe trans-shipment warehouse with 420,000 *yuan* share capital. At Songshulin we set up a branch cooperative with share capital of 340,000 *yuan*. The surplus accumulated by the transport team increased its capital to 750,000 *yuan*. The head and branch cooperatives expanded their share capital by 1,232,000 *yuan*, making a new total of 2,520,000 *yuan*. The membership was 1,112 (each member represented one household). The largest investor had shares to the value of 5,000 *yuan*. There were nineteen units of the cooperative within the boundaries of the district (including production, transport, and consumption). Apart from the cooperatives, there was no other private commerce. Southern district is 60 *li* long and 40 *li* broad. It has 1,544 households with 7,128 people. Altogether there are 1,469 oxen, 635 donkeys, 60 horses, 22 mules, and 4,445 sheep. Arable land covers 54,408 *mu*. The wheat harvest was 872.5 *dan*. The harvest of coarse grains was 9,084.16 *dan*, equivalent to 5,662.43 *dan* of hulled grain. The output from subsidiary undertakings was equivalent to 334.25 *dan* of hulled grain. The full total was 6,869.18 *dan*. In 1942 we paid 2,480 *dan* of grain tax leaving 4,389.18 *dan*. The average amount of grain per head was 0.6 *dan*. Animal fodder totalled 1,500 *dan*.

This spring the government mobilized to get 34,000 *yuan* for education expenses and for sentry fees for the self-defence army, 8,000 *yuan* for share capital for production at Gaomaowan, and 20,000 *yuan* for bank savings bonds. The total was 62,000 *yuan* to be raised in three parts. Each time each household would have to attend a meeting for collection and lose the work of one of its members. This would happen three times and each time the work of 1,500 would be lost. The work of each person was valued at 30 yuan so the total loss of earnings would be 135,000 yuan. Added to the 62,000 yuan, the full burden on the people would have been 197,000 yuan. Therefore the cooperative paid the 62,000 yuan, on behalf of the people, saving the 135,000 yuan which would have been lost. We helped the people's production at a particularly busy agricultural time. We also handed over 1,050 packs of salt each worth 240 yuan as salt tax on behalf of the people. The total value of this was 252,000 yuan. Reducing the amount of work time lost by the people influenced their attitude towards the cooperative, and we increased share capital by 420,000 yuan. We plan to pay next year's salt tax on their behalf.

We organized 600 peasant women to do spinning. Each day each person spun 2 liang of yarn. The total of raw cotton spun each day was 75 jin, and the people should get half of it. Each jin of yarn was reckoned as worth 150 yuan. The profit per day was 5,250 yuan and the profit for the year was 1,890,000 yuan. This year they spun 5,000 jin of raw cotton. In the first half of the year cotton was low-priced. Combining both halves each jin cost 70 yuan. The people earned 2,500 jin of raw cotton, equal to 175,000 yuan. The cooperative arranged advances of 20,000 yuan for spinning-wheels. After deducting this 20,000 yuan, the people earned 155,000 yuan. Now we are expanding the amount of spinning done by women. In the past there was no spinning done in Southern district. Now large numbers of women are taking part, but there are problems of raw materials. Finally, this year we sold 200,000 jin of charcoal for the people at 2 yuan per jin. The people got 400,000 yuan.

The above facts relate what the cooperative has done. We have not divided out the dividend so far this year on account of the floods. The cooperative has lost 58 buildings[4] with a value of 400,000 yuan, equipment worth 300,000 yuan, goods worth 400,000 yuan, and the Fuchang Storehouse at a value of 200,000 yuan. Total losses were 1,300,000 yuan. The Government later helped us borrow 500,000 yuan and we went to Dingbian county three times to sell goods making a gross profit of 300,000 yuan. At present we again have repair expenses of 240,000 yuan and we are expanding share capital.

As regards the organization of the cooperative, each village elects one or two representatives. Cooperative affairs are handled by the twelve-man management committee held on the sixth day of each month. All questions concerning management and cadres are determined at the management committee meetings.

---

[4] The report uses the term jian meaning a division of building, usually taken as a room.

Supplementary notes:
(1) At present the cooperative has 135 buildings[5] and fifty-five stone-built cave houses[6] worth 2,890,000 *yuan* at current values, liquid capital of 1,500,000 *yuan*, and equipment and livestock worth 1,020,000 *yuan*.
(2) The experience and lessons of the cooperative are explained in the page on the Southern District Cooperative in the volume *Materials on Yan'an's Economic Construction*.

13 December 1942

The above document leaves a gap of two years between the eighth and ninth periods, and there seem to be some omissions. Enquiries were made and the following report came back:

CONCERNING THE PROBLEM OF PERIODIZATION OF THE SOUTHERN DISTRICT
COOPERATIVE

Operations began in December 1936 and the first meeting of all cooperative members was held after three months. Altogether three such meetings were held at three-monthly intervals. Then they were changed to once every six months and a further three meetings were held. After the sixth meeting, there was a gap of eight months and then the first meeting of representatives was held (at the end of 1939). Afterwards the second meeting of representatives was held in July 1940, and the third in August 1941. We planned to hold the fourth meeting in July this year but because of floods it was difficult to draw up the accounts so we extended the period. Before 1939 the period between meetings was short and all the members attended. This was because our scope and membership were both small. Later, meetings of representatives were held once a year because our membership was too large, our undertakings had expanded and drawing up accounts was not easy.

In our previous report we omitted to refer to the second representative meeting of July 1940 and so the eighth period was lengthened into two years.

The previous report was made without proper drafting. If there are still questions on this material please instruct for further reports.

Wang Pi'nian[7]
Liu Jianzhang
15 December

Below is the report of the comrades of the Yan'an county Party Committee on the Southern District Cooperative. It is reproduced here for study.

[5] *jian.*   [6] Typical buildings of the loess region of north China.
[7] The 1949 version gives the name as Wang Pizhang.

DEVELOPMENT OF COOPERATIVES

Looking at the process of development of the Liulin District Cooperative we can see:

(1) Cooperative operations are not limited to consumption but are also
related to production, credit and transport, making them a coherent
whole. The head cooperative and its branches make a total of
sixteen.

On the production side there is the textile-mill, the leather-
workshop, the felt-workshop, the oil-pressing shop, and the
flour-mill.

On the transport side there is the transport team with over a
hundred animals. The cooperative's capital investment is 500,000
yuan.

Because the Liulin District Cooperative operates by uniting several
economic functions together, its scope is wide, its capital is large,
its activities are big, its development is fast, and it has solved many
problems in the supply of daily commodities for the people. Other
cooperatives in this county are limited to consumption. Compared
to a cooperative which also carries out production and transport,
their capital and scope are small and their development retarded.

(2) The policy for management of cooperatives by the people was put
forward by adopting the experience of Liulin. This cooperative's
share capital expanded, absorbed the capital of small merchants
and drew them in to take part in the work. All the work of the
cooperative was discussed and decided by the cooperative members. The people were deeply involved with the cooperative. They
did not consider it to be run by officials but by themselves.

(3) The cooperative solves problems in the supply of daily necessities
for the masses, such as bolts of cloth, salt, matches, ploughshares,
etc. at lower than market price. Taking matches and salt alone, the
annual savings for the people are more than 80,000 yuan. Naturally
the people wish to buy things at the cooperative. The cooperative
can supply the entire needs of the people of Liulin district in these
four daily necessities.

(4) The cooperative helps the masses out of urgent difficulties such as
those created by marriages or funerals by allowing them to borrow
funds temporarily, either giving credit against bolts of cloth or
taking something as a pledge. It sets a time limit for repayment. This
fills the role of a credit cooperative, solving major difficulties for the
people. Because the cooperative does this at a time of urgent need
when no help can be found elsewhere, it creates trust among the
people, who consider the cooperative really helps them.

(5) The cooperative has a variety of ways of expanding share capital:

(i) Buying shares with ready cash.

(ii) Taking out shares in return for goods: a chicken, a pair of shoes, some sheepskins, some hemp ropes can all be exchanged for shares at equivalent value.

(iii) Absorbing the capital of small merchants.

(iv) Helping the masses pay burdens from the government and making this a way of taking out shares. After the government issues its demands, the cooperative turns them into a call for buying shares (to the same amount) and itself pays the taxes. For example, in 1942 the people of the district had to pay 250,000 *yuan* to the government as a cash substitute for tax salt. This was treated as share capital and paid to the cooperative. The cooperative paid the salt tax to the government, making a profit from the handling of the cash. The people also got a dividend. Government bonds, education costs, sentry costs, and so forth were collected in this way and paid by the cooperative. The government was paid, the cooperative's share capital increased and its operations expanded. The people profited and they had less troubles. They also received dividends as shareholders.

(v) Increasing share capital through making timely responses to the needs of the moment of the people. For example, when they wanted to expand spinning and weaving, they put forward the slogan of raising share capital to do so. In 1941 the cooperative experimented with paying tax grain for the people. For each *dan* of the previous year's grain tax the people bought shares for cash. The cooperative used the cash to expand its operations. In the following year when the grain tax was allocated among the people, it was paid by the cooperative from the profits it had obtained. This was done for forty or so households, for whom paying grain tax was almost like not paying. They became shareholders in the cooperative able to get a dividend every year. They were very happy, their enthusiasm for production increased and they got even more grain.

(vi) Paying a dividend on taking out shares. People taking out shares for 40 *yuan* were issued a pair of socks valued at 20 *yuan*. In this way the people were encouraged to buy shares.

(6) The cooperative is in a very good geographical position since it is in Liulin district which is close to the large commercial market in Yan'an. Liulin has much forest land. Many people sell timber and charcoal, which raises their income and thus there is a lot of liquid capital in the villages which can be absorbed in the purchase of shares. At the same time, being near a market, the turnover of capital is very quick. These are objective factors.

(7) The scope of the cooperative's activities is very wide. It has estab-

lished relations with the Border Region Bank, the Guanghua Store and the various official organizations in Yan'an. Sometimes it can borrow capital or do a lot of work for the official organizations and the cooperative has been able to develop through this mutual help.

(8) The cadres have not been transferred much and they pay attention to investigation and research. Director Liu has not been transferred to other work since he was appointed. He has been able to concentrate exclusively on his work, on research and on thinking of ways of doing things. At the same time, he also pays great attention to investigating objective conditions. For example, he often investigated such things as the annual consumption per individual of bolts of cotton, salt, matches and so forth so as to solve the people's problems.

Here is an example to show the relationship between the cooperative and the people. In 1941 the peasant Bai Da of Lüfengpo in Liulin district had to hand over 60 yuan for national salvation grain tax. Beforehand he paid it to the cooperative as share capital. At the appointed time the cooperative paid the government on his behalf. Later the dividend was added to the original capital of 60 yuan bringing it up to 200 yuan. He bought four ploughshares from the cooperative and saved 15 yuan on each (that is, they were sold at 15 yuan less than the market price), making a total saving of 60 yuan. He bought five packs of matches saving 5 yuan on each, a total of 25 yuan. At the end of the twelfth lunar month in 1941, he bought goods worth 1,000 yuan at the cooperative but only paid 500 yuan saving 500 yuan. Subsequently, the market prices of these goods rose by 550 yuan. Including the previous purchases of ploughshares and matches he saved a total of 635 yuan. Originally he had to pay 60 yuan in grain tax, now it has become share capital of 200 yuan and he saved 635 yuan on the purchase of goods. This has really made the cooperative belong to the people, facilitating their dealings and looking after their interests. There are many examples like this.

The Cooperative Situation throughout the County

Table 5.1   Number of cooperatives in Yan'an county, 1941 and July 1942

	1941	1942
Branch cooperatives	18	30
District cooperatives	8	8
Total	26	38

Table 5.2 *Capital (in yuan) invested in cooperatives in Yan'an county, 1941 and 1942 (half year)*

	1941	1942 (for half year)
District cooperatives	264,207.56	312,207.56
Branch cooperatives	193,340.00	978,507.14
Total	457,547.56	1,290,714.70

Within six months capital increased by 833,167.14 yuan. The fastest increase in capital was in the branch cooperatives, which are directly organized by the people with the support of the district cooperatives. Therefore the people are very enthusiastic about taking shares.

The average taken from 1,290,000 yuan works out at 20 yuan per head of the population of the county. This is not much so the role of the cooperatives in the entire county is still a minor one.

Important experience
(1) Persist in the policy of management by the people and non-interference by the government. We inspected the cooperatives in July this year and called for an increase in share capital. Substantial capital should be held by the cooperatives.
(2) Cooperative cadres should not be lightly transferred to other posts. Let them be settled in their posts, concentrating on their work. Guarantee their livelihood. Cooperatives should adopt the method of assigning personal shares [da shenfen]. That is, each member of the cooperative's personnel should be equivalent to a number of shares depending on his ability and work. For example, if someone is made equivalent to shares of 5,000 yuan, he is paid the interest due on shares of 5,000 yuan at the time of settling accounts. This becomes his salary and he does not receive any other income.
(3) Enlarging the scope of cooperative undertakings should not be limited to consumption alone but should include production, transport, credit and so forth. This is an inevitable trend in cooperative development henceforth. That is to say, we must run comprehensive cooperatives.
(4) Concentrate on making a good job of one or two cooperatives and gaining experience. Gradually expand to other areas. For example, we are preparing to turn the Songshulin Cooperative of Jinpen district into a second Liulin Cooperative.
These are opinions on our future work.

6

ON THE DEVELOPMENT OF THE
SALT INDUSTRY

Salt is the great resource of the Border Region. It is the mainstay which balances imports and exports, stabilizes the currency, and regulates commodity prices. A large proportion of the people rely on salt [as a form of] exchange for goods from outside. A relatively large proportion of the troops and working personnel rely on salt for their livelihood or to supplement their livelihood. Salt is also a major source of government financial revenue. Therefore salt plays an extremely important role in the Border Region. Since the War of Resistance began, the supply of salt from the sea has been cut off and the supply from the Huai area and from Shanxi has been reduced. The southwest relies on salt from Sichuan and the northwest and the eastern areas[1] on salt from Ningxia and Qinghai. Salt from our Border Region has thus come to occupy an important position and the transport and sale of salt increases annually. In 1938 our salt exports were only 70,000 packs (each pack is 150 jin and each jin is 24 liang). In 1939 there was a sudden increase to 190,000 packs. In 1940, the figure was 230,000 packs, and in 1941 there was another abrupt increase to 299,068 packs. By September 1942 the total was 155,790 packs and it is estimated that another 70,000–80,000 packs can be sold in the last three months making a total of 230,000–240,000 packs. These statistics reflect two important facts: the first is the external demand, and the second is our hard work. Some comrades cannot see that external demand is determined by the War of Resistance and that within certain limits salt can be sold. Therefore they propose that things should follow their own course and that there is no need for the

---

[1] Mao here uses the phrase zhongyuan which was used historically to indicate the eastern areas of Shaanxi province.

Party and government to interfere. Other comrades merely ascribe the yearly increase in the sale of salt to external demand and do not recognize that the leadership of the Party and government is a great factor in that increase. We began to pay attention to the salt industry in autumn 1940. As well as the objective factor of the external salt famine and depletion of salt stocks which made 1941 salt sales particularly good, the abrupt increase from 230,000 packs in 1940 to 299,000 packs in 1941 was also due to the subjective factor that we implemented the policy of supervising transport in that year. Apart from the fact that external demand was not as urgent as in 1941, the sudden drop to 230,000–240,000 packs in 1942 from the previous year's 299,000 was due to our abandonment of the policy of supervising transport (putting an end to the many plans made by the people for transporting salt). If we do not learn a lesson from this, we shall repeat past mistakes in future work. Certainly there were defects in the salt-industry work for 1941. The original plan to transport 600,000 packs was too big. The Border Region still does not have such a great transport capacity. The achievement in producing 700,000 packs of salt was good, but the quality [of the salt] was too poor. Supervision of transport was correct but it was unnecessary to mobilize everyone everywhere. There were also many abuses in the organization and method of mobilization which did not accord with the actual situation. All these things were shortcomings and mistakes in our work in 1941. Nevertheless, adopting a policy of active development of the salt industry was entirely correct. Belittling, misunderstanding and even opposing this policy is entirely wrong.

What should be done in 1943? First we must determine a policy for active development. In the current situation in the Border Region, we certainly cannot adopt a negative approach towards salt which is a major factor in solving financial problems (the publicly-run salt industry and the salt tax), in balancing imports and exports, and in stabilizing the currency and commodity prices. Therefore we must enlarge the already established Salt Company into the main force for allying public and private salt industry and for expanding public and private production, transport and sales. And we must improve the quality of salt produced so as to promote sales. We must restore transport supervision and organize all possible transport capacity among the people to expand salt transport. We must draw in porters from outside areas to transport and sell more. We must build roads, and arrange for inns, warehouses and fodder to help transport. The Salt Company should gradually gain control of outside sales in order to avoid the anarchic situation produced by lack of public and private coordination. These are our general policies for the active development of the salt industry in 1943. Concrete arrangements should be as follows:

(1) Expand the Salt Company and increase its capital. Under the direction of the Commodities Bureau raise share capital from the various official organizations, the troops and private individuals. Develop salt transport, expand salt sales. Regulate salt prices. Guarantee that the company transports 40,000 packs in 1943, and with this salt as a basis buy as much salt from the people as possible to carry out partial unification of salt sales to outside areas. Afterwards, depending on the situation, gradually achieve complete unification so as to prevent outside manipulation and guarantee the interests of the government and the people.

(2) In 1943 plan to produce 400,000 packs of salt and to transport 300,000–360,000 packs. Moreover strive to exceed this. As regards production, continue the policy of supervision by officials and production by the people. Ensure that the salt is mostly or entirely top-quality and do not allow inferior-quality to be produced again. As regards transport, plan for the Salt Company system to transport 40,000 packs, draw in porters from outside to move 50,000 packs, and organize the manpower and animal power of the Border Region to move 210,000–260,000 packs making a total of 300,000–360,000 packs.

(3) The organization of the manpower and animal power of the Border Region to transport 210,000–260,000 packs is an immense, arduous and meticulous piece of organizational and mass work. It should be directed by the Reconstruction Department and supervised by the government at various levels, the Party committees at each level having the responsibility for checking up and helping. Mobilization to transport salt must have a degree of coercion but it certainly must avoid command-

ism which causes damage. We must chiefly adopt the policy of using propaganda and persuasion. The organization to transport salt must take the forms of transport cooperatives and transport teams. Propagandize the masses to buy shares voluntarily. Some can provide manpower and some can provide draught animals. Some can provide both. Some can provide running costs and some, in special circumstances, can be exempted from providing anything. We can organize transport teams among people who have rich experience in portering, together with the necessary animals. The Party and government at county, district and township level should actively direct the rational, fair and healthy organization of these transport teams. They should set off smoothly, do the necessary work along the way and ensure the safety of the personnel and animals. On return pay attention to the distribution of the cooperative's profits and guarantee the interests of the people involved and of all the cooperative members. Salt transport must not violate the agricultural seasons. We must strengthen the organization of labour mutual-aid cooperatives (exchange labour) so that after the transport team has set off the cooperative members do not lose agricultural production through lack of manpower and animal power. As regards the salt-transport organizations (cooperatives and teams) of the Sui-Mi special military area and the three eastern counties, we should allow the masses greater freedom and reduce coercion. The transport cooperatives and teams of all places must be built up on a basis of benefiting the cooperative members. The duties of the Party and government lie in making these benefits increase daily, otherwise we will certainly be defeated. The Reconstruction Department, the sub-regions and counties should teach the people through the most successful examples of salt transport by the masses. They should propagandize them widely for imitation so as to be certain that the plan for salt-transport in 1943 will be completed and will also bring large direct benefits for the people.

(4) The enterprises of the Commodities Bureau and the people's cooperatives in all places must closely coordinate with the people's transport cooperatives and teams, and strive to ensure that the animals used by the people to transport salt are able to transport other goods on their return journey. Only then can the

people's salt-transport undertaking expand and the whole of salt transport develop, and only then will the whole salt-transport plan be completed.

(5) The key sector in developing the salt industry is transport, and the major condition for transport is communications. In 1943 the government should allocate 2 million *yuan* under the direction of the Reconstruction Department for the building of two cart-roads between Yan'an and Dingbian, and Dingbian and Qingyang, and for repairing the road from Yan'an to Fuxian. Furthermore the Commodities Bureau should set up inns with stables and trans-shipment warehouses along the main salt-transport routes, and dig water-storage holes in places lacking water. The Reconstruction Department and Commodities Bureau together should plant alfalfa widely along the routes and also provide fodder in other ways. So long as there are roads, inns, grass and water, transport costs can be greatly cut, the volume of transport can be greatly increased, and the three forms of transport – porters from outside, people from the area and the Salt Company – can all develop. Plans to improve the means of transport should also be directed by the Reconstruction Department. Carts and handcarts should be built according to road conditions in order to increase salt transport. Provided the roads are well built, it is much better for the government to use more carts and the people to use more handcarts than to use pack-animals.

(6) In 1943 the salt tax is fixed as 100,000 packs. Those who live near will provide transport, those who live far away will provide a substitute, and some will provide a mixture of both. However, the salt tax and the development of the salt industry are two different matters. So long as we can definitely export 300,000–360,000 packs, it does not matter whether we accept actual salt or substitute payments for salt tax.

If we can complete our plans for planting cotton and spinning and weaving in 1943, we can reduce our imports of raw cotton, cotton yarn and cotton cloth. If we can export 300,000–360,000 packs of salt in 1943 at an average value of 10 *yuan* Border Region currency per *jin* (each donkey pack is 150 *jin*), our income will be between 450 million *yuan* and 540 million *yuan*. Thus by reducing one and increasing the other, the Border

139

Region's problem of balancing imports and exports will be entirely solved. The following material reflects the people's experience in the transport of salt during 1941.

A RECORD OF LU ZHONGCAI'S LONG MARCH

Report on the first experiences in salt transport of Chengguan district, Fuxian county, as told by the deputy leader of Chengguan district, Lu Zhongcai. Supplemented by Wang Yuxian and Kong Zhaoqing. Recorded by Gao Kelin, 13 August 1941.

(1) For the first salt transport, Chengguan district should have provided fifty pack animals. In fact it provided twenty-eight. The reason the plan was not fulfilled was the lack of animals (at the very most we could mobilize forty). Some animals were hidden away and not kept at home. The district government did not handle things firmly as it was busy with grain loans and government bonds.

(2) We set off on 18 July and returned home on 11 August, a total of twenty-five days. It took twelve days to get from Fuxian to Dingbian, one day to get to Yanchi and load up, and twelve days to return. The longest stage was 90 *li*. The route, stage names and conditions during each stage was as follows:

  (i) From Fuxian to Zhangcunyi, 50 *li*. Five gullies[2] and the road was difficult. Good water and grass.

  (ii) Zhangcunyi to Lannipo, altogether five stages, each 70 *li*. Road good. Cut grass to feed the animals.

  (iii) Lannipo to Lijiabian. 20 *li* of mountains and 40 *li* of gullies. Road difficult. Fodder no good.

  (iv) Lijiabian to Lujiajiao. 30 *li* of gullies and 5 *li* of mountains. Most difficult to travel. Fodder no good.

  (v) Lujiajiao to Luanshitouchuan. Travelling in gullies. There were military stations. Fodder was sold (each 100 *jin* of mountain grass 30 *yuan*, of valley grass 50 *yuan*, and wheat hay 40 *yuan*).

  (vi) Luanshitouchuan to Sanlimiao, 80 *li*. There were military stations. Dry grass cost 50 *yuan* for 100 *jin*. Forty *li* of mountains, very precipitous. Difficult to travel. Water difficult (salt water not drinkable). Saw a salt-porter whose donkey had fallen to its death.

  (vii) Sanlimiao to Liangzhuang, 80 *li*.

  (viii) Liangzhuang to Dingbian 90 *li*. There were military stations. Fodder 50 to 100 *yuan* per 100 *jin*. No water.

  (ix) Dingbian to Yanchi, 40 *li*. One day there and back. Sandy road difficult to travel.

[2] Gullies in loess country are like cracks in the earth's surface with precipitous earth cliffs on either side.

(3) Difficulties along the route were:

(i) During three of the five stages from Zhangcunyi to Lannipo, locusts [zhameng] were biting. It was best for men and animals to travel in the evening.

(ii) During the two stages from Sanlimiao to Liangzhuang and thence to Dingbian there was no water. Men and animals were thirsty.

(iii) There were a lot of thieves at Dingbian. Animals, money, clothing and tools often taken.

(iv) Beyond Luanshitouchuan since salt-transport animals from various counties converge, there are often several thousands or hundreds of animals travelling together. Thus there are problems of inn space, fodder, water, and especially of room to rest animals. Things can easily go wrong and cause trouble.

(4) Life on the road:

Chengguan district sent twenty-eight animals and fourteen men. Along the way we cooked for ourselves. Each meal required 7 *sheng* of millet, roughly 25 *jin*. Everyone felt that 'We eat more when we have set out'. Inn charges ranged from 3 *yuan* at the lowest to 8 *yuan* at the most. It depended entirely on whether you had a good or bad relationship with the manager of the inn. When travelling we sang and told stories, many of them about Duke Xiang seeking a wife. Everyone was very happy and no one felt burdened. Animal fodder was cut in rotation. It was plentiful and could not all be eaten up. The masses along the route were very good, and there was no problem in getting grain and fodder – though we chiefly relied on ourselves. Sometimes there were quarrels, mainly because the animals had eaten someone's crops. Only in one place did the manager of an inn give us bad grain.

(5) Points that arose during the journey:

Good:

(i) None of the animals had any illness. Those from the First and Third townships were thin when we set off but returned fat. This was because of the care of the porters, and careful feeding.

(ii) None of the porters had any illness. Everyone was very fit and in good spirits. No one grew thinner. They just got a little sunburned.

(iii) Nothing was left behind along the way and the animals did not eat people's crops [sic]. This was mainly because deputy district head Lu Zhongcai's was an old porter. He was experienced, responsible, and meticulous. Everyone else was very active and thus we were successful.

Bad:

(i) Du Hai, head of the village council of the First administrative village of the Third township, sold a good donkey and bought a bad one to go. As a result the donkey was exhausted, did not carry packs, and we wasted 165 *yuan* in travel expenses. Third township

141

also sent another bad animal (it had bad loins) and Jianjuntaicun of Fourth township sent a donkey with a bad leg. Neither carried salt and each wasted 165 *yuan* in travel expenses. Furthermore, the same village sent a donkey with a rotten saddle with the result that its back was hurt through the pressure of its load. The head of Second township had two donkeys. He sent a bad one with a poor saddle and frame. This caused a lot of bother along the way. The district-level government did not make a careful inspection of these matters before we set out. Some were known about but not corrected. As a result only twenty-five of the twenty-eight donkeys carried salt. The other three travelled without loads, not contributing one bit to the value of salt carried and wasting from 500 to 600 *yuan* in travel costs. All in, the total loss was over 1,500 *yuan*. This is a valuable warning for district and township cadres.

(ii) The head of the village council of Jianjuntaicun in Fourth township did not obey deputy district head Lu Zhongcai's instructions. He did not bring good fodder for the animals (oats [*yumai*] and broad beans [*candou*]) and instead used kaoliang and other poor substitutes. As a result the animals from that township sometimes lay down when travelling because of their poor fodder. We are preparing to struggle against that village head and punish him.

(iii) The porter Yang Wanbao from Fourth township was a real trouble-maker on the way. He pretended to be ill and skulked off home. He created wild rumours, 'two people had died, deputy district head Lu and a man called Wang . . . There was nothing to eat along the way . . . The donkeys' backs had all been ruined under their loads . . . The inns could not sell grain . . .' so that many people back in the town felt unhappy. The district head did not pay sufficient attention to this. In future he should be alert.

(iv) Some families sent bad donkeys which carried less, only about 110 *jin*. One family from Jianjuntaicun in Fourth district changed their donkey's halter for a bad one when they sent it off. They anticipated the donkey would die and had made up their minds to write everything off. The donkey from the head of Second township was only 10 *li* from home on the way back when it lay down. He was unwilling to send a good donkey to take over. He defaulted on his responsibility as he thought the donkey would surely die and could not return. So he did not come and take over.

(v) Twelve donkeys carried too much and 40 to 50 *jin* were given to a donkey without a load. When we got to the tax inspection office at Sunkeyaoxian they confiscated 50 *jin* of salt and one sack (value 20 *yuan*) because we had no certificate.

(6) Costs, losses and gains:

(i) Average expenses per donkey were: 2 *dou* of beans value 60 *yuan*;

142

each man had 1.5 *dou* of grain and as each man looked after two donkeys this equalled 0.75 *dou* per donkey with a value of 35 *yuan*; travelling costs were 70 *yuan*. The total was 165 *yuan*. In addition there was salt capital [*yanben*] of 20 *yuan*. The average cost per donkey was thus 185 *yuan*.

 (ii) On average each donkey from First township carried 130 *jin*, and from Second, Third and Fourth townships 110 *jin*. At present market prices of 200 *yuan* per 100 *jin* salt, each load was worth from 220 to 260 *yuan*.

(iii) At current prices, after expenses are deducted, earnings per donkey load ranged from 35 to 75 *yuan*. Note: (a) If each donkey were able to carry 150 *jin*, the guaranteed income per donkey at current prices would be above 100 *yuan*. (b) Reports on amounts carried were given by the porters who were certainly holding something in reserve – most donkeys here can carry 150 *jin*. (c) At the same time the principle is clear that so long as you have good donkeys you can earn more. The worse the donkeys the less you earn, and you can even make a loss.

(7) Experience and lessons:

Experience:

 (i) The victorious return of this salt-transport team from Chengguan district, Fuxian, proves that the Party and government's plans, estimates and methods for salt transport are entirely correct. The doubts, lack of trust and considerations that it would be a burden by various comrades are all erroneous and shallow outlooks.

 (ii) We smashed the fears of some cadres and masses about going to Sanbian for salt ('men and animals will die . . . they will go and not return'). On the contrary, the animals carrying salt returned fatter, and the men were healthier and merely a little sunburned.

(iii) We proved that salt transport can earn money, and smashed the inaccurate reckless talk that we 'certainly would lose capital', 'each donkey would lose 100 *yuan*', and 'it is the greatest burden ever imposed in the Border Region'.

(iv) We showed that certain cadres at district and township level, particularly at township level, did not do their work responsibly (they did not inspect carefully), were prepared to cover-up things that were wrong (village and township heads could send poor animals and were not investigated), were corrupt (used poor kaoliang instead of beans), and had become tails following behind the masses.

 (v) The cadres played a decisive role. Deputy district head Lu Zhongcai was experienced, lively and responsible. Each time we reached a place or something happened, he held a discussion meeting of the porters – he even discussed how much salt each donkey should carry. As a result neither men nor animals came to any harm and on the contrary ended up stronger and in better spirits than when they set out.

Lessons:

(i) The district and township cadres did not pay attention to and investigate at the right time the troublemaker from Fourth township, Yang Wanbao who skulked off home and created rumours. They did not talk to him and did not report to higher levels. As a result a rumour spread among the people of the district that two people had died – deputy district head Lu and somebody Wang – and that three donkeys had died. This made people very uneasy.

(ii) There were problems along the way (some stages were hard going, one or two had many locusts, and two had little water) but they could be overcome. On bad roads we had to be more careful. Where there were locusts we travelled in the evening. Where there was little water we drank more on getting up in the morning and carried water with us. With patience all difficulties could be overcome.

(iii) The better the donkeys, the more we can earn. If we could earn 75 *yuan* for each donkey that carried 130 *jin* this time, we can earn 115 *yuan* for donkeys carrying 150 *jin*. The worse the donkeys the less we can earn, and we can even make a loss. For example, Chengguan district sent three poor donkeys (one with bad loins, one with bad legs, and one was exhausted). As a result they did not carry salt. Each donkey wasted 165 *yuan* in travelling expenses and the total loss including porters was over 1,000 *yuan*. At the same time this showed that work must be done carefully and you cannot muddle through. If the district and township had carefully inspected the donkeys sent this time, worked conscientiously, and not given any favours, we would not have made these losses since everyone would have known about the poor donkeys.

(iv) If we had not stayed at inns along the way and let the animals out to pasture not buying hay, we could have saved over 50 *yuan* per donkey. What we save becomes earnings.

(v) We must pay more attention to the national laws. Because we were not careful we had 50 *jin* of salt and one sack confiscated. This was an unnecessary loss. (This report was published in the *Liberation Daily* 14, 15 September 1941.)

144

7

ON THE DEVELOPMENT OF
SELF-SUPPORTING INDUSTRY

The agriculture, animal husbandry, handicraft industry, cooperatives and salt industry discussed above are all economic undertakings by the people. The Party and government give guidance and help within the bounds of possibility and need so that these things can develop and the requirements of the people can be met. At the same time, the portion handed over to the government by the people in the form of taxes ensures a part of the government's needs (for example, grain tax, salt tax and other taxes) and the portion handed over in the form of trade ensures another part of the government's needs (for example, raw cotton, cotton yarn, cotton cloth, wool, etc.). Their basic nature is that of undertakings run by the people. Only in the case of the salt industry, where 40,000 packs of salt are transported and sold under the control of the government's Salt Company and the 5,000 or so packs are consumed directly by government personnel, does a part (about one-seventh of the whole) belong to the public sector of the economy.

As a whole the undertakings of the public sector of the economy consist of the following three kinds: (1) the salt industry, industry and commerce run by the government; (2) the agriculture, industry and commerce run by the army; and (3) the agriculture, industry and commerce of the official organizations of the Party and government. These all directly ensure the supply of the living and other expenses of the Party, government and army personnel. According to accounts for 1942 and the budget for 1943, the amount supplied in this way exceeds the amount handed over by the people in the form of taxes (including the grain tax). Therefore publicly-run economic undertakings have become the greater of the two large sources

145

ensuring financial supplies. Their importance cannot be over-stated.

The reasons we pay attention to publicly-run economic construction are both historical and contemporary. During the civil war, the Party Central established some publicly-run industry and commerce in the Jiangxi Soviet in order to meet the needs of the war. At that time, we initiated the growing of vegetables and raising of pigs by the various official organizations and schools so as to make up for the lack of provisions. Only the army did not have experience in production. Also, since the peasants of Jiangxi were comparatively rich and numerous, it was not yet necessary for us ourselves to set-to to provide grain. These are historical reasons. Since the War of Resistance began, we have found ourselves in a very special situation. At first the Guomindang provided a very small amount of rations for our army. Subsequently it cut them off entirely. The Border Region was blockaded, leaving us no alternative but to become self-supporting in supplying the needs of the War of Resistance. These are contemporary reasons.

After the War of Resistance began, attention was turned to publicly-run economic construction in 1938. Since we could not cover the costs of our army we began a production movement. However, at that time we only ordered some of the troops to take part in production, growing vegetables, raising pigs, cutting wood, making shoes and so forth on a trial basis. The aim was simply to rely on this as a way of improving the livelihood of the soldiers. We still did not plan to rely on it as a way of providing general finance and supplies. Later we saw how successful the soldiers were in this experiment. They could do a lot of productive work during their rests from training, and their living standards really improved. After this happened there was a reduction in the instances of desertion. On seeing this success, we applied the experience widely among the troops garrisoned in the Border Region. An order was issued from the Garrison Office [liushouchu] calling on the troops to learn from this example. But we still aimed at improving livelihood and not at meeting general needs. At that time, the government started to pay attention to setting up several small factories, but the official organizations and schools were not even called on to grow vegetables

146

and raise pigs. In 1939, the Guomindang issued the *Methods to Restrict the Activities of Alien Parties* and relations between the Guomindang and the Communist Party worsened. The number of official organizations and schools in the Border Region also increased. Although there was a small amount of subsidy for expenses from outside, it was already far from sufficient. We were facing a serious situation in finance and supplies. For these reasons we were forced to devise a movement for all-round mobilization to become economically self-supporting. We then raised the following questions at the congress for cadre mobilization. Do you want to starve to death? Shall we disband? Or shall we set-to ourselves? No one approved of starving to death, and no one approved of disbanding. Let us set-to ourselves – this was our answer. We pointed out this simple principle: in the final analysis, how did ancient man survive if not by getting down to it himself? Why is it that we, the sons and grandsons of these ancient men, do not even have this spark of intelligence? We also pointed out: it is very common for an exploited peasant household in a feudal society with three or four or even seven or eight mouths to feed to rely on the production of only one labour power. Such a family must not only support itself but must also pay 50 to 80 per cent of its income in rent and taxes to others. Why are we not as good as such a family? Our army is made up entirely of labour power, there are no women, no old and young. Nor is there the burden of rent and taxes. How could hunger arise? We have these powerful organs of government. Why cannot they provide their own clothing, food, housing and equipment? We reflected for a while on the reasons why ancient man and today's poor peasant were able to survive, and moreover to live better than wild animals. Without doubt it was because each had a pair of hands, and extended their hands using tools. We again considered ourselves. In fact each of us has a pair of hands, and we can extend them with tools. This period of reflection was very important. Thereafter our problems were immediately solved. In sum we affirmed that we were able to overcome economic difficulties. Our response to all problems in this respect were the three words 'set-to ourselves'. This time the tasks we set were no longer the same as those of 1938. We no longer wanted merely to improve our livelihood, but also

wanted to meet some of our general needs. The scope of mobilization was not limited to the army and we called on all forces,
official organizations and schools to carry out production. We
implemented a call for a large-scale production movement. *The
Song of Opening up New Land* was a new song from that period,
and so was *The Production Chorus*. This call not only mobilized
the several tens of thousands of personnel in the Party, government, army and schools, but also mobilized the common folk of
the Border Region. In that year the common folk opened up over
1 million mu of new land. This call also reached all over north
China. Many units of the Eighth Route Army at the battlefront
also carried out production during breaks in the fighting. This
was the first stage of our movement for production self-
sufficiency. This stage included the three whole years of 1938,
1939 and 1940. During this stage the government's industrial
construction advanced and the army, official organizations and
schools developed agricultural production.

From 1941 until this Senior Cadres' Conference (December
1942) has been the second stage. The foundation for self-
supporting production had already been firmly laid. During
these two years, personnel increased and many people unable to
find enough to eat outside came to the Border Region seeking
food. The 359 Brigade also came to strengthen defences along
the Yellow River. The troops have grown in number and support
from outside has completely ceased. There are only two sources
for the government's living and operating expenses, the people
and the government itself. As a result of two years' hard work the
proportion of the total amount coming from the government
itself is greater than that coming from the people. Experience
during this stage makes us feel grateful to those people who
blockaded us. For the blockade as well as having its negative
drawbacks also brought about a positive side, which was to
encourage us to be determined to set-to ourselves. As a result we
achieved our goal of overcoming difficulties and gained experience in running economic enterprises. The old saying 'Hardship
and distress help you to success' is something we have come to
understand entirely and consciously.

During the first of the two stages we have gone through, the
troops, official organizations and schools placed emphasis on

agriculture and the government developed industry. During the second stage we stressed commerce in order to provide for the critical needs of the moment. With the exception of those troops, official organizations and schools which persisted in the policy of putting agriculture in a prime position, the rest developed business skills and did not place such heavy emphasis on agriculture as in the first stage. However, the government, troops, official organizations and schools all developed industry and handicrafts. After this Senior Cadres' Conference we will enter a new stage of development. In the new stage our economic base will already be rather firm and our experience fairly wide. We should put agriculture in first place, industry, handicrafts, transport and animal husbandry in second place, and commerce in third place. Since commerce can only help in an emergency, we cannot and should not attempt to lay a long-lasting foundation upon it.

Distinctions between the government, the army, and the official organizations and schools in the public sector of the economy can only be made in terms of management and not in terms of an economic nature. Therefore in the following discussion on self-supporting industry we shall treat the industry run by all three as a whole, and when discussing the self-supporting economy of the army and the official organizations and schools, we shall again look at their industrial production separately. However, since industry run by the government is the largest part of all publicly-run industry (government textile mills produce 56 per cent of the 22,000 bolts of cloth produced annually by all publicly-run textile mills; the output of government paper factories is 70 per cent of all publicly-run paper production; the output of government soap factories is 70 per cent of all Border Region soap production), it is rational to deal with all self-supporting industry alongside that run by the government.

Why should unified, self-supporting industry be run in such a dispersed way? The main reason is that the labour force is divided among the various branches of the Party, government and army. If it were centralized, we would destroy their activism. For example, we encouraged 359 Brigade to set up the Daguang Textile Mill and did not order it to combine with a government mill because most of the several hundred employees at the mill were selected from the officers and men of 359 Brigade. They work to produce the bedding and clothing requirements of the Brigade and their enthusiasm is high. If we centralized, we would destroy this enthusiasm. Another important reason for dispersed operation is that raw materials are in many different locations and this causes transport problems. For example, in order to meet the needs of the Party, government and army personnel of Guanzhong, Longdong, Sanbian, and Suide the bedding and clothing industry finds it best to produce cloth (or buy it) on the spot, and to make it up on the spot. It certainly should not concentrate its making up in Yan'an alone. Thus we use the activism of the various branches to undertake production to meet their own needs. Adopting the policy of 'dispersed operation' is correct and ideas aimed at centralizing everything are wrong. However, enterprises of the same kind carried out within the same area should be centralized as much as possible. Unlimited dispersal is not profitable. At present we are already carrying out or about to carry out centralization of this kind. One example is the handing over to government control of the Tuanjie Textile Mill of the Central Committee's Central Administration Bureau [Zhongyang Guanliju] and the Jiaotong Textile Mill of the Rear Services Department [houqin bu]. Perhaps this process of dispersal at first and centralization later cannot be avoided. Dispersal makes it possible to use the activism of various branches when setting something up, and centralization enables the various branches to get better supplies. But it is very important that dispersed management does not lead to forgetting centralized leadership. This facilitates unified planning, balanced supplies, and essential arrangements in rational management and distribution. Up to now we have had great shortcomings in this respect and they must be corrected in future. To sum up, our policy is 'centralized leadership and dispersed operation'. Not only is industry like this, agriculture and commerce are too.

At this point we must distinguish between two forms of publicly-run agriculture, industry and commerce, the large and the small. Large should be centralized and small should be dispersed. Examples of things for which we should encourage dispersed operation include agricultural work such as growing vegetables, raising pigs, cutting wood and making charcoal, and handicrafts such as shoemaking, knitting, or small mills when both are run by one or more provision units [huoshi danwei] to provide for their own daily food, bedding and clothing needs and to make up deficiencies in running expenses; or cooperatives and small-scale commerce operated to provide for consumption costs or to earn a small profit to cover office expenses. These things must be dispersed, being carried out and developed everywhere. They cannot be centralized and should not be. This is one kind. However, there is another kind. Examples of this are such things as large agricultural plans to provide a definite amount of grain for a whole brigade or regiment of troops – that is the military farming [tun tian] plan; large agricultural stations run to meet the grain and vegetable requirements of many official organizations; large workshops and factories run to provide for the bedding, clothing and daily requirements of a whole brigade, a regiment, or a large number of official organizations; and large-scale commerce run to meet the operating costs of such large units. All these things must have a unified plan, centralized control, and strict regulation of expenditure. We cannot allow them to lack coordination and operate without restraint. However, agriculture, industry and commerce which should be under centralized leadership must not be put entirely in the hands of one single official organization for the whole Border Region. Instead the unified plan drawn up by such an official organization (at present the Border Region Finance and Economy Committee and its office) according to the needs of the whole and the parts and the possibilities for operation, is handed over to the Party, government and army systems for separate implementation. Within the Party, government and army systems, there is also a unified plan with division in operation. These are the features of the policy of 'centralized leadership and dispersed operation' in the publicly-run sector of the economy of the Border Region.

In the five years since 1938, the public sector of the economy has made some very great achievements. These achievements are worth treasuring for ourselves and for our nation. That is, we have established a new model for the national economy. The reason that this is a new model is that it is neither the old

Bismarckian model of the national economy nor the new Soviet model of the national economy but it is the national economy of the New Democracy or the Three People's Principles.

Our publicly-run, self-supporting industry has not yet reached the stage of supplying fully all our needs. We still cannot talk of using surplus capacity to meet the needs of the people. As yet those needs can only be met by the Party and government providing organizational stimulus and the people setting-to themselves. At present all our efforts are aimed at meeting the needs of self-sufficiency within two or three years, particularly the need for cotton cloth. We must not indulge in the fantasy that in present circumstances we can have tremendous development. That will only do harm.

Below I shall discuss our publicly-run economic undertakings over the past five years item-by-item beginning with self-supporting industry.

We first began to pay attention to the construction of publicly-run industry in 1938. In that year the Border Region successively established the Refugee Textile Mill, the paper factory, the bedding and clothing factory, the agricultural implements factory, and the Eighth Route Army medicine factory. Later on most of these factories each provided an important stimulus. At the time the industrialist Mr Shen Hong voluntarily moved his ten privately-owned machines to the Border Region to serve the Eighth Route Army, and Mr Shen himself came to the Border Region to work. Thereafter many scientific and technical personnel also came to the Border Region to work, enabling the Border Region to gather a pool of scientific and technical talent as the guiding force in the establishment of industry.

In 1939 the blockade of the Border Region economy began. Imports of industrial products were limited. The Party Central issued the calls to 'set-to ourselves' and to be 'self-reliant'. After the Border Region Government held the agricultural exhibition in January, it held an industrial exhibition on Labour Day, which stimulated enthusiasm to develop industry. The government and the Rear Services Department sent people to Xi'an to select and buy machines and materials. They also organized spinning and weaving cooperatives and oil-pressing and tile-making producer cooperatives in Yan'an and Ansai. Although the machines and materials bought from Xi'an were insufficient, they became one of the major material strengths in the development of Border Region industry over the past few years. In that year we also set up the Xinhua Chemical Factory and the Guanghua Medicine Factory, and began to explore the thick coal-seams at Shilipu in Yan'an county.

The development of industry in 1940 was carried out under the policy of becoming 'semi-self-sufficient' in production. It was decided to make the development of light industry the key feature. In January we held the second industrial exhibition and reviewed the strength of our factories. The Border Region Bank lent 1 million yuan to expand factory capital, to set up proper factory sites and to continue buying materials. In February the Central Committee put forward the policy of 'centralized leadership and dispersed operation'. In September Commander Zhu promoted the wool-spinning movement and developed some wool-spinning and weaving undertakings. Very many large official organizations and schools and troop units planned actively to set up factories. They sent people to existing factories to study techniques. They studied methods of control and fixed plans for the rapid development of industry in 1941.

In 1941 the Central Committee put forward the policy of 'moving from semi-self-sufficiency to complete self-sufficiency'. Under this policy the Bank increased its loan by 3 million yuan and the government also invested 500,000 yuan in the publicly-run factories. Many official organizations and troop units also set aside funds to establish factories. On the Eighth of March Festival[1] we held a production exhibition. In December the large Bank building was completed and we held another industrial exhibition presided over by the Bank. The following list gives the factories set up by the official organizations and schools directly under the Central Committee in 1942 so as to show the efforts made by the various units to develop industry at this time. These industries are all handicraft factories, none large and some very small.

(1) The Xin Zhongguo Textile Mill, the Shiyan Factory, the wooden implements factory, the carpentry factory, the first and

---

[1] That is, International Women's Day.

153

second charcoal factories, the tile factory, and the bedding and clothing factory run by the Finance and Economy Office directly under the Central Committee. Total capital over 200,000 yuan. More than 220 employees.

(2) The Shengli Wool Factory and Shengli Carpentry Factory set up by the Central Organization Department [Zhongyang Zuzhibu].

(3) The Qiyi Mill set up by the Central Propaganda Department [Zhongyang Xuanchuanbu].

(4) The Tuanjie Textile Mill set up by the Marxism-Leninism Institute.

(5) The Sun Yat-sen Textile Mill set up by the Central Party School.

(6) The blanket factory, mill, alcohol factory, glass factory and machine factory set up by the National Sciences Institute.

(7) The factories run by the Lu Hsun Academy, the North Shaanxi Public School [Shaangong], the Youth League cadres and the Women's University.

(8) The Xinhua Carpentry Factory and the bedding and clothing factory run by the Central Printing and Publishing Department.

(9) The Yanyuan Paper Factory run by the instruction brigade (jiaodao dadui).

The above lists twenty-seven factories run by the systems directly controlled by the Central Committee with a total of 447 employees and more than 400,000 yuan capital. Most were set up with the aim of achieving economic self-sufficiency.

These apart, there are several small factories run by the Economic Construction Department [Jingjianbu], the Garrison Office, the Public Security headquarters, the Border Region Finance and Economy Office, 359 Brigade and various special offices. The Daguang Textile Mill of 359 Brigade has a fairly large output. The various regiments of 359 Brigade also have their own small-scale cotton or wool-spinning and weaving workshops.

The industry constructed from 1938 to 1941 is now expanding. Development during 1941 was particularly vigorous and provided a foundation for the work of 1942. However throughout the period construction was carried out rather blindly. Many personnel lacked conscious awareness. They only thought of the present and not of the future. They only thought of dispersed operation and not of unified leadership. They had an entirely anarchic outlook. As a result some factories closed down as soon as they were built, some announced they were closing down after a short period of operation and some merged with other factories. Only a portion of them have continued to exist. To take textile enterprises near Yan'an, by 1942 only three large factories, the Refugee, the Jiaotong and the Tuanjie and two small factories, the Xinghua and the Gongyi remained. This winding path could not be avoided at the time, since one can only gain experience from paths that one has already travelled. But having gained experience from this stage, it would be better to avoid following a similar winding path in new industrial construction.

In 1942 the Reconstruction Department laid down the policy of 'consolidating existing publicly-run factories and developing rural handicrafts'. Government investment in industry was 1,700,000 yuan. Rural handicrafts run by the people had already greatly expanded before this year. In Suide, for example, there were 600–700 cotton cloth hand-looms. Blanket-making, leather-tanning and ironwork had also developed in other places. The public and private textile industry has developed particularly quickly and it has a lot of problems. In order to ensure the development of the textile industry, we have reduced the import tax on raw cotton and foreign yarn to 1 per cent and increased the import tax on bolts of cloth to 15 per cent. In Suide the bank organized the 'the Yongchang Native Cloth Producing and Selling Company' with capital of 2 million yuan. It issues raw cotton and collects yarn and cloth, encouraging the peasant women to spin yarn and weave cloth. Since cloth-weaving by peasant households has expanded, much of the cloth produced by privately-run, small-scale, capitalist textile production cooperatives can no longer be sold. They also have difficulties with the supply of native yarn. They have no choice but to reduce their scope of operation, or to become fragmented, distributing their equipment among the people and transforming themselves into family subsidiaries. Since publicly-run textile mills chiefly supply for public use, they can maintain themselves. But they also have problems with the supply of raw cotton and yarn. This year the Zhenhua main factory and branch factory of the publicly-run paper industry completed the task of supplying the Publications Office with 3,000 rolls of paper made from *malan* grass. The Lihua first and second factories originally planned to produce 2,500 rolls but did not succeed. This year's output will not exceed 500 rolls. Other publicly-run paper factories experience great difficulty since there is no market for their paper. The products of the publicly-run woollen industry such as blankets are aimed at solving problems of finance. The government does not use them itself. Some are exported and others are sold to the troops. The fine-spun woollen thread produced is particularly well received and brings a good profit. Beginning in September, the Jiaotong, Xinghua and Tuanjie textile mills, and the first and second Lihua paper factories were all handed over to the control of the Border Region Government from the Central Committee and the Rear Services Department systems. In order to ensure raw materials for spinning and weaving in 1943, we have begun to buy cotton from the three eastern counties this year. We plan to buy 750,000 *jin*. To ensure the supply of raw materials for paper manufacture, we have raised a levy of 730,000 *jin* of *malan* grass from the counties of Ganquan, Yan'an, Ansai, Anding, and so forth. The factories should wait until they have carried out the policy of better workers and simpler administration before dealing with the recruitment of personnel.

The year 1942, and particularly this Senior Cadres' Conference, is an important landmark in beginning to get rid of blindness and anarchy, and for introducing consciousness and unified and planned operation into the whole of the public sector of the Border Region economy, and especially into publicly-run industry. Although the Central Committee put forward the principle of 'centralized leadership and dispersed operation' long ago in February 1940, only in 1942 has it attracted comrades' attention. It has only obtained unanimous acceptance at this Senior Cadres' Conference. Five years of practical experience has made us progress a lot. After this conference, the whole public sector, industry included, must be reorganized so that it develops healthily.

Above I have given a simple outline of the history of industry in the Border Region over the past five years. By December 1942 we have seven kinds of industry, textiles, bedding and clothing, paper, printing, chemical, tools and coal and charcoal.[2] There are seven textile mills[3] with 26,900,000 yuan capital and 1,427 employees; eight bedding, clothing and shoe factories with 1,001,100 yuan capital and 405 employees; twelve paper factories with 4,100,000 yuan capital and 437 employees: three printing factories with 5,200,000 yuan capital and 379 employees; twelve chemical factories (medicine, soap, leather, pottery, petrol, etc.) with 17,030,000 yuan capital and 674 employees; nine tool factories with 3,662,792 yuan capital and 237 employees; and twelve coal and charcoal factories with 1,777,070 yuan capital and 432 employees. The total figures are sixty-two factories with 59,670,962 yuan capital and 3,991 employees.[4] Although our industry is still very small and mainly takes the form of handicrafts with not much machine industry, nevertheless it has taken five years of effort, laid down an initial foundation and played a part in ensuring supplies and regulating commodity prices. Developing from this foundation, it can certainly plan an even greater role.

Our most important self-supporting industries are the textile industry and the bedding and clothing industry. These are what the several tens of thousands of troops and personnel in the official organizations and schools rely upon each year for their cloth, bedding and clothing. Without them we would be frozen. In 1942 our textile industry was already capable of producing over 22,000 bolts of cloth. However we needed 40,000–50,000 bolts and we can only reach our goal of self-sufficiency through great efforts. If we want to develop textiles, we must carry out the following policies.

(1) We must raise cotton-cloth import duty and protect native cloth. At the same time, the troops and official organizations and schools must use only native cloth produced in the Border Region.

[2] Both the 1947 and 1949 editions here give the term *shitan* which may be a misprint for *shihui*, lime. However in the following discussion the term used is *meitan* which probably refers to coal and charcoal. I have translated *shitan* as 'coal and charcoal' in what follows, noting its occurrence in case 'lime' was intended.

[3] The 1949 edition gives the number as eighteen.

[4] Totalling up the figures quoted gives sixty-three factories.

(2) We must generally encourage peasant women to spin cotton yarn and woollen thread to guarantee supplies of yarn and thread to the factories. At the same time, we can raise the income of the masses.

(3) We must solve problems of supply and distribution. No matter whether publicly-run, privately-run or family subsidiary, the ability to develop is chiefly related to whether problems of supply and distribution can be solved. As regards raw materials, we are still not self-sufficient in raw cotton and cotton yarn, and the sources are not dependable. Since communications are not very good either, there are problems in distribution. We must arrange things so that yarn-spinners can buy raw cotton whenever they want it, and cloth-weavers can buy yarn whenever they want it. As regards finished products, the markets for cotton cloth and woollen products are not stable. We must arrange things so that producers can sell their products at any time at suitable market-prices. These problems must be solved by the combined strength of the financial organs, commercial organs and the people's cooperatives.

(4) As for problems in the supply of clothing and bedding, we must act according to the methods implemented by the Finance Department in 1942 so as to economize on costs and get clothing at the right time.

Our papermaking industry can already produce over 5,000 rolls of *malan* paper per year. In 1943 we can increase this to 7,000 rolls, which is entirely sufficient for our printing needs. However, we must: (1) unify the production and supply of paper. *Malan* paper is not suitable for general use apart from printing. It cannot be sold if the printing departments do not want it. At present we have the following situation: if the printing factories do not use enough, the paper factories cannot sell and have to stockpile, capital turnover is sluggish and this influences production. In order to solve this contradiction between supply and demand in 1943, we should unify purchase and supply, and make precise economic relationships between particular official organizations and paper factories. (2) We must improve the quality of the paper. With existing equipment and technical conditions the quality of the paper can be improved at a greater cost in work and raw materials. From the point of view of function and significance, a slightly greater cost is worthwhile. On the other hand we must study improvements in papermaking implements so as to raise production efficiency.

Our printing industry is a modernized cultural tool, and a large quantity of books and papers depend on it. In 1942 printing shops of the Central Committee, Eighth Route Army and Northwest Bureau printed 51,600,000 characters. In 1943 this can be increased to 53,600,000. However, we must increase equipment and ensure the supply of paper.

Our chemical industry includes medicine, soap, leather, pottery, glass, alcohol, matches, petrol and so forth. The Eighth Route Army and Guanghua medicine factories can produce some of the Western and Chinese medicines needed for military and public use, but we are still not entirely self-sufficient. In 1943 we should study the medicinal materials produced in the Border Region, and set up the means for buying raw materials so as to increase the production of necessary medicines. The Xinhua and Daguang factories make soap. Their production increases daily and their quality is good. As well as meeting our own needs, they can sell outside. In 1943 the Xinhua factory can produce 420,000 pieces of soap valued at 7 million *yuan*. And it has prospects of development. The scale of leather-tanning is small and the cost of materials high. It cannot develop much. If we could use plant materials produced in the Border Region to manufacture leather for military use then there would be some prospect of development. There are three small pottery kilns making pottery for daily and industrial uses. Glass has already been successfully trial-produced and we have decided to set up a factory. We can also make our own alcohol for industrial and medical use. We have still not been able to solve the problem of supply of phosphorous for making matches. We are now investigating the possibility of getting it from animal bones. Apart from these, there is petrol from Yanchang which supplies a little each year for military use. The white wax it contains can be supplied for daily use. In sum, the chemical industry must choose to expand and introduce the supply of things which are urgently needed or are profitable and possible. It should not bother with the rest.

Our tool-manufacturing industry supplies spinning-machinery, weaving-machinery, cotton-bowing and crushing machinery, papermaking equipment, horse-carts, carpenters' tools, agricultural implements and so forth. They are mainly handicraft tools but are extremely important. We must do research into improvements, and provide for expansion.

Our coal industry[5] is concentrated in Yan'an and Guanzhong. Its output is chiefly for daily use. Although it is small-scale, it is very important.

The Border Region lacks iron, which impedes the manufacture and improvement of industrial and agricultural tools. At present we are holding trials in Guanzhong and there are hopes of success. If we can make iron, we can solve a major problem of the Border Region.

The above discussion has roughly covered the whole of publicly-run, self-sufficient industry. Textiles, papermaking, bedding and clothing, printing, chemical, toolmaking and coal all have reasonable prospects for development. Their first target is to meet the needs of the army and government, and their second is to supply some of the people's needs. We should make the following improvements in 1943 in order to meet these targets.

(1) Increase capital (the amount to be decided). Each official organization concerned should draw up concrete plans for consideration by the Finance and Economy Office [of the Border Region Government – Caijing Banshichu] with the aim of investing in each of the various industries and in certain investigation and research undertakings, in order to promote the development of self-sufficient industry in a planned way.

(2) Establish a unified leadership for the whole of self-supporting industry, overcome the serious anarchy which exists now. The principle of 'centralized leadership and dispersed operation' put forward earlier is correct but it has not been thoroughly implemented. As a result, there is lack of planning, excessive dispersal in production, lack of work inspection and waste of manpower and materials among the industries run by the Reconstruction Department, the Finance Department, the troops and the official organizations. In 1943 we should set up

[5] The term *shitan* is used again.

unified leadership under the Finance and Economy Office and first make all self-supporting industry have a unified plan, no matter which branch it controls. In the unified plan we should calculate as a whole the supplies of raw materials, grain and straw, the totals for production and the coordination of sales. In supplying raw materials we must deal with the problem of many factories facing regular raw-material crises because the region is spread out and these materials are not concentrated, or because supply comes from outside. In supplying grain and hay, we should provide the factories with the grain and hay they need as calculated by the Finance Department so as to save distracting the responsible people at each factory from their concentration on looking after production. In respect of the problems of production and sales, the Finance Department and the official organization concerned should, under the unified plan of the Finance and Economy Office, give each factory responsibility to produce a definite amount so that whatever is needed is produced in the quantity required and the finished products are accepted by a definite organ at the right time solving the contradiction between production and supply. In the unified plan we must realize mutual aid between enterprises and get rid of departmentalism, which gives rise to independence from each other or even hinderance of each other. We must also realize unified inspection, giving encouragement and criticism so that the poor catch up with the good. In sum, the problem of unified leadership is the central problem in advancing self-supporting industry during 1943. We must make thorough efforts to solve it.

(3) Establish the system of economic accounting [*jingji hesuanzhi*], overcome the muddled situation within the enterprises. To achieve this we must do the following. First, each factory unit should have independent capital (liquid and fixed) so that it can handle the capital itself and its production is not frequently hindered through capital problems. Second, income and expenditure in each factory unit should be handled according to fixed regulations and procedures, putting an end to the confused situation where income and expenditure are not clear and procedures are not settled. Third, according to the actual situation in the factories, some should adopt the cost-accounting system [*chengben kuaijizhi*] and some need not for the time

being. However, all factories must calculate costs. Fourth, each factory should have regulations for inspecting the rate of progress in completing the annual and monthly plans. They should not let things slide by doing without inspections for long periods. Fifth, each factory should have regulations for economizing on raw materials and looking after tools, and for fostering the practice of doing these things. All these points are the chief elements of the system of economic accounting. Once we have a strict accounting system, we can examine fully whether an enterprise is profitably operated or not.

(4) Improve factory organization and administration, overcome the tendency to build organizations like those of government organs [jiguanhua] and relaxation of discipline. The first thing we must reform is the irrational phenomenon of excessive staffing in factories. At present many of our factories are extremely irrationally organized. There are too many personnel, the organization is too large, the ratio between administrative personnel and those directly involved in production is not right, and systems for administering large factories are being used in our small factories. These phenomena must be quickly corrected so that all factories carry out 'enterprization' [qiyehua].[6] All factories should shrink or grow according to their economic prosperity. All salaries should be paid from the factories' own profit and not from tax grain, government clothing and government grants. Second, we should implement the ten-hour work system and the progressive piecework wages system [jijian leijin gongzizhi] so as to raise work enthusiasm and increase production. The eight-hour system is something to be implemented in future with the development of large-scale industry. At present we should universally implement the ten-hour system and make employees understand that this is a requirement of the War of Resistance. An egalitarian system of wages destroys the distinction between skilled labour and unskilled labour and the distinction between industriousness and laziness, thus lowering work enthusiasm. We can only stimulate labour enthusiasm and increase the quantity and quality of production by replacing it

[6] 'Enterprization' is contrasted with factory organization along the lines of a government organ [jiguanhua]. It implies for example the use of the economic accounting system rather than a budgetary system as in the latter.

with a progressive piecework wages system. For the moment industrial production in the army cannot adopt the piecework wages system and should have the piecework incentive system [jijian jiangli zhidu]. Next, we should improve the work of the workers' congress [zhigonghui] and launch a Zhao Zhankui[7] movement in every factory. Work done by the workers' congresses which is not suitable for raising labour discipline and activism must be changed. Within a factory, the work of the administration, Party branch and workers' congress must be united towards common ends. These common ends are to save as much as possible on costs (raw materials, tools and other expenses), to make as many and as good products as possible, and to sell them as quickly and as profitably as possible. These tasks of lower costs, better products and faster sales are the tasks shared by the administration, Party branch and workers' congress, all three of which should unite as one. Working methods which divide their work into three separate areas are entirely wrong. The three sides must organize a unified committee, in the first place to put administrative personnel, administrative work, and production plans on the right track. The task of the Party and the workers' congress is to ensure completion of the production plans. Finally the factory should reward the workers and employees with the greatest achievements, and criticize or punish workers and employees who commit errors. Without a suitable system of rewards and punishments, we cannot ensure the improvement of labour discipline and labour enthusiasm.

(5) Strengthen and enlarge textile mills, increase output of bolts of cotton cloth, struggle to achieve complete self-sufficiency in cotton cloth used by the government in 1944. Improve woollen goods and, after supplying the army's needs, increase the amount exported. In the bedding and clothing industry fix standards for the cotton cloth used and the methods of making up. Ensure that cotton garments and bedding can be used for two years.

(6) Put papermaking factories in order, improve the quality of paper. Ensure it is fully satisfactory for printing and office use. Make us entirely self-sufficient in paper for printing and office use in 1944.

[7] A model worker.

(7) Increase production of coal and oil, ensure self-sufficiency and also some exports. Set up ways of making or buying phosphorous so that match-factories can be established. As for other industries, continue with or enlarge those which are urgently needed or profitable. All those which do not match the principle of ensuring supplies or are unprofitable should be merged or closed down.

8

ON THE DEVELOPMENT OF THE
PRODUCTIVE UNDERTAKINGS OF
THE TROOPS

Which of the three branches of the public sector of our economy – the government, the army and the official organizations – is ultimately the most important in terms of directly meeting requirements most quickly and in greatest quantity? Our experience of the past few years shows that it is the army. The army's productive undertakings have become the most important part of the public sector of our economy because the army is the body which is relatively most organized and has most labour power. So long as it has no direct fighting duties, it can use all its time outside training doing work. And under our present backward technical conditions, labour is the decisive factor in economic undertakings.

The production movement in the garrison forces of the Shaan-Gan-Ning Border Region began in 1938, and one year before that in the official organizations and schools. A joint production movement of the army and the official organizations and schools together began in 1939. In 1940, 359 Brigade took on the duty of defence on the Yellow River and joined in the production movement. In 1941 and 1942, the army increased its responsibility for self-supporting production just like the official organizations and schools. However, the tasks taken on by the army were greater and occupied the most important position in the total volume of self-supporting production. It would have been impossible if during these years the army had not for the most part provided its own means of livelihood and running costs and instead had relied on the government. Responding to the Party Central and Northwest Bureau's call for 'production self-sufficiency', the army has fulfilled its production tasks in the midst of the urgent work of fighting, guarding and training. The objective circumstances of some troop units are better than those of others; some have more duties than others, some have worked harder than others, and some have employed better methods of production than others. As a result their respective level of achievement has varied. Nevertheless, in general they have all fulfilled their tasks. With very little capital and backward techniques, they have all developed agriculture, handicrafts, transport and commerce. Some have even set up relatively large-scale textile and papermaking factories. During these two years, the capital invested by the government in the army's productive undertakings has not exceeded 6 –7 million yuan in total. However, in that time they have both ensured supplies worth over 300 million yuan and they have accumulated roughly 80 million yuan capital from their agriculture, industry and commerce. They have opened up several tens of thousands of mu of land, and supplied rich experience for the whole of production construction. They have not only played a political and military role in the protection of the Border Region but have also played a role in directly providing a large amount of financial supplies and in helping to develop the Border Region economy.

Let us take a look at the self-supporting production of a certain company in a certain regiment. The income and expenditure of this company during 1941 are shown in Table 8.1.

With the exception of 750 yuan production capital from upper levels, miscellaneous payments of 360 yuan from the office, supplementary production payments of 2,855 yuan and supplementary provisions payments of 3,771 yuan given by the regimental supplies office, a total of 7,736 yuan, the expenditure of 52,530 yuan [sic] shown [Table 8.1] was met by the company's own production of 44,794 yuan. This excludes the capital accumulated for use in production the following year.

According to these figures, each regiment of ten companies can be self-supporting up to 440,440 yuan [sic].

Furthermore, there is still the self-supporting production run by the regimental headquarters [shown in Table 8.2]. The total value of production of the companies, battalions and regiments is

Table 8.1   *Income and expenditure of a regimental company in 1941*

1941 Income (*yuan*)		1941 Expenditure (*yuan*)	
Transport of coal and charcoal (*shitan*)	698.20	Miscellaneous expenses	1,312.00
Transport of salt	772.45	2 mules	2,850.00
Sawn planks	3,256.40	1 donkey	574.00
Wooden beams	630.00	600 sweat shirts	600.00
Pig sales	738.02	Shoes (2 pairs per man)	405.50
Stables	2,256.00	87 towels	128.00
Corn sales	998.20	Tobacco	179.00
Export business	935.60	Basins	90.00
Miscellaneous business	481.25	Production tools	181.00
Oil (840 *jin*)	16,800.00	Oil	16,880.00
Meat (1,610 *jin*)	16,100.00	Meat	16,100.00
Vegetables (4,690 *jin*)	4,690.00	Vegetables	4,690.00
Charcoal (5,000 *jin*)	500.00	Charcoal	500.00
Firewood (2,555 *jin*)	2,555.00	Firewood	2,555.00
Received production capital	750.00	Supplementary provisions	3,771.00
Miscellaneous office payments	360.00	5 months' pay	567.50
Supplementary production payments	3,885.00	Rifle-cleaning	22.00
		Summer clothing	100.00
Supplementary provisions payments	3,771.00	New Year costs	146.00
		Office	339.00
		Horse feed [?*magan*]	620.00
Total	59,147.12	Total	52,530.00
Net income 6,537.12 *yuan*[1]			

[1] The sum of the income column is in fact 601,77.12 and the expenditure column 52,610 giving a net income of 7,567.12 *yuan*. The tables probably contain a number of typographical errors which are carried over in the discussion. There are discrepancies between the 1947 and 1949 editions.

Table 8.2   *The values (in yuan) of self-supporting production by regimental headquarters*

Regimental headquarters	197,426
Directly controlled forces	27,149
1st Battalion headquarters	18,629
2nd Battalion headquarters	12,777
3rd Battalion headquarters	7,408
Total	263,389

703,828 *yuan*. The regiment's total annual expenditure (including grain and a proportion of clothing and bedding) is 896,838 *yuan*, which leaves a shortfall of 185,510 *yuan* [*sic*] to be supplemented from upper levels. As a result the regiment's own self-supporting production accounts for 79 per cent of consumption and supplements from above account for 21 per cent. If we add the large amount of self-supporting production carried out by the brigade headquarters, the proportion for the whole brigade far exceeds 80 per cent.

The following material is a summary by the Garrison Office of five years' production by the garrison army. We can see the general situation in self-supporting production by the army.

A SUMMARY OF FIVE YEARS' PRODUCTION BY THE GARRISON ARMY

(a) Outline

In the new and difficult environment since the War of Resistance and following Chairman Mao's call for production, the garrison army began the production movement in the autumn of 1938. At the time, production was not yet aimed at self-sufficiency and was merely making up for deficiencies in the necessities of life. We could only give each member of the forces 0.05 *yuan* for vegetables and 1.5 *jin* of grain per day. At the market-prices of the time each *yuan* could buy 30–40 *jin* of vegetables, 2 *jin* of edible oil, or 100 *jin* of firewood. With a hundred men in a company, each day they had 5 *yuan* for vegetables. If they bought vegetables, they could not buy oil, salt and firewood. If they bought oil, salt and firewood, they could not buy vegetables. Pork was even further beyond their reach. As for their clothing and bedding, you could rarely see a soldier whose clothing was not darned and patched. Bullet bags were so tattered they could no longer carry bullets, which had to be put in pouches. Some wore padded clothes in summer and some wore shorts in winter. Some went on parade barefoot in the snow and some could not even find a broken old leather bag for leg wrappings. These were the material conditions of the troops then.

The methods used in the production movement at that time were: (i) to set up cooperatives; (ii) to plant lots of vegetables; (iii) to set up grinding-mills, to raise pigs and sheep, to make bean curd and to grow bean sprouts; (iv) to mobilize every soldier to learn to make shoes; (v) to knit woollen clothes, socks, shoes and gloves; (vi) to promote economy and prevent waste. The result of half a year's production in 1938 exceeded the plan, and the soldiers' life was greatly improved. For example, they ensured self-sufficiency in vegetables, each week they had two pork meals, they partly met requirements for woollen clothes, socks, gloves and shoes, and they supplemented the supply of bullet bags, pouches, leather bags and leg-wrappings.

The significant achievements in production of the latter half of 1938 raised the troops' enthusiasm for, and trust in, production. So in 1939 even greater tasks for self-supporting production could be put forward, reducing the burden on the people of the Border Region. In 1939 it was stipulated that the troops in their agricultural work should plant grain as well as vegetables so as to fulfil the task of producing 4,700 dan of grain. Most production in 1939 was agricultural and 25,136 mu of new land was opened up over the whole year. At first it was estimated that 2 dou of hulled grain could be harvested per mu giving a total of 4,986 dan. But because the new land was just being broken in, there were not enough agricultural tools, leadership experience was not even and some of the land suffered natural disasters, only 2,590 dan of hulled grain was harvested. At this time the troops still had little capital and commerce had not yet developed.

In 1940 the production tasks for the troops stipulated that each section should provide grain for one-and-a-half months, a total of 3,400 dan. In that year the troops opened up 20,679.7 mu of land which should have given 4,136 dan of hulled grain. Because the harvest was poor, they only got 2,400 dan. In order to fulfil its duties, each section also took-on salt transport, digging liquorice root and felling trees (in Guanzhong they also did some commercial work). The garrison army earned a total profit of 2,236,516.16 yuan from this supplementary production. This, together with the agricultural harvest, provided grain for one-and-a-half months and also met part of the supplements for equipment.

In 1941 the operating budget for all troops was 4,479,536.40 yuan and the task for production was to provide 400,000 yuan. However, the result was entirely different. The requirement for operating expenses was much greater and the task for self-supporting production was much greater than originally estimated. Chiefly as a result of the call by Commander Zhu to select six battalions to get salt, we got a total of 56,966 packs of salt valued at 236,408.90 yuan. In agriculture 14,794.6 mu were opened up and 1,170 dan of miscellaneous grains harvested. In commerce the total profit was 12,019,592.72 yuan. Because of price inflation, the value of paper money fell. Regular expenses and clothing and bedding expenses for the whole year were 7,881,757.17 yuan. (All this excludes the income and expenditure of one regiment and the forces in Guanzhong.) The average daily expenses for provisions per man over the whole year was 0.50 yuan. Apart from the 0.10 yuan issued by the State, we provided 0.40 yuan ourselves, a total of 2,592,000 yuan. The total for the above regular expenses, bedding and clothing expenses and provisions expenses was 10,473,757.17 yuan,

5,673,804.35 yuan above the original budget. There was still a surplus after payments were made from production income.

In 1942 the budget for expenses (excluding grain, clothing and bedding) was 5,833,636 yuan and we took on the task of helping central expenses with 2,500,000 yuan. The year's production plan was for 12,400,000 yuan. By August (statistics for the later period not yet available), commerce had earned a profit of 38,969,230.20 yuan and industry had a profit of 431,773.40 yuan, giving a total of 39,401,004.60 yuan.

By June we had received 1,440,058.60 yuan running expenses, and supplementary expenses for the first issue of summer clothing of 206,825 yuan. Actual expenditure was running expenses 7,750,598.85 yuan, supplements for bedding and clothing 3,067,730.60 yuan, and supplements for provisions (the State issued 0.70 yuan per man per day and the actual cost was 3.00 yuan) over the half-year, 9,180,000 yuan. Most of the winter clothing and bedding for the latter half of the year was provided by the brigades and regiments themselves. The second issue of summer clothing, half of the padded clothing, 40 per cent of the bedding, and bindings, bullet bags, grenade pouches, padded cotton shoes, and light shoes, these eight items had a total value of 12,641,200 yuan. Other things like charcoal for heating in winter were provided by each unit itself. As for animal fodder, in 1941 we provided two months' horse-feed ourselves. In 1942 the Finance Department issued eight months' hay for horses, leaving two months' unaccounted for. In general we cut two months' supply of grass ourselves, saving roughly 1,200,000 yuan. Furthermore, in 1942 the budget for horse fodder was 11,000 dan. According to the regulations of the Finance Department 1 dou of hulled grain is equivalent to 2 dou of horse fodder. But this is insufficient and it is necessary to increase the annual amount by 2,750 dan which comes to 1,375,000 yuan at 500 yuan per dan.

The outcome of five years' production has been that, besides meeting annual running expenses, clothing and bedding expenses and provisions expenses, current financial assets include 24 million yuan commercial capital, 556 transport animals (excluding plough oxen, and excluding the First and Fifth regiments) with a value of 11,232,000 yuan, and factory capital of 712,000 yuan. The combined total is 35,944,000 yuan.

(Note: The above summary does not include 359 Brigade and the peace preservation corps, [bao'an budui].)

(b) Lessons

(1) The reason why the forces of the Border Region have been able to carry out self-supporting production and solve great problems over the past few years is their immense labour power and better organizational

strength, and the fact that the Border Region also has rich resources to develop. This experience proves that the troops can be entirely self-sufficient. Because the troops have solved the problem of self-sufficiency over the past few years and increased their faith in production, they have realized that self-sufficiency is one of the major tasks in building-up the army, and is one of the best methods of overcoming hardships and coming through a difficult period.

(2) The production construction of the troops is part of the economic construction of the whole Border Region. Although in the past the troops did well in working hard to fulfil production tasks, ideologically they did not emphasize the relationship with the construction of the Border Region. Therefore they still had a shallow understanding of the development of the agricultural and industrial base. They were not good enough at working hard to establish a secure foundation. Their thinking on unified construction was also muddled. There was even a lack of coordination between units and incidences of serious breaches of command discipline. These shortcomings must be resolutely and ruthlessly corrected.

(3) Under conditions of backward production methods, the production base must chiefly be built up depending on the labour power and economic base of each unit. Therefore the government's financial and economic policy should look after the productive undertakings of these units. Within the confines of the government's unified policy, they should be allowed full development and profitability. Only this way can the development of productive undertakings have greater organization, greater strength, greater unity, greater rationality, and greater ability to fight the blockade in a unified way. The greatest shortcoming of the troops in production is to pay most attention to commerce and to neglect agriculture. In future they must improve and encourage agricultural production.

(4) In their productive work, the troops should grasp ideological leadership tightly and set up and strengthen the regulations and leadership organs in production. They should correct and guard against cadres doing things without coordination, becoming decadent, eating and living well, spending recklessly, not economizing, not stressing effective results, and adopting other corrupt practices.

The above sums up our opinions.

The self-supporting production of 359 Brigade is the best among the various units in the garrison forces. In the first place the leading comrades of 359 Brigade have grasped the strategy of agriculture first, industry and transport second, and commerce third. They have taken advantage of their lack of active duties, the suitable environment of Nanniwan for agriculture and of the

Suide special military area for light industry. They have mobilized the large amount of labour power and within three years have completed large assignments for economic self-sufficiency. In particular they have grasped the policy of taking agriculture as the core so that the economic base rests on a secure foundation. Second, the troops of 359 Brigade have carried out the following concrete economic construction: (i) Their grain production in 1940 was a failure, but they were not disheartened. They persevered in 1941 and got tremendous results. In 1942 they strengthened this foundation. They opened up 25,000 mu of land and planted grain, vegetables, hemp and tobacco, meeting the troops' requirements of vegetables, lamp-oil, hemp for shoes and tobacco, and supplementing supplies of grain, vegetable-oil, horse beans and fodder. Thus after only two years' work, they laid the foundation of the agricultural economy of all the companies in the brigade. Furthermore, the period of labour for all the officers and men was no more than two months per year. Ten months were left for troop exercises, and training was not impeded. According to the new method thought out by the brigade, each company sets up a specialist agricultural labour group of six or seven men and the masses of soldiers only provide extensive assistance during the busy agricultural seasons. In this way training time is even greater. (ii) They have used the farms to develop animal husbandry. In 1942 the whole brigade maintained 2,000 pigs which met the troops' requirements for meat and oil. Since the troops ate more meat, they saved grain. In addition they organized groups of men to gather firewood, make charcoal and saw planks, which not only provided for their own fuel and building needs but also provided a surplus for sale. (iii) They also built up industry and handicrafts. In 1941 they assigned some soldiers and rear-service personnel to establish the Daguang Textile Mill and Daguang Soap Factory. Now there are 'Daguang' products on the market in addition to those they consume themselves. They set up ten salt-wells in Suide and Nanniwan, one charcoal-pit, two carpentry factories, three iron-factories, six mills, eight flour-mills and one oil-press. They also mobilized the soldiers during their spare time after training to spin woollen thread, to make various kinds of utensils from willow and elm wands, to make writing-boards from birch bark, to make vegetable-boxes and to make lamplighters. This work done by the soldiers not only benefited the whole but also profited the individuals. The brigade stipulated that four-fifths of all the products of handicraft labour done using publicly-owned tools should come under public ownership and one-fifth should belong to the private individual, and that two-thirds of that produced not using publicly-owned tools should come under public ownership and one-third should belong to the private individual. This method provided commodities for public use and was also equivalent to raising the soldiers' pay. (iv) They established a strong transport undertaking. Now they have a transport team which owns 600 pack-mules and is fully engaged in the transport of salt and goods. Along the road between Suide, Sanbian and Yan'an they have set up ten stables and settled a group of older and weaker personnel. (v) Their commercial organ is the Daguang Store, which has ten branches besides the main shop. The profit in the first nine months of 1942 was over 6 million *yuan*. However, this commerce only makes up 10 per cent of the brigade's total production of 60 million *yuan* (at Yan'an market-prices). (vi) The brigade has implemented a unified production plan, and regulations for production and supply. The production plan for the whole brigade is fixed by the brigade headquarters. Some undertakings are directly run by the brigade headquarters such as large-scale industry, transport and commerce. Others are run by the regiments and companies such as agriculture, animal husbandry, small industry and commerce. Inspections are carried out at each level from brigade down to individual companies. The regulations for production are also fixed by the brigade headquarters. The arrangements for soldiers spinning woollen thread described above is an example of this. The regulations for supply also preserve unity. Although the agricultural, industrial, transport and commercial undertakings are each run separately, all expenditure above a certain level must be approved from above. Lower levels cannot spend freely. This prevents instances where free spending of the fruits of production bring unequal blessings or waste. It ensures the unity of the whole brigade. (vii) They have not only developed large amounts of production, but have also carried out the policy of strict economy rigorously. For example, they laid down that they would issue three suits of summer clothing every two years and two suits of padded clothing every three years, and that new bedding and clothing would only be issued in exchange for old. They also issued needles and thread to the soldiers so that they could repair clothes themselves. Thereafter bedding and clothing lasted longer, and the soldiers took greater care of them, greatly reducing these expenses. As mentioned above, they ordered the soldiers to make writing-boards from birch bark, vegetable-boxes and lamplighters, and issued wool to the soldiers to knit socks, gloves and so forth. This not only increased the supply of daily necessities but also economized on purchases of these things. All building construction and tool repairs for the whole brigade is done by the troops and none is contracted out. All these things have not only economized on expenditure but have also developed care for public property among the officers and men, attention to results, opposition to waste and a simple style of work that rejects ostentation.

The following material is a summary of the three years' production by 359 Brigade drawn up by its leading comrades. It shows us the actual situation in the brigade's agriculture, industry and commerce.

A SUMMARY OF PRODUCTION AND CONSTRUCTION IN 359 BRIGADE OVER THE
PAST THREE YEARS

In the three years since this brigade has returned to take up the defence of the Border Region, the implementation of the economic policy of self-reliance and self-sufficiency has been a new creation in building up the army. With the exception of grain received from the government, we have achieved 82 per cent self-sufficiency in all other expenses through carrying out this policy. In this way we overcame difficulties with material resources, improved our troops' provisions, consolidated our forces, promoted the physical strength of the soldiers, consolidated army discipline and strengthened the ties between the army and the people. The following outlines our experience over the past three years in agricultural, industrial and commercial operations.

(A) Agriculture

In response to the call for a production movement, we began agricultural production in 1940. We planned to plough and plant enough land to be self-sufficient for two months' grain, to be entirely self-sufficient

174

in vegetables from the summer onwards, and to raise enough pigs to cover our meat requirement for the New Year festivities. However, since the areas where we were stationed in Suide, Mizhi and Wuqi counties were heavily populated with little spare land, we had to travel to places over 100 *li* away (Jiulishan and Qingjian) to open up new land and wasted a lot of time in travel. Although enthusiastic and taking trouble, we did not investigate carefully nor plan suitably. As a result the harvest did not match the capital spent on tools and seeds. However, the vegetables planted near where we were stationed enabled us to be self-sufficient for these after the summer. Each provisions unit was issued 0.10 *yuan* provisions expenses per man per day, barely enough to buy oil and salt. The troops had to go up to 100 *li* away carrying charcoal for sale. They earned enough to make more charcoal and a surplus to buy pigs for raising. These productive activities laid the foundations for the companies to improve provisions. Apart from opening up all the public unused land (public cemeteries, the neighbourhood of temples, odd pieces of land near cities, stretches of old unused road, old military defence works, etc.) around the towns of Suide, Mizhi, Jiaxian, Wuqi and Qingjian where we were stationed and along the river defences, we also rented land from the local inhabitants to plant vegetables. The spirit of bitter struggle and hard work of the commanders and troops gained great sympathy and understanding from people of all walks of life. Some of the landlords from whom we rented land (like the landlords and rich peasants of Yihezhen) would not accept our rent payments. Other poor peasants voluntarily granted temporary tenant rights. This came from the deep sympathy and concern of the people for the army. For those stationed in poor agricultural regions, particularly those where the climate only suited summer and autumn crops, agricultural production was not only necessary to solve difficulties in running expenses, but was also essential to maintain the correct relationship with the people. From the end of 1939 to the spring of 1940, the troops did not have enough expenses for provisions and were short of vegetables. Personnel sent out to buy sometimes resorted to the serious actions of forced purchase or purchase at unfair prices. In carrying out agricultural production, we ensured a good political influence among the people with the exception of the small number of people in the county towns who relied on market gardening for their livelihood and spoke angrily of the poor defence forces who offered no profit.

We solved the following problems with our production in 1940. (i) We became self-sufficient in vegetables after May. (ii) We added pig-raising to self-sufficiency in vegetables and improved provisions in the latter half of the year so that each man could eat 1 *jin* of meat per month. (iii) Each provisions unit made their own agricultural implements and

raised over ten pigs. (iv) We proved the old saying: 'If you have vegetables you have half a year's grain, if you have no vegetables you have
half a year's famine.' The troops' grain was sufficient. (v) Planting grain
meant opening up new land. In the first year we got no profit from grain
since it was too far from the places we were stationed. We could not
weed at the right time and we wasted too much effort in travel. For these
reasons, the planned grain harvest was not realized.

In 1941 the troops found land they could farm and implemented the
policy of farming which the commander-in-chief himself ordered. Each
man on average farmed 6 mu of land. Each mu needed seven days' work
including opening up, planting seed, weeding and harvesting. Six mu
required forty-two days' work, from which was obtained roughly 3 dou
(lower-middle harvest) of hulled millet, and hay, also worth 3 dou
hulled grain. The grain and hay together could be exchanged for one
suit of padded clothing. If an upper-middle harvest could be obtained,
the return would increase by one-quarter. Various secondary crops
such as corn, hemp and sesame also gave a harvest the same as that of
millet. Around the edges of the 6 mu we could plant many subsidiary
crops such as castor, pumpkins, beans and so forth giving good harvests. In addition, each man planted half a mu to provide vegetables for
a whole year. Also among the products were hot peppers, garlic,
onions, lamp-oil, tobacco, grass rope for sandals, and so forth. Since we
had field crops, it was easy to raise domestic animals such as pigs, cows,
sheep, chickens, ducks, rabbits, etc. As pig-raising was most profitable,
it was the major subsidiary. Reckoning at one pig for every five men, a
hundred men could raise twenty pigs. As well as this they could raise
three sows. Every year each sow can have two litters of at the very least
four piglets. With no swine fever and no untoward events, they could
produce twenty-four pigs per year. Killing pigs at a rate of two a month,
we would have to kill twenty-four a year. The pig-breeding rate would
counterbalance the slaughter rate and there would still be surplus
piglets. From birth to slaughter, piglets can grow 5 liang per day on
average. In actual practice the annual average was indeed one pig per
five men.

As a result of agricultural production, there was a lot of vegetable
refuse. Since we were grinding flour, we got the chaff remains from the
husking, and since we were making beancurd we got the bean residues,
etc. We could raise the pigs using waste and gain great benefits. Now
the entire brigade has achieved all of the above. The wealth obtained
from agriculture and animal husbandry by each provisions unit is
increasing. All this wealth is controlled by the party branch, supervised
by all the soldiers and used rationally according to the regulations
laid down at high levels. As yet there is no summary for 1942, but
harvests will definitely be no less than last year.

Reviewing the agricultural production movement, we can make the following summary of its merits and shortcomings.

Merits

(1) The troops carried out political mobilization concerning the performance of the tasks so that all personnel realized that the slogan of self-sufficiency in production put forward by Chairman Mao was of great significance in maintaining unity in the War of Resistance and in passing through an economic crisis. The commander-in-chief himself led the way after his return to the Border Region and strengthened the soldiers' enthusiasm and endurance.

(2) Improvements in real livelihood made us feel the advantages of the production movement.

(3) The brigade and regiments fixed the whole of the annual production plan, stipulated the production tasks for the companies, and conscientiously supervised the regiments' guidance and supervision of the companies' production.

(4) The companies organized production committees to discuss and arrange the implementation of production tasks, to inspect and examine the economy (the companies' economies are entirely public) and to ensure the implementation of the supply regulations.

(5) Now every company is enjoying a self-sufficient, rich peasant family standard of living because of its agricultural production.

Shortcomings

(1) We have not paid full attention to production tools, we have not organized and employed plough oxen and we have not selected some soldiers (from among the cooks) to specialize in farming throughout the year. We have generally adopted the method of all-round mobilization, wasting time and impeding troop-training.

(2) Some cadres have taken a negative attitude towards farming and do not strive to get a larger harvest by extending the land farmed.

(3) We have not been conscientious in gathering manure.

(4) We have no cadres specially directing production.

According to experience, we must use oxen for ploughing, carting manure and harvesting (using ox-carts), prepare sufficient tools, assign cadres with special responsibility for directing production (a deputy battalion leader for production and company leaders with special duties), assign soldiers (from among the cooks) to carry out agricultural production throughout the year, mobilize all the officers and men to take part at planting, weeding and harvesting times, and stipulate the number of workdays so as to use a fixed amount of time. In this way the total work per man to farm 6 *mu* and cut a year's firewood will not exceed two months, and we shall not only get grain but will also

177

become entirely self-sufficient for all daily vegetables, meat, straw, shoes, firewood, shoes and socks. The last few items alone make up one-third of all running expenses so they cannot be considered a small problem. The grain harvest can sustain 2,000 men.

The above is a brief summary of the brigade's agricultural production.

The following list shows how much work and time it would cost a provisions unit for a hundred men to travel over 60 li to make its purchases if it did not plant vegetables itself.

Monthly vegetable consumption (1 jin per man per day)	3,000 jin
Number of purchases (each time buying 100 jin)	30 times
Labour days per purchase (each time using 2 men)	4 days
Actual days per purchase (there and back 2 days)	2 days
Labour days per month	120 days
Actual days per month	60 days
Labour days per year	1,440 days
Actual days per year	720 days

Using this table alone we can explode the lie that 'agricultural production is profitless and hinders training'.

(B) Industry

There follows a summary of our experience in establishing and developing the Daguang Textile Mill and of other handicrafts.

(1) Motivation and intention

The troops need clothing and bedding every year. The raw materials for bedding and clothing are the chief problems in supply work. In the winter of 1939 after the troops returned to the defence of the Border Region, we had difficulties in buying these raw materials and also had no money. In response to the call by Chairman Mao for self-reliance, self-sufficiency and overcoming difficulties to build up the Border Region, we made a long-term plan to run a textile mill.

(2) Trial beginnings

We began to think of running a textile mill in September 1940. At the time there was a man from Hebei in the short-term training class set up by the supply department who could weave cloth. We set up a small wooden loom, bought some foreign yarn and tried it out. Within ten days all the yarn was woven and the cloth was quite good. We could weave 100 feet per day [Chinese measurement] and costs worked out one-third cheaper than buying cloth.

Since there were weavers among the troops we decided to set up a factory and undertook the following: (i) we bought wood and built nineteen small looms in our own machine-repair shop, and we bought four metal looms from Shanxi; (ii) we bought yarn from local merchants on credit; (iii) we selected twenty skilled men from places like Gaoyang in Hebei who were among the troops.

In this way the factory got going. It was not only profitable and convenient, but also solved problems in buying cloth.

In December 1940 we decided to enlarge the factory in order to achieve self-sufficiency in cloth for the whole brigade.

Early in 1941 we abolished service personnel at all levels throughout the brigade, and collected together over a hundred youths as apprentices to study weaving.

We again bought two iron looms from the northwest of Shanxi and made a further eleven large wooden ones ourselves. In February and March we made another sixteen large wooden looms, and fourteen more towards the end of March. We thus had sixty-six looms of all kinds. At the same time we made spinning-wheels and other essential small implements.

As regards raw materials, in 1941 the government issued the brigade with 400,000 *yuan* capital for production. Of this, 250,000 *yuan* was divided among the regiments. Of the remaining 150,000 *yuan*, 100,000 was spent buying 300 bales of yarn (each bale was 7 *jin* 14 *liang* and cost 280–90 *yuan*) and some things that had to be bought (such as the wire for the looms which we could not make ourselves and had to purchase outside).

Administered by the supply department accountants, the workers divided into yarn-starchers, weavers, thread-joiners [*luoxian*], and threaders [*daxian*]. Each group had twenty to thirty men. About ten skilled men became master workmen and took charge of the technical work in starching and reeling the yarn. Intelligent youths studied weaving, and the less bright and the younger did threading and thread-joining.

As soon as the looms started working, we became aware of a need for more labour power. So taking the name, the Daguang Textile Mill, we employed fifty young boys and girls from the Suide areas as apprentices. We also took captured bandits and people who had committed mistakes from the military courts. In this way we assembled our labour force. There were then over 200 workers administered by the military training unit and the supply department. They were divided into four platoons and twelve squads (including one women's platoon; each platoon had three squads of ten or more people).

The factory was roughly taking shape. But there were still two difficult problems to be solved, first the supply of capital and raw materials, and second the control, education and training of the workers.

(a) The problem of the supply of capital and raw materials
In May 1941 we borrowed 200,000 *yuan* from the Border Region Bank but it still did not provide support for long. After that we had to make friends, build up relationships, liaise with rich merchants and buy raw materials on credit, making repayments at fixed periods.

179

Before May 1941, most foreign yarn was bought from Shanxi. After-wards, because supplies were cut off, we could only buy from Xi'an and Yan'an (Shenxin and Guanghe brands). We also bought raw cotton from Xi'an and Yan'an.

The supply of local yarn came as a result of the government's encour-agement of local women to spin. At first the wage for spinning 1 *jin* of yarn was from 3 to 7 *yuan* (raw cotton cost 4 *yuan* per *jin*), and it was divided into three grades. In July and August this was changed to issuing 1½ *jin* of prepared cotton in return for 1 *jin* of yarn. In February and March of 1942 this was again changed into 2 *jin* or 2 *jin* 2 *liang* for 1 *jin* of yarn.

Because the supply of yarn from the people was insufficient and of poor quality, we set up our own yarn-spinning factory with four cotton-bowing machines and forty spinning machines in October 1941. By July 1942 we still lacked skilled workers and the cotton bowed by the machines could not all be used on the machines (the raw cotton was poor). Now only the four bowing machines are still going and spinning has stopped.

(b) The problem of controlling, educating and training the workers

The number of workers has increased but there are many different elements and they are not easy to control. The young service personnel in particular were used to a free life and had not taken part in labour before they left home. At first they would fight, curse and carry-on every day. They would say 'We've seen all the officers, big and small' and would not accept any controls.

Most of the women from the villages had come because of marriage problems. They had been sent to the factory by the women's aid com-mittee or the government. Whenever they talked of marriage, some cried and some laughed. They often asked for help in solving their marriage problems.

Persuading captured bandits to work was difficult.

Many of the people being punished for mistakes were company and platoon cadres who maintained their old character, were unwilling to work and were troublemakers.

From January to March 1941, the head of the supply department tried hard to correct them and achieved some success.

During this time, approximately twenty skilled workers acted as master-workers and taught the youths in the weaving group. First they used the small looms (needed little strength and easy to manage). The master-worker did all the preliminaries and told them how to start the loom, how to connect broken threads, how to handle the shuttle, and how to coordinate hand and foot. At the beginning they only wove for two or three hours a day. After one or two months, this group had mastered these looms and moved onto the large wooden ones, and another group came to learn. Thus group-by-group the teaching went on until March 1941.

The work of joining the threads and threading was easy to learn and only needed patience. Once you had learned to join the threads properly, you were all right. But it needed practice. When unpractised, the results were not good enough for weaving.

When the work began and the young apprentices sat at the looms or did their joining and threading, their backsides ached after a short time, yarn easily broke, tempers rose, there was little patience and they wasted a lot of thread and broke some looms. So before March 1941, products were no good.

Apart from strengthening technical training and raising technical skills, the chief way of dealing with this was political encouragement and education in revolutionary labour discipline. This made the workers consciously realize the important significance of production, made them patient in their work and improved their enthusiasm for production and their labour discipline.

Various methods of education were used to implement military discipline. The head of the supply department, He Weizhong, the head of the military training unit and the branch Party secretary personally came to give guidance every day, explaining that production at the rear was equal to fighting at the front, that they should accept organization, that work was glorious and that they were the working class. We proposed a competition with emulation between apprentices and emulation between male and female workers. We implemented a system of rewards and punishments and a system for getting time off. At the same time each person was given some writing materials every month, and we bought some entertainment equipment.

Thereafter the workers felt that to work was glorious. After work they wanted to study culture and politics and to live a military life. As a result life became organized on military lines. In this way we gradually set up the soldier-worker system, and the factory got going in the right way. Before breakfast there were early-morning exercises and running. After breakfast they went to work. In winter and spring there was a ten-hour day.

We then encountered new difficulties.

The factory site was a hired house. As it was not convenient for work, we built ten or so cave houses ourselves for the workers to live in. Unexpectedly the cave houses were moist and damp, the workers developed sores and many of them could not work. So we changed the new caves into storerooms and the workers moved into the hired house. In June we began to build five stone cave houses for the looms and these were not completed until October. During this period there was nowhere to put the looms. The only thing we could do was put them in the courtyards and work under tents. In May and June there was early morning dew and it rained often. Wet thread is no good for weaving. In July the weather was hot and the sun strong. The threads became very dry which was also no good for weaving. The only thing we could do then was cover the looms in wet army blankets and pour water on the ground. But this only worked for two or three hours and, as can be imagined, gave a lot of trouble.

The months from June to September passed in this way. The new caves were completed in October and we also built one-storey houses with a total of twenty-seven rooms for the workers to live in. Only then were all these problems overcome.

As for raising the workers' technical level, after June the youths gradually became skilled, and some even exceeded the master-workers.

In the first week when they were apprentices they generally only worked for two or three hours a day and made four or five feet of cloth. After two or three weeks they worked for seven or eight hours a day and could weave 10 to 40 feet. After April they could do 40 to 50 feet, and by May, 60 to 70. After June, they had all become skilled workers and the best could weave 120 to 130 feet a day. During this time the quality of cloth continuously improved.

We can say that after June 1941 the factory was consolidated and began to develop, having overcome all kinds of difficulties.

(3) Establishing the soldier-worker system

The factory expanded and needed to be regularized. It was very inconvenient for the administrators from the military training unit. And so under the supply department we set up a factory head and a commissar to provide leadership, and drew-up a draft outline for the administration of the factory.

Under the leadership of the head and commissar, the administration was divided into four sections, labour, operations, accounts and general work. These sections divided the tasks and worked together, each with its own responsibility. We stipulated a variety of regulations for meetings, minutes, reports, inspection, livelihood, pay (according to technical skill with the top rate of 10 yuan) and for rewards and punishment. We settled the times for work, study, rest and relaxation. We fixed the scope for democratic life and all kinds of principles – for the workshops, dormitories, canteen, days off, leaving the premises and so forth.

By October 1941, everything was properly set up.

After October we felt that the wooden looms were not as good as the iron ones. The cloth the latter produced was of good quality and needed less work. We planned gradually to replace the wooden looms with iron ones. Between January and October 1942 we built iron looms ourselves. However, as one had to be strong and skilful to weave with these looms and there were not enough workers like that, we could not convert entirely to iron looms and we did not build any more. The total was forty-five iron looms and sixty-two wooden looms. Apart from this, we bought thirteen wooden looms for weaving woollen blankets and woollen goods from the Longwan Factory (in spring 1942) and built thirteen wooden looms ourselves. This gave a total of 133 looms. On average we produced about 1,000 bolts of wide cloth, 500 woollen towels and 100 blankets per month.

After May 1942 the pay system was changed into a piecework system giving 70–80 yuan per month at the most (roughly one-tenth of wages in a privately-run factory), and 20–30 yuan at the least. This increased the workers' enthusiasm to produce. Some workers did not take their noon rest and did not stop work at the end of the working day but kept on working. After some persuasion and education, we overcame this excessive enthusiasm.

We persisted in the soldier-worker system. The factory workers also grew vegetables and raised pigs for their food.

In the winter of 1942 we stopped work for one month to make padded clothing.

In 1941 after all expenses, the factory made a profit of 3,900,000 yuan. In the first ten months of 1942, the profit was 8 million yuan. The value of the factory site, looms, yarn and raw cotton is 5 million yuan (yarn and cotton 1 million yuan). We intend to invest several million more to maintain reproduction.

In sum the lessons of experience in running industry are as follows:
(i) The profit earned by the soldier-workers working in textiles, that is the Daguang Mill led by the brigade supply department, is the largest of all the profits earned by the various industrial enterprises. In 1941 the total number of employees was 250 and in 1942 it was 225. After all expenses, its profit in 1941 was 3,900,000 yuan equivalent to the price of 4,000 dan of millet at year-end prices (300 jin per dan). Profit by October 1942 was 8 million yuan, again equivalent to 4,000 dan of millet at current prices in Suide. The average net profit per worker was roughly 18 dan.

In the light of two years' experience and the present circumstances, we shall invest 25,000 yuan per head for the 225 employees of the factory during 1943, not counting buildings and tools, making a total of 5,625,000 yuan. The cloth required for uniforms will be bought from the factory. In this way production for 1943 will earn a net profit per man of 20 dan of millet (because of inflation, it is best to take millet as the standard).

Each regiment has a cloth-weaving factory which can produce enough cloth for a hundred men.

In addition, apart from undertakings purely for producing equipment and clothing for the troops such as shoemaking, clothes-making and leather-tanning, the brigade also has roughly 200 blacksmiths and carpenters. In the light of the past two to three years' experience and the prospects for the continued development of the Border Region economy, these craftsmen could make an annual profit roughly equivalent to 6 *dan* of millet in return for an investment of 1,000 *yuan* per man.

There is also a papermaking factory and an oil-pressing shop which use as raw materials the sesame seeds and straw coming from the troops' agriculture and *malan* grass cut by the soldier-workers, for which the factories pay a cheap price. These enterprises employ sixty people with an average net profit per head of 6 *dan* of millet.

(ii) Besides agriculture, effective operation of the system of soldier-workers is a way of realizing self-sufficiency and solves both commodity and financial problems. Commerce is definitely not as reliable as agriculture and industry. Commerce relies on others, not on oneself, so it is not suitable to do too much of it.

(iii) Shortcomings are: in running a large factory there is a lot of expense and waste, and there is no fixed amount of capital. This influences reproduction. Therefore in future we must strive to set up a fixed amount of capital.

(iv) In the past we did not take the whole Border Region economy into consideration. Nor did we make a unified plan for the troops' agricultural and industrial production. We could not interlock agriculture, industry, transport and commerce. This was a great failing. Henceforth, we should have unified plans and interrelated management.

The above is a summary of our opinions.

(C) Commerce

Our commerce began with a cooperative and it took six years to develop into large-scale commerce.

In 1937, the brigade was sent across the Yellow River to the area around Guoxian to fight the enemy. After the loss of Taiyuan, commerce was disrupted and city goods could not be moved into the countryside. The common folk did not dare to travel to buy goods. As a result there were great shortages in daily necessities. Oil and salt were out of supply for a while. Both the army and the people had to eat plain food. In these circumstances we set up a cooperative at the request of the people. We allocated animals to go to Ningwu and elsewhere for salt. The supply department put up 300 *yuan* to buy goods belonging to merchants which were stored in the countryside. We contracted the merchant, Li Maolin, from Yangwu as manager and set up business at Yangwu. It was called '359 Brigade Army-People Cooperative'. The aim was simply to solve difficulties in the supply of salt, oil and so forth, and to handle other necessary goods. At the time the currency had not yet lost value so, although the capital was small, business was success-ful. In the short period of six months from October 1937 to April 1938 when the troops moved east, we gained great sympathy among the people of the county. Thousands of people praised us saying that if it were not for the cooperative, they would have died without being killed by the enemy. Making a profit was not the aim at the time, so although business was good we did not earn any money. At the end in April, the capital and profit of 490 *yuan* was handed over to the troops and used.

In May 1938, the cooperative personnel went to the Shanxi-Chahar-Hebei Border Region with the troops. When they got to Lingqiu there was another shortage of daily necessities. Both the people and the army suffered. They wanted to continue with the cooperative but had no capital and could think of no way. In August, the cooperative personnel went to the county town of Laiyu county to build up relations with merchants. Through friendly connections they bought goods worth 3,042 *yuan* on credit. Most of it consisted of bolts of cloth, writing-materials, paper, soap and so forth totalling eleven packs. They returned to Donghenanzhen east of Lingqiu and set up a shop. The suppliers of the goods also came along. Within five days the goods were entirely sold and they got a net profit of 800 *yuan*. They paid the suppliers 2,042 *yuan* and presented 1,000 *yuan* to the front-line troops for buying provisions. With the 800 *yuan* left over, they returned with the suppliers to Laiyuan to get more goods. This process was repeated several times up until December when the bill for goods was fully repaid. From August to December the operations of the cooperative provided supplies of oil, salt and cloth needed by the people of the Lingqiu region and earned 2,800 *yuan* to supplement the troops' expenses. In addition there remained goods worth 1,500 *yuan*.

In January 1939, we moved the 1,500 *yuan*'s worth of goods to Xiaguanzhen. We mainly dealt in oil and salt, on the one hand supply-ing the troops and on the other helping the ordinary folk. Since the troops were continuously engaging the enemy at this time, we had over 1,000 wounded. It was not easy to get Western medicines and nutritious foods so the cooperative set up good relations with various merchants and through them got Western medicine, milk, arrowroot and so forth from Tianjin, Beijing, Baoding and other places. This ensured the supply of necessities for the wounded. In September 1939 the brigade received the order to take on the defence of the Yellow River between Shanxi and Shaanxi. The cooperative was closed down. The nine months' business brought in 9,400 *yuan*. When the troops set off they had no money so 5,400 *yuan* was paid out in expenses. The remaining goods worth 4,000 *yuan* were brought west with the troops in five donkey packs. In October we got to Wuliwan in Suide in the Border Region, we sold them for 20,000 yuan and we sent people to Loufan, Wenshui and Jiaocheng to buy writing-materials and cloth. By the end of the year we had 31,000 yuan in goods and cash.

In January 1940 the cooperative moved to Nanguan in Suide. At that time the troops' economy was in great difficulties. We could only rely on the earnings of the cooperative to help pay expenses, so we felt the name 'Army-People Cooperative' was not suitable and changed it into the 'Daguang Store' showing that its goal had changed into making a profit. During that year we built up friendships with some merchants and bought goods either for cash or on credit. We bought writing-materials, cloth, paper, shoes, socks, towels and so forth, and made a profit in the market. We worked hard and by the year-end earned 191,700 yuan. We apportioned 101,700 yuan to the troops to help with the expenses, and kept 90,000 yuan as capital for 1941.

In 1941 the brigade decided to expand its commercial activities as a supplement to the major undertakings in agriculture, industry and transport in order to meet the urgent requirements of the troops. Besides the existing 90,000 yuan capital, a further 250,000 yuan was given from the 400,000 yuan issued to the brigade by the Finance Department for production capital. In addition all the small shops run by the regiments were closed, and their capital of 60,000 yuan collected together. The total capital was 400,000 yuan. Beginning in January 1941 we set up ten branch shops. After a year's operation we got a profit of 2,982,377 yuan of which 982,377 yuan was used to supplement the troops' expenses and 2 million was kept as the store's capital.

In 1942, the store and ten branch shops got a profit of 6,720,080 yuan from operations during spring, summer and autumn. Two million yuan were used to supplement expenditure for the troops and the remaining sum of 4,720,080 yuan continues in use.

The lessons of experience are:

(i) We helped the ordinary folk to buy cloth, paper, oil, salt and other necessities, and we strengthened relations between the army and the people.

(ii) We helped the troops to buy daily necessities by making it possible for the soldiers' income of 1 yuan to purchase soap, towels, toothbrushes, toothpaste etc. at a time when the Eighth Route Army was in difficult economic circumstances. On the other hand, the troops rightfully bought daily necessities with their money which reduced improper and wasteful behaviour among the troops.

(iii) Building friendships is very important. If we had not had good relations with the merchants of Laiyuan, we could not have bought goods.

(iv) Surplus income supplemented expenditure for our forces.

(v) We sold local products and put limits on goods from outside.

However, since we did not inspect strictly and provide firm leadership, some shops could not carry out this work in a planned and integrated manner. They only looked after narrow departmental interests and neglected all-round economic construction.

(vi) Before 1940 we did not know much about setting up a commercial information network, and only knew how to work hard. As a result we suffered quite a few losses from rises and falls in prices. In 1941 we set up such a network to report on the situation in various places and built up liaison with some big merchants. We learned of rises and falls in prices at the right time. Therefore we did not make losses of this kind in 1941 and 1942.

(vii) We liaised and worked together with local experienced merchants able to operate outside the Border Region. When we encountered difficulties in the supply of raw materials for spinning and weaving, we obtained great help. However, we also encountered some rogue merchants who used us to carry out their own business, damaging our operations.

(viii) There were too many people working in the store not earning their keep and adding to expenses.

(ix) Frequent contact with merchants from outside enabled us to understand each other's policies and attitudes, reducing misunderstandings and building friendships.

(x) We tested the cadres' Party spirit, thought and ability.

(xi) Only with strict administration and a complete system of regulations could the store reduce waste.

(xii) To help stabilize the currency, in 1940 the store changed Guanghua banknotes.[2]

(xiii) Comprehensive preparations, correct and lively application of trading policies, staying within the scope of non-prohibited goods, selling local products and selling necessities solved difficulties in the supply of goods for the army and provided a profit.

(xiv) With the aim of earning money, after January 1941 all the brigade and regimental cooperatives became part of the Daguang Store. The organization took Suide as its centre and set up branches in Suide, Mizhi, Jiaxian, Wuqi, Anding, Yanchuan and Yanchang. The brigade had the Daguang Store, and the regiments had the branches.

(xv) Most personnel in the shops were soldiers given payments accord-

---

[2] These notes were issued by the semi-official Guanghua Trading Company from 1938 to 1941. During that period the Guomindang currency was the official currency of the Border Region but the communists could not get any small denomination notes which were very necessary for the poor area they were operating in. The Guanghua issue which totalled around 300,000 yuan (Guomindang currency) over the four years was intended to cover this deficiency. See Foreman (1945), p. 81 and Stein (1945), pp. 156–7.

ing to their jobs. Employees were paid a wage according to their ability, strengths and weaknesses.

(xvi) Most of the goods were bought from northwestern Shanxi during 1941. Afterwards because of the enemy's mopping-up campaigns and the economic blockade (the decline of the nationalist currency and the use of the puppet currency), commodity prices rose. In addition because of our problems with capital, we could not get much money to buy goods. Therefore using the slogan 'resist the enemy's goods and sell local products', we sold the cloth we wove ourselves, and the leather shoes, woollen towels and cloth shoes we produced ourselves. We also sold Daguang soap in even greater quantities. To prevent unprincipled merchants from raising market-prices and to promote the Border Region currency we changed Guanghua banknotes, and lowered the rising market-prices. For example, the salt we extracted ourselves we sold at 2 *jin* 4 *liang* per *yuan* compared to the market-price of 1 *jin* 4 *liang* per *yuan*. Thus we enabled the ordinary folk to buy at cheaper prices. So we can say that in a certain period our aim was not to earn money but to stabilize prices and secure the people's livelihood.

(xvii) 'If you knew what would happen in three days' time, you would be rich for thousands of years.' It seems as if trading is a question of finding the right way by accident. If you find a good opportunity, then you can earn money. In fact it is not so. Trading relies entirely on correct estimation, understanding of the situation locally and elsewhere, and understanding the difference between imports and exports. Then you can forecast the rises and falls in commodity prices, and fix the policies for attention in a certain period.

(xviii) A stable currency and secure finances are the primary conditions for developing business. During the past three years the sudden rises and falls in the value of the Border Region currency and the disruption of finances has influenced trading in commodities and made everything difficult. Another aspect is that this situation has enabled speculative merchants to deal in currency notes. They have earned a lot of money and influenced the economy of the Border Region.

(xix) The various regimental shops have in practice not thoroughly implemented centralized leadership and have competed with each other. They have lacked coordination which is an unhealthy tendency.

(xx) The various regiments have set up an accounting system run by specialists who keep the accounts. However since too many of them were merchants in the past, they did not use new methods of recording and still used the old. (The summary ends here.)

A concrete plan for agricultural production in 1943 has been prepared by 359 Brigade. It is really clear and definite and may be supplied to all units for consideration. The text follows.

359 BRIGADE'S 1943 AGRICULTURAL PRODUCTION PLAN

The military farming system of the troops stationed in the Border Region is one of the basic duties of our army in carrying out the policy of the anti-Japanese national united front and in establishing new democratic politics. Persisting in carrying out this duty enables us to lighten the people's burdens, improve the quality of the army and achieve close unity with the people from a position of self-reliance and self-sufficiency. Therefore, in the light of the experience and achievements in carrying out the call from upper levels for production during the past three years, the brigade has drawn up the following plan to strengthen the implementation of this call and to increase the quantity of production in 1943.

(A) How should we organize the troops' agricultural production?
(1) All the defence areas where the regiments and troops are stationed have arable land, so we stipulate that each provisions unit should carry out agricultural production according to its manpower and the land situation.
(2) In circumstances where the army is stationed in one place, each provisions unit only needs three cooks for every hundred men. Therefore each provisions unit can select six or seven strong comrades with agricultural experience from among the cooks to specialize in farming.
(3) The deputy battalion head with responsibility for production in each battalion, the head of the special duties in each company, and the deputy officers with responsibility for production in the brigade and regiments have the task of planning and inspection. During spring ploughing, summer weeding and autumn harvesting, they should organize and lead all personnel to take part.
(4) We stipulate that the provisions unit of each combat company, apart from supplying all their own vegetables, should plant 600 mu of grain. [Table 8.3] lays down the tasks each unit can shoulder.

(B) The year's plan relies on the spring. This winter we must prepare for the work of the coming spring
(1) Each provisions unit must make a clear register of the land to be planted, how much mountain land, how much river land, how much land that has been farmed, and how much uncultivated land. It must also work out what is going to be planted and how much work, seed and so forth will be required for planting, hoeing and harvesting.
(2) Farming requires oxen, ploughs, and other agricultural tools such as hoes, rakes, baskets and sickles. These should be fully prepared in winter. Actual requirements per provisions unit are three plough oxen, three ploughs and sixty other implements.

Table 8.3 Agricultural tasks assigned to units

Troop units	A	B	C	D	E	F	G	H	Total
Number of production units	5	2	1	17	16	13	6	5	65
Area to be planted (mu)	3,000	1,200	600	10,200	9,600	7,800	3,600	3,000	39,000
Number of men to be selected from among the cooks	30	12	6	102	96	78	36	30	390

Table 8.4 Preparatory work necessary by spring 1944

Units	A	B	C	D	E	F	G	H	Total
Number of production units	5	2	1	17	16	13	6	5	65
Number of plough oxen	15	6	3	51	48	39	18	15	195
Number of ploughs	15	6	3	51	48	39	18	15	195
Number of other implements	300	120	60	1,020	960	780	360	300	3,900
Amount of manure in dan	12,000	4,800	2,400	40,800	38,400	31,200	14,400	12,000	156,000

(3) If you do not use manure, the crops do not grow well. Every unit must collect manure. All nightsoil, animal manure, and wood and straw ashes must be gathered. Pay attention to control of lavatories, pig-sties, sheep-pens, and oxen and horse-stables. We must put at least 4 dan of manure on each mu of land. In many places there are grass roots from flooded land and tree leaves. These can be moved to the farmed land for burning.

[Table 8.4] lists the amount of preparatory work to be undertaken by all units and by the brigade as a whole.

(C) How much money is needed and how many workdays?
(1) Oxen, ploughs and other implements all cost money to buy or make. This is capital. In addition there is manure and seeds which come to at least 800 yuan for 600 mu. Total capital for 600 mu, and for the land formed by the units and for the brigade as a whole, is shown [in Tables 8.5 and 8.6].

Table 8.5   *Capital needed to farm*
600 mu

Item	Cost (yuan)
Oxen	12,000
Ploughs	600
Other implements	6,000
Manure & seed	800
Ox fodder	2,700
Total	22,100

NB (i) Each ox is reckoned at 4,000 yuan.
    (ii) Each plough at 200 yuan.
    (iii) Each implement at 100 yuan.
    (iv) Ox fodder at 900 yuan per animal.

(2) How many workdays are required on 600 mu from opening up the land and sowing seed to harvesting? It is estimated that opening land and sowing seed requires 500 days; preparation and spreading of manure, 800 days; three weedings, 1,800 days; and harvesting, 450 days. This makes 3,550 days in all. Note: six cooks farming 600 mu throughout the year can do at least 1,000 workdays; 3,550 work days minus 1,000 leaves 2,550. Each provisions unit has a hundred men so each man has to do twenty-five days' agricultural labour during the year.

(D) The type of crops and the harvest
(1) Find out what is the most suitable grain to be planted according to

191

Table 8.6 *Capital needed for the land farmed by the units and by the brigade as a whole (yuan)*

Unit	A	B	C	D	E	F	G	H	Total
Oxen	60,000	24,000	12,000	204,000	192,000	156,000	72,000	60,000	780,000
Ploughs	3,000	1,200	600	10,200	9,600	7,800	3,600	3,000	39,000
Other implements	30,000	1,000	6,000	102,000	96,000	78,000	36,000	30,000	379,000
Seed, manure	4,000	1,600	800	13,600	12,800	10,400	4,800	4,000	52,000
Ox fodder	13,500	5,400	2,700	45,900	43,200	35,100	16,200	13,500	175,500
Total	110,500	33,200	22,100	375,700	353,600	287,300	132,600	110,500	1,425,500

the land. In general, plant spiked millet [gu (zi)], millet [su], gaoliang, maize [baogu], beans, rice and so forth. In addition, also consider the needs of the troops and plant hemp for sandals, lamp-oil and cooking-oil. Some units can plant cotton.

The seventh regiment can plant 200 mu of cotton. Estimating a harvest of 30 jin of cotton per mu, the total will be 6,000 jin. At a value of 50 yuan per jin this will be equal to 300,000 yuan.

Each company in the special duties battalion [tewuying] should plant 80 mu of cotton in addition to its 600 mu of grain. This can give an estimated harvest of 2,400 jin worth 120,000 yuan. The battalion head-quarters can plant 20 mu giving 600 jin worth 30,000 yuan.

(2) Reckoning at 4 dou of hulled grain for every 3 mu, 600 mu can produce 80 dan of hulled grain, and the 39,000 mu of the whole brigade can produce 5,200 dan. At a value of 1,250 yuan per dan, the crop from 600 mu will be worth 100,000 yuan, and that of the brigade's 39,000 mu, 6.5 million yuan.

(3) In each 600 mu, it is estimated that 300 will be planted to spiked millet. Each mu will produce 300 jin of hay giving a total of 90,000 jin. At a value of 1 yuan per jin, 600 mu will produce hay worth 90,000 yuan, and the whole brigade will produce hay worth 5,850,000 yuan.

The harvest totals are given [in Tables 8.7 and 8.8].

Table 8.7   Harvest total on 600 mu

Hulled grain	80 dan
Value of grain per dan	1.250 yuan
Total grain value	100,000 yuan
Hay	90,000 jin
Value of hay per 100 jin	100 yuan
Total value of hay	90,000 yuan
Total value grain & hay	190,000 yuan

After each regiment and unit has received this plan, it should at once call a meeting of production cadres to discuss implementation. The general plan for the regiment or unit and the plan for each provisions unit (including their own plans for vegetables, edible oil, lamp-oil, hemp for making sandals and so forth for which they have been self-sufficient for three years) should be reported upwards by the end of November. It is important that this should be obeyed.

(End of plan.)

The above materials show us that the army's self-supporting production has undoubtedly achieved a great deal. What have these achievements depended on? They have depended on the

Table 8.8 *Harvest for 359 Brigade*

Unit	A	B	C	D	E	F	G	H	Total
Area planted in mu	3,000	1,200	600	10,200	9,600	7,800	3,600	3,000	39,000
Grain which could be harvested in dan	400	160	80	1,360	1,280	1,040	480	400	5,200
Hay (10,000 jin)	45	18	9	153	144	117	54	45	585
Value of grain crops (10,000 yuan)	50	20	10	170	160	130	60	50	650
Value of hay crops (10,000 yuan)	45	18	9	153	144	117	54	45	585
Total value of crops (10,000 yuan)	95	38	19	323	304	247	114	95	1,235

active leadership of the cadres and the labour enthusiasm of the troops. The cadres have given active leadership to the production movement consciously in order to overcome difficulties in the course of the revolution. The troops have taken part in productive labour consciously in order to overcome difficulties in the course of the revolution. If these two groups had not had this conscious awareness, if they had not felt that their work was not for others but for themselves, not for some worthless cause but for the sacred cause of the revolution, there would have been no way for them to fulfil these difficult production tasks. If they had felt they were hired labourers, if they had felt that the production they carried out had no relationship to their own interests and no relationship to the common revolutionary cause, there would have been no way to fulfil these production tasks.

Above we have discussed the fine experience and great achievements of our army in self-supporting production. Below we shall again discuss the shortcomings in our work.

Our work has shortcomings, and these shortcomings are not only found in the army but also in the official organizations and schools. Some of these shortcomings were unavoidable in the past. However, after five years' experience we should be able to correct them. Some have already become serious abuses. If we do not correct them, they will hinder the interests of the Party and the revolution.

What are these shortcomings?

First, in order to solve urgent problems of self-sufficiency quickly some army units and some official organizations and schools have relatively or specially stressed commerce and neglected agriculture and industry. They do not realize that only agriculture and industry produce value. Commerce is merely a medium for circulation. It cannot produce any value itself. Warned by experience, the production task for all forces and official organizations and schools in 1943 is gradually to transfer the main emphasis to agriculture, industry and transport. In our present circumstances, agriculture is particularly important since the majority of the things we need are agriculture products (staple grain, miscellaneous grain, vegetables, hemp, meat, vegetable-oil, animal-oil, cotton, horse-fodder, timber, firewood, etc.). Agricultural products can also be exported in exchange for industrial products. If we also undertake some possible and necessary handicrafts (spinning yarn, spinning wool, making shoes, weaving woollen thread and garments, digging coal, sawing wood, pressing oil, etc.) and large light industry (textiles, papermaking), we can meet the majority of our daily requirements and produce enough for trading.

The second shortcoming is that we lack unified planning and unified inspection. Lower levels act without coordination and upper levels either do not have or lack sufficient unified direction, planning and inspection of policy principles and work content. As a result the various branches do not know what they should not do, or do know but still do it. Thus instances of lack of coordination or struggling for independence often occur. Incidents have arisen where policy principles and government orders have been broken, where the people's interests have been damaged, where various economic units have not only not cooperated but have competed and hindered each other, where the upper levels have been deceived and not the lower levels, or where both have been deceived, where things have been kept back or where lies have been told. There has been great waste, reckless spending, concentration on show and not on results. Particularly serious are cases of the evils of bribery and corruption among cadres. Some cadres have been enticed by material things and are not loyal to the sacred cause of communism, having become completely corrupt. Other cadres have been poisoned, and can only get back to health by drying out in the sun. All these bad things and all this corruption have occurred to a lesser or greater extent among some parts of the army and in some official organizations and schools. Henceforth, all upper-level leadership organs in the army and the official organizations and schools must place emphasis on looking after the whole situation and on grasping policy. They must provide unified planning and inspection for the productive activities of all subordinate units. They certainly must not permit the abuses described above to occur again. If they do occur again, they must be strictly disciplined. Less important cases should be criticized and serious ones punished. We certainly cannot condone them or, to use a flattering term, 'have a liberal policy'. These are the three work styles[3] for rectification in economic work. We must carry them out without the slightest delay.

The third shortcoming is that in the production activities of many army units, official organizations and schools, the cadres responsible for administration and control do not take many pains. A minority even pay no attention at all and merely entrust everything to the supply organ or to the general office. This is because they still do not understand the importance of economic work. And the reason they still do not understand it is because they have been poisoned by the deceitful corrupting words of metaphysicists like Dong Zhongshu,[4] 'Conform to the requirements and do not seek gain, be concerned with the way and do not plan for merit', and have not yet cast them fully aside. It is also because they consider politics, Party and army affairs come first and are most important, while economic work, although also important, is not important to the same degree. They feel that they themselves do not have to divide their attention or to give much attention by being concerned. However, these attitudes are entirely wrong. In the present situation in the Shaan-Gan-Ning Border Region, the great majority of people have work to do. If you talk of revolution, then in the final analysis apart from economic work and educational work (including theoretical education, political education, military education, cultural education, technical education, professional education and national education) what other work is worthy of the names central or primary work? Is there any other work that is more revolutionary? True, there is other work and a lot of it, but the central or primary work for the majority of comrades in the present situation in the Border Region is certainly economic work and educational work. All other work is only significant in the context of these two. If we conscientiously carry out these two items of work, we can consider that we have done well in supporting the war at the front and in helping the people of the great rear areas. Of the two, education (or study) cannot be carried out alone. We are not in a time when 'official rank lies in study'. We cannot go and 'conform to the requirements and

[3] That is, unified direction, planning and inspection.
[4] The Han dynasty philosopher responsible for restoring the old learning after the burning of the books during the Qin dynasty.

illuminate the way' with hungry stomachs. We must get food to eat. We must pay attention to economic work. Talking of education or study separately from economic work is merely using superfluous and empty words. Talking of 'revolution' separately from economic work is like making revolution against the Finance Department and against yourselves. The enemy will not be in the least hurt by you. Because we have many comrades with leadership responsibilities who still take the attitude of neglecting or not paying much attention to economic work, many other comrades copy them, being willing to do Party, government, army and educational work, or to work in literature and art but unwilling to do economic work. Some female comrades are unwilling to marry economic workers, implying that they consider them dishonourable. They consider that marrying the head of a mule-and-horse-team would be an insult and they would rather marry a political-worker. In fact all these viewpoints are very wrong and do not match the situation in this time and place. We must make a new division of labour. We need some revolutionary specialists who are separate from production affairs. We also require some doctors, literature and art workers, and so forth. But we do not want many people like this. If there are too many then danger arises. If those who eat are many and those who produce are few, if those who are employed suffer and those who benefit are comfortable, we shall collapse. Therefore many cadres must be transferred from their present work or study to economic posts. Chief responsible cadres at all levels in the Party, government and army must at the same time pay full attention to leading economic work. They must investigate and study the content of economic work, be responsible for making plans for economic work, allocate cadres for economic work, inspect the results of economic work, and never again entrust this extremely important work to the supply departments or general offices alone and wash their hands of it.

The fourth shortcoming is that in the past some army units and official organizations have not had a division of labour between levels when allocating production tasks. All levels from brigade to company and from upper level to lower level have been permitted to run commerce without any limits. Thus many defects have arisen. Henceforth most commerce, industry and transport should be concentrated in brigades, in regiments working in independent areas and in upper-level organs. Furthermore these must work according to correct principles. Trade with the outside must be united under the direction of the Commodities Bureau. Units under regiments working in an independent area, units at battalion level or below, and most lower-level organs should be instructed to carry out agriculture, handicrafts that can be done by troops or miscellaneous personnel and business or trading of the consumer cooperative type. They are not allowed to do other work.

In the light of achievements and shortcomings over the past five years, the concrete tasks for the various units of the army in 1943 are as follows.

(1) With the exception of most of the grain and some of the bedding and clothing which are supplied by the government, the great majority of army units should provide 80 per cent of their own supplies. Some units (such as 359 Brigade) should provide 100 per cent. Only those in special circumstances (such as the cavalry) can be allowed to bear a lighter production burden, and they too should think of ways to provide more in 1944. All forces should prepare to increase self-sufficiency in grain and clothing and bedding in 1944 so as to reduce the burden on the people and to let them build up their strength.

(2) With the exception of 359 Brigade, which is already fully carrying out the military farming system, or the cavalry, which would find it difficult because of special circumstances to implement that system at once, and of those with garrison duties, all other forces should carry out the policy of military farming in individual units or several units together so as to increase agricultural production.

(3) All units from top to bottom should carry out production in an organized, led and planned way. Set up production committees at all levels from brigade to company, and carry out collective planning and inspection at each level. Study improvements in production techniques so as to increase production and improve supplies. Correct all irregular phenomena.

(4) Select cadres strong in politics and ability to administer production and supply work in each department. Existing economic cadres should be examined. Incompetents and those

who have committed corrupt and decadent errors must be transferred. Particularly serious cases must be punished. Every unit must set up a deputy battalion head with responsibility for production and personnel to administer production in companies. These people should specially control production and the distribution of tasks for whole battalions and whole companies. Brigade units and regimental units should establish deputy officers with responsibility for production to administer the production work of the units themselves. The commanding officer of each level must personally plan and inspect economic work.

(5) All economic and financial work of the Party, government and army in each sub-region should carry out coordinated cost-accounting under the leadership of the finance sub-committee of the sub-region. In order to stimulate the activism of the production and working personnel of all units, it should permit them to spend a suitable amount of the results of their production on improving their livelihood. Everything apart from this should be distributed in a coordinated way so as to avoid the problem of unequal benefits. Some coordinated distribution should be applied throughout the Border Region as a whole, some within the sub-regions, some within the various systems, and some within units. It can be decided according to the nature of production and the economic situation.

(6) Implement the policy of 'giving consideration to both the army and the people'. The economic activities of the army, Party, and government should harmonize with the economic activities of the people. Anything which damages the people's interests or causes them dissatisfaction is not allowed.

(7) Production and education cannot be out of balance. All units must carefully plan both kinds of work and their mutual relationships. Correctly share out the time for each so that production and education in 1943 can be greater and better than in 1942. We have had five years' experience and it is entirely possible to achieve this aim.

(8) The core of the army's political work is to ensure the fulfilment of its production and education plans, to ensure that while it is carrying out these plans there are correct relationships with the Party, government, and people, to ensure the correct rela-

tionship between upper and lower levels within the army itself, and to ensure the purity of economic cadres. If political work does not fulfil its own task in these areas, then it will be defeated.

9

ON THE DEVELOPMENT OF THE PRODUCTIVE UNDERTAKINGS OF OFFICIAL ORGANIZATIONS AND SCHOOLS

Within the three branches of the public sector of the economy, production by the troops and by the official organizations and schools is directly intended to meet their own living- and running-costs. Production by governmental organs is also included in this. For example, the personnel working in the various departments and offices of the Border Region government run agricultural, handicraft and commercial undertakings. These directly supplement deficiencies in the running-expenses of the organs and in clothing, bedding and food for the personnel. By contrast the salt industry, industry and agriculture established as government enterprises are not intended to provide running-expenses but to meet the needs of the whole Party, government and army.

In Yan'an and the Border Region, the official organizations of the Party and government, leading organs of the mass organizations and many schools have pursued agriculture, industry and commerce under the slogans 'set-to ourselves' and 'self-reliance'. This is a broad mass-movement, and it has solved many big problems of finance and supply. It is only just second to the army's production and it is worth our while to sum up its experience carefully, to point out its achievements and short-comings and to determine the work-plan for 1943.

The army's production movement began in 1938 and gained some experience. In 1939 we spread this experience into all official organizations and schools. In February 1939 we held a Production Mobilization Conference. We organized production committees to be leading organs for the production movement and we stipulated different production tasks according to the different circumstances of the work and study of each official organization and school and the strength of their labour force. For example, we laid down that working personnel in districts and townships should be fully self-sufficient in grain and other organizations from the centre down to the county, should be either one-half or one-third self-sufficient according to the strength and size of their labour force. In total we asked them to open up 100,200 mu of land and to harvest 13,000 dan of hulled grain. Besides this we decided that all official organizations and schools should be entirely self-sufficient in vegetables, should raise pigs for meat and should use the straw from their grain crops to provide part of the fodder for horses. At the time there were roughly 20,000 people in the official organizations and schools of the whole Border Region. We issued average production expenses of 2.60 yuan per head, a total of over 49,000 yuan. This provided capital to buy plough-oxen and agricultural tools. After they had found land and bought oxen and tools, everyone was mobilized for the spring ploughing. Most of these people were intellectuals and youths who had never previously taken part in production. Together with cadres from worker and peasant backgrounds and service personnel, cooks and grooms, they were organized into production groups to open up the land. All hilltops near Yan'an with unused land became covered with men and women opening them up. They automatically showed labour discipline and declared competitions in clearing land. The strong took up hoes and the weak grew vegetables and raised pigs, or took food and water to the workers.

The gains from this production movement were: (i) the official organizations and schools of the whole Border Region opened up 113,414 mu of land, harvested 11,325.63 dan of grain (equivalent to 5,830.17 dan of hulled grain) and harvested roughly 1,200,00 jin of vegetables. At prevailing market-prices the two harvests were worth over 368,000 yuan (over 10,179,000 yuan at 1942 prices). This provided one-quarter of the grain requirements of 20,000 people, one-half of the horse fodder and some of the vegetables and meat. (ii) It enabled over 10,000 intellectuals and young people to understand from their own experience what physical labour is. This tempered them. (iii) When the common folk of the Border Region saw or heard that all working personnel and young students in all the Party and government official organizations – from Party Central Committee members to young service personnel – were all going up into the mountains to farm, they were moved. Everyone was keen to open up land and it became an exceptional year for doing so.

On the other hand, the stipulated task for grain production was not fulfilled in this year because of lack of labour experience and because the application of manure, seed planting and weeding was not done at the right time. Also, in some areas there was drought and so forth. As a result, although a lot of land was opened up, the harvest was not large and only 45 per cent of the original grain target of 13,000 *dan* of hulled grain was achieved. Secondly, the error of egalitarianism was committed in leadership and organization. The different nature of each organization and school was not considered. Some were given tasks that were too great such as the call for district and township cadres to be self-sufficient in grain. In fact they only achieved one-quarter. Some put off and spoilt their work or study in order to carry out production with the result that it was uneconomic. In some cases male and female comrades too physically weak to do hard work were forced to labour and their health suffered. Some units could in fact have undertaken industry and commerce but this was not pointed out at the time, and they purely and simply concentrated on agriculture.

In 1940 we corrected these shortcomings. First we reduced the agricultural production tasks. Apart from self-sufficiency in vegetables and meat, we stipulated that the official organizations and schools should be only from one-seventh to one-sixth or one-quarter self-sufficient in grain according to their different circumstances. We did not ask weak males nor any females to do physical labour. No person over fifty or under fifteen took part in production. We permitted the hiring of experienced peasants to join-in or to direct production. In addition the Finance Department issued 50,000 *yuan* to the official organizations and schools as capital to allow them to undertake industry and commerce and to develop animal husbandry, raising pigs and sheep. Therefore in agricultural production during 1940 we did not increase cultivated land beyond the existing amount. Some units lacked labour power and adopted the method of taking ordinary folk on as tenants. Some gave part of their grain-producing land to others and concentrated on planting vegetables and raising pigs. In addition some schools moved to other places in north China. Therefore the 1940 harvest only amounted to 3,000 *dan* of hulled grain and 900,000 *jin* of vegetables, worth 3 million *yuan* at the market-prices of the time.

The commerce we ran began with cooperatives. In 1939 each official organization and school had a consumers' cooperative and some had opened restaurants. By the first half of 1940 there were thirty cooperatives and restaurants with more than 60,000 *yuan* capital. The largest had 10,000 *yuan* and the smallest not more than a few hundred *yuan*. Their aim was to supply daily necessities for the organization or school itself. At the same time they sold to outsiders for a slight profit as a means of improving their livelihood. They had still not become commercial undertakings to meet general needs. However, they gave initial tempering to cadres running commerce, and accumulated some commercial experience and a small amount of capital.

In the two years of 1939 and 1940, the organizations and schools generally did not undertake industry. They only set up some flour mills for their own needs, and the rear services' Jiaotong Store set up a smithy for horseshoes. These can be considered the beginnings of their handicraft production.

The above was the first period in self-sufficient production for the organizations and schools. Below we turn to the second period.

In the winter of 1940 the production tasks of the organizations and schools rapidly changed as a result of the economic blockade of the Border Region, the cutting-off of outside aid, the extreme financial difficulties, and the unavoidable need to move quickly from semi-self-sufficiency to full self-sufficiency in finance and supplies.

At the time (with the exception of the troops) the various organs of the Party, government, army and mass organizations and the personnel of the schools could not all take up agriculture and the task of achieving self-sufficiency was extremely difficult. On the one hand we wanted to rely on developing production to ensure daily and monthly supplies. At the same time we wanted to accumulate capital to establish a foundation for future self-sufficiency.

In order to get through this difficult situation, the Party and government adopted necessary steps. First we improved the organizations for leading production. In succession we established the Finance and Economy Office directly under the Central Committee, the Rear Services Economic Construction Office, the Finance and Economy Office at top level in the Border Region Government, and ordered each sub-region and county to set up production committees. Second, between the winter of 1940 and the spring of 1941 the government paid out 700,000 *yuan* and the Border Region Bank lent 3 million *yuan* to increase the production capital of the various branches. This was handed to the various bodies leading self-sufficient production for issuing downwards, to be added to the capital accumulated by the organizations themselves in the first period. Thereupon everyone made new arrangements, selected personnel, chose undertakings and put industry and commerce to the fore. Agriculture was then placed in a subordinate position.

Below we shall discuss the experience of the various organizations and schools in industry, commerce and agriculture during this period.

The starting point for the industry of the organizations and schools was textiles. Since the Border Region had wool, the personnel of the organizations and schools spun wool by hand after work and study during the winter of 1940. For a while it became a movement and everybody began to spin. But since there was not enough raw material and spinning skills were poor, the woollen threads were uneven and too much labour was wasted. After March 1941 this was gradually stopped and we applied ourselves to setting up handicraft textile mills. In the first half of 1941 each large organization and school selected service personnel and messengers to go to the Refugee Textile Mill run by the government to study spinning and weaving. Like bamboo shoots after spring rain, more than ten textile mills grew up within a short time. The shortcoming was that there was no planning. By the latter half of the year because they had no ensured supply of raw materials or market for yarn, or because they lacked sufficient liquid capital or were poorly administered, some had closed, some had merged and some had temporarily closed. For example, the Xin Zhongguo Textile Mill of the Finance and Economy Office directly under the Central Committee first merged with the Shengli Mill of the Central Organization Department and then merged with the Tuanjie Mill run by the Marxism-Leninism Institute. Then using the name of Tuanjie Textile Mill, it was run in a centralized way and got more profit. The wool-spinning factory run by the Lu Xun Academy and the Women's University was closed down and its capital used elsewhere. The Tuanjie Textile Mill of the Financial and Economy Office under the Central Committee and the Jiaotong Mill run by the Rear Services could not fully employ their production capacity because of all kinds of difficulties. They alternately worked and closed down for a while until they eventually got on the right track. Thus the process of moving from a hand-spinning movement of several thousands of people to the setting up of handicraft factories, from the setting up of over ten small textile mills and wool-spinning factories to the final merger into two factories, the Jiaotong and the Tuanjie, was a process of moving from blindness to consciousness in which there was continuous groping forward through research, improvement in techniques and improvement in administration. This process on the one hand illustrated the hard-working spirit of the various organizations and schools and on the other illustrated our complete lack of experience in running industry at that time. By 1942 the Jiaotong produced 3,336 bolts of cloth and the Tuanjie produced 2,736, becoming major factories in the Border Region. They are the valuable creation of the process of hard work and groping the way forward.

Besides textile mills, the organizations and schools directly under the Central Committee have successively set up many handicraft factories for such things as bedding and clothing, shoes, coal and charcoal, carpentry, papermaking, pottery, flour-milling and oil-pressing, silk weaving and making iron implements. Their aim has been self-sufficiency. The capital for these factories came either from commercial capital, or from bank loans, or from the closure of the wool-spinning factories. Warned by the experience with textiles, these factories were not run in such an entirely disorganized way. They were rather more orderly with several organizations and schools cooperating, or with cooperation with the common folk or with the Bank. But it was not all plain sailing. Most only laid a firm foundation after following a winding path from initial loss of capital through continued support to final profit.

In the years 1941 and 1942, the system under the Central Committee's Finance and Economy Office [Zhong-cai xitong] set up a total of twenty-seven large and small handicraft factories with total capital of over 400,000 yuan and with 477 employees. Among them there were eight textile mills with 217,000 yuan capital and 161 employees, three coal and charcoal factories with 70,000 yuan capital and sixty-eight employees, three mills with 15,000 yuan capital and twenty-one employees, two bedding and clothing factories with forty-eight employees (capital details not available), three carpentry factories with 35,000 yuan capital and seven employees, one shoe factory with 10,000 yuan capital and thirty-eight employees, and one papermaking workshop with 20,000 yuan capital and twenty-nine employees. In addition there were six small factories individually producing machinery, glass, alcohol, pottery, oil-lamps and blankets. (There are no statistics on capital and employees for these factories. The first three were experimental undertakings by the Natural Sciences Institute.) All the above factories were reorganized in September 1941 when the official organizations and schools directly under the Central Committee carried out their first drive for better troops and simpler administration. They were transferred to the direct control of the Central Administration Bureau (the Finance and Economy Office directly under the Central Committee was dissolved and we set up the Central Administration Bureau attached to the Central Work Department [Zhongyang Bangongting]). Their number was reduced from twenty-seven by closure or merger to nineteen. In particular the merging of the eight textile mills into two, the Tuanjie and the Shiyan, enabled concentration of management and improvement in operation. Thus we were able to move from a situation where eight mills either lost capital or just maintained themselves to one of a profit of 1,600,000 yuan in October 1942.

Self-sufficient industry run by the Rear Services system was started in the winter of 1940 just like that run by the central financial system. After two years' operation, 1941 and 1942, there was one textile mill, two papermaking factories, three charcoal factories, two carpentry factories, two silk-weaving factories, and one factory each for coal [shitan], refined salt, pottery, bedding and clothing, writing-brushes, ironwork, flour-milling, shoes and hemp-weaving, a total of nineteen altogether. There are no statistics yet for the amount of capital, number of employees and amount of production of these factories. Although the profit earned by these undertakings is not great (in the first ten months of 1942 it was 200,000 yuan), their great merits are: (i) they are run in a centralized way by the Rear Services and are not run freely in a dispersed way as by the various official organizations and schools. Thus leadership and inspection are thorough, and mistakes are quickly corrected. (ii) They constitute a wide range of operation. Unlike the Central Committee's Finance and Economy Office system's initial concentration on textiles through the establishment of eight factories, the Rear Services has at all times only run one factory, the Jiaotong Textile Mill, and thus had spare capacity to do other things. (iii) They are entirely aimed at ensuring supplies. Although they do not earn money, they have provided a supply of many necessary goods.

In October 1942 we carried out a thorough drive for better troops and simpler administration. The Central Administration Bureau and Rear Services systems were combined, and their industries administered in a unified way. We also carried out further reorganization. The Tuanjie and Jiaotong textile mills and the bedding and clothing factories were transferred to the Finance Department. The medicine, alcohol, iron, and glass-making factories were transferred to the Garrison Office. The Natural Sciences Institute and all the things that went with it were handed over to the government. All remaining factories were closed, or merged and handed over to the control of the Central Administration Bureau. By December 1942 there were three carpentry factories, two papermaking factories, five charcoal-factories, one shoe-factory, one oil-pressing factory, one flour-mill, three grinding-mills, one cart-factory, one wine-factory and three blanket-workshops, a total of twenty-one large and small handicraft factories and workshops. These can ensure all supplies of coal, shoes and flour, the manufacture and repair of all wooden and galvanized-iron implements, and some of the paper and edible-oil requirements for the whole of the Central Administration Bureau system. Bedding and clothing are supplied by the government. This is the outcome of the activism in industrial production over the past two years of the Central Administration Bureau (prior to September 1941 the Central Committee's Finance and Economy Office) and the Rear Services.

The above experience shows that under present circumstances it is essential for the official organizations and schools to run handicrafts. The aim is not to earn money but to ensure supplies of necessities. However, organizations and schools cannot set up any kind of factory they want to. They should choose in a planned way which ones to run, according to the nature of the industry and the situation in the official organization or school. They should reduce the number of errors created by blindly groping around. Existing factories should be organized into systems according to area and official organization. Cut-backs, mergers and transfers can reduce waste and enable them to play an even greater role in providing supplies.

As mentioned above, our comrades lacked experience of running commerce in the same way as they did of running industry. They had previously only managed a few cooperatives. We wished to turn to relying on a profit from commerce in order to provide a large proportion of supplies. What had to be done? Once again it was a process of moving from blindness to consciousness in order to find an answer to this question.

During 1941 and 1942 commerce started off with the aim of rapidly overcoming difficulties. Therefore we had no choice but to use the bulk of the capital of each official organization and school to trade for a quick profit.

In the year from autumn 1940 to autumn 1941 we mainly operated large stores. Some official organizations and schools enlarged their existing low-capital, small-profit cooperatives, small shops and stalls, increasing capital and staff, joining chambers of commerce and running proper commercial undertakings. For example, the Jiaotong Store of the military base was at first a small cigarette-shop set up at the entrance to the base at Qilipu in Yan'an. In August 1939 it moved to the new market in Yan'an and as well as selling general goods set up a Chinese medicine shop and a horseshoe-shop. Its capital increased from a few hundred *yuan* to 20,000 *yuan*. Another example is the Hezuo Store which grew from the cooperative of the Anti-Japanese University. In June 1940 it moved to the new market and set up branch stores at the three branch schools of the Anti-Japanese University. Its capital increased from 80 *yuan* to 19,000 *yuan*. The Rear Services Store was at first a small stall with 30 *yuan* capital. By September 1940 it had expanded and its capital had grown to 20,000 *yuan*. As well as selling goods it also set up a dyeing shop. Originally many official organizations and schools did not have shops. Around this time they too collected capital and people together and set up business either independently or in partnerships. At the time the business done by all the publicly-run stores depended on trading goods mainly from Suide, Dingbian and Fuxian counties, in particular the cloth, paper, writing-materials required by the official organizations, schools and troops themselves, and the matches, raw cotton and so forth required by the common folk. During this period the official organizations and schools set up over sixty large and small stores in Yan'an, Suide and Dingbian, not including those run by the army. In addition, there were many that did not set up premises but depended on one or two people and a few animals to trade goods along the roads, calling it 'floating trade'. According to statistics for October 1941 the stores under the control of the Rear Services' committee for store administration were the Xibei Store, the Xibei Vegetable Cooperative, and fourteen large and small stores including the Xinghua, the Hezuo, the Jiaotong, the Xinxin, the Xingmin, the Minxing, the Baihuo, the Junmin, and so forth. The Central Administration Bureau had twenty stores.

We really relied on commerce to pass through a serious crisis during that year. It solved great problems of supply. For example, during the first half of 1941 the Central Committee's Finance and Economy Office and the official organizations and schools relied on the twenty large and small stores run by 113 staff with 296,800 *yuan* capital to earn a profit of 256,000 *yuan*

211

which supplied 48 per cent of their daily running-expenses. The Rear Services system with capital of 706,000 *yuan* made 810,000 *yuan* profit in the same period which supplied 45 per cent of their daily running-costs.

However commerce during this period had one great fault which was excessive dispersal and no centralized leadership. Furthermore, almost all of it was trade in general goods. These faults came from the urgent need to solve difficulties in running-costs for each official organization and school. Each acted without coordination, competed with others and even disobeyed Party policy, influencing prices and currency. Simultaneously, there was price inflation, the Border Region banknotes lost value and the external blockade intensified. Suddenly, dealing in export and import of general goods had a gloomy future and the various official organizations and schools which relied on this for their running-expenses also found themselves with problems. In this situation, it was urgently necessary to transform the commerce run by the official organizations and schools and by the army. This transformation began in the latter half of 1941. In the spring of 1942 the Border Region carried out an initial drive for better troops and simpler administration. It was then decided to organize all commerce into proper enterprises [*qiyehua*]. On the one hand each system put its existing stores in order, organized a joint committee for publicly-run commerce, unified the leadership of publicly-run stores, and strictly carried out laws, commands and policies. On the other hand they expanded the scope of commercial activity, carrying out many kinds of business such as salt-shops, mule and horse supplies, trans-shipment agencies, merchant warehousing, slaughtering and so forth. The method of operation also changed. In some cases stores were merged, in others capital was invested in private stores or in cooperatives and the official organization or school did not run its own trade. In other cases capital was invested in the government's Salt Company or in the Guanghua Store. Thereafter the fault of having too many shops competing with each other was avoided, and the function of providing the running-costs of the official organizations and schools could be restored. For example, as a result of reorganization according to this policy the Central Administration Bureau and Rear Services systems reduced the number of their shops from thirty-eight with 196 staff to twenty-five with 105 staff by October 1942. In the first ten months of 1942 the two systems earned a profit of 16,440,000 yuan with capital of 8 million yuan. This accounted for 68 per cent of all production income. Also during 1942 the production committees of the various departments and offices of the Border Region Government earned 600,000 yuan from agriculture and commerce, of this commerce accounted for 350,000 yuan or 58 per cent. Official organizations at sub-region and county level originally put agriculture first, but by 1942 commerce was the most important.

In 1943 financial and economic leadership will be united [yiyuanhua]. External trade will be unified under the Commodities Bureau. Every official organization and school must carry out a thorough drive for better troops and simplified administration. As a result the commerce run by the official organizations and schools must be regulated by the Commodities Bureau, must share in running transport for local products and salt, and must allocate some capital for cooperation with the Commodities Bureau. In this way publicly-run commerce will be more rational.

The agricultural production of the official organizations and schools also made progress in 1941 and 1942. In these two years there were great achievements in the areas of grain, vegetables, charcoal and labour after work.

Some official organizations and schools were still growing grain entirely independently in 1941, some had already changed to forming partnerships with the common folk, and some ran agricultural stations (including both independent operation and partnerships). Independent operation had changed somewhat. The entire personnel no longer went up the mountains to farm. Instead, those who went were chiefly those doing miscellaneous duties organized into production teams accompanied by some of the physically stronger personnel. For example, the production teams of the various official organizations in the Rear Services system planted 5,200 mu of grain in 1941, and the Central Party School planted 800 mu. Those in partnership with the common folk included the Central Organization Department which planted 840 mu and divided the grain at a ratio of 2:8, 2 to the government and 8 to the private individuals, and the hay at a ratio of 7:3, 7 to the government and 3 to the individuals. The agricultural stations included the two stations run by the Secretariat of the Border Region Government on a partnership basis. There were also the independent stations run at Nanniwan by teams selected from the miscellaneous duties personnel of the official organizations and schools equipped with oxen and tools. These included two from the Rear Services and one each from the Central Committee's Finance and Economy Office, the Central Organization Department and the Youth League cadres. Official organizations of the sub-regions and counties also adopted both independent operation and partnerships.

In 1942 the drive for better troops and simpler administration was carried out. Many official organizations and schools in Yan'an were merged. As a result, self-supporting vegetable production continued but all grain production was only carried out either at agricultural stations or in partnerships.

Although partnerships have some of the character of exploitation, the common folk, in particular the immigrants and refugees, appreciate it very much since the government supplies seed, plough oxen and agricultural implements, and the taxes are not high. This method has a role to play in encouraging immigration and in adjusting the use of labour power. The Party School provides an example:

The general office of the Party School planted 300 mu in partnership with four immigrants. These four were all very strong. The Party School sent one man responsible for leadership and inspection. The arrangements were for the Party School to supply the agricultural tools, a hoe, a pick and a sickle per man, to lend two oxen and to give the seed. They also lent grain at a rate of 4 sheng of hulled grain per 3 mu making 4 dan for 300 mu. It was agreed to repay in the autumn of the following year. The division of the grain and hay harvest was laid down as 20 per cent of the spiked millet [gu (zi)] for the government and 80 per cent for the private individuals, 30 per cent of coarse millet [meizi] for the government and 70 per cent for the private individuals, and 40 per cent of the miscellaneous grains for the government and 60 per cent for the private individuals. All the hay went to the Party School. This year the Party School received 10,500 jin of hay, 8.37 dan of spiked millet, 10.17 dan of coarse millet, 6.9 dou of black beans [heidou] 4.2 dou of hemp-seed [*xiao mazi*], 1 *dou* of sesame [?*lao mazi*] and 2 *dou* of adzuki beans [*xiaodou*], valued at a total of 31,925 *yuan* in Border Region money. The four partners received 33.48 *dan* of spiked millet, 22.4 *dan* of coarse millet, 7.5 *dou* of black beans, 6.3 *dou* of hemp-seed, 1.5 *dou* of sesame, and 3 *dou* of adzuki beans, valued at a total of 46,805 *yuan*. This is a good example of giving consideration to both public and private interests.

There is also new experience in building up agricultural stations. Since the personnel selected from the official organizations and schools are not strong labour powers, have limits on their working-time and are not skilled in agricultural techniques, they will waste their capital if they only concentrate on farming. In 1942 we adopted the following two methods. One was independent operation which included subsidiary undertakings such as animal husbandry, wood-plank sawing and so forth as well as planting grain. This was like the method adopted by 359 Brigade. The other was to form partnerships and involved going into partnership with the common folk on stations that already had some foundation, and setting up another new station oneself. In the first year the new station brings no profit but in the second year it has some foundation and can also be changed into a partnership. The Secretariat of the Border Region Government provides an example. According to the comrades there:

We have two stations, one to the east, the other to the south. Their size, method of operation and harvest are much the same. In 1942 the southern station planted 288 *mu* of river land, 324 *mu* of previously farmed hill land and 408 *mu* of newly opened land. Altogether the harvest was 244 *dan* of grain. Since beans and corn formed the bulk, this was equivalent to 146.6 *dan* of hulled grain. Taking each *dan* at 1,300 *yuan* this was worth 190,230 *yuan* [*sic*]. We also harvested 14,000 *jin* of hay worth 14,000 *yuan*, and 20,000 *jin* of vegetables worth 20,000 *yuan*. The total value for these three items was 224,320 *yuan*. Originally we had 128 sheep. In 1942, eighty-one lambs were raised, worth 10,000 *yuan*. We bought pigs for 3,482 *yuan*, and we also had thirteen worth 400 *yuan* each. The total of all the above items is 243,002 *yuan*.

As we have adopted the method of partnership operation all our expenditures were taken from the amount harvested including all expenses for the five men we assigned. We went into partnership with twelve households, totalling forty-five people. They had nineteen

215

whole-labour powers, thirteen half-labour powers and thirteen children not able to work. Altogether their share was 68 *dan* of grain equivalent to 40.8 *dan* of hulled grain with a total value of 53,040 *yuan* at 1,300 *yuan* per *dan*. They also received 7,000 *jin* of hay worth 7,000 *yuan*. The two items came to 60,040 *yuan*. Our own five men (one was crippled and looked after general running, two cooked, planted vegetables and crops, and two looked after sheep and did general work) four oxen, one mule and five dogs received 30 *dan* of grain for eating equivalent to 18 *dan* of hulled grain worth 23,400 *yuan* and 50 *jin* of edible oil worth 1,300 *yuan* at 26 *yuan* per *jin*. In addition, repairs to implements, ploughs, clothing and supplementary payments came to 20,000 *yuan*. The total of all the above expenditure was 104,740 *yuan* giving a surplus of 138,262 *yuan*. Adding on the roughly 110,000 *yuan* from the eastern station, the return on the two stations was roughly 250,000 *yuan*.

The two stations are nominally run by the Secretariat and the Civil Affairs, Finance, Education and Reconstruction Departments. In practice, they only send out ten people of whom two are hired labourers, one is a cripple and seven are surplus personnel. The government has a production committee to control the two stations. In practice usually only one person runs things. This year thanks to floods and strong winds we were 150 *dan* short on our harvest, worth 117,000 *yuan*. We were also swindled on the seeds we bought for turnips and cabbage which were the wrong kind. This lost 30,000 *yuan*. These two items came to 147,000 *yuan* and total losses for the two stations were roughly 200,000 *yuan*. This means that without natural disasters and the wrong seeds we could get 200,000 *yuan* more. The working personnel in the Civil Affairs, Finance, Education, Reconstruction Departments and the Secretariat number around 400. The income of 250,000 *yuan* is thus an average of 625 *yuan* per head. Although the harvest this year is below norm, they have laid the foundations for next year and provided a livelihood for twelve immigrant households. Furthermore, relying on this foundation, next year we are preparing to expand the ploughed land at the southern station by 900 *mu* so as to settle down surplus personnel. The two original stations will still be run as partnerships.

The methods adopted by the county-level official organizations also include both individual operation and partnerships. For example, the top-rank official organizations in Yan'an county have planted a total of 630 *mu*. Of these over 270 *mu* are farmed in partnership with two households. These have five labour powers and the county committee has only assigned two people to work on the station. The remaining 360 *mu* are farmed by criminals. In 1942, excluding the amount distributed to the partners, they received a total of 75 *dan* of grain, equivalent to 45 *dan* of hulled grain with a value of 58,500 *yuan*. With the addition of hay worth 3,000 *yuan*, the total was 61,500 *yuan*.

As the above examples show, independent operation, partnerships and a combination of both are correct. We should pay attention to this experience when determining the grain production tasks for 1943.

A very great task in agricultural work is the growing of vegetables, since grain is also provided by the grain tax. If vegetables are not grown then over 20,000 people will be semi-starved. The saying 'no vegetables is like half a year's famine' is completely true.

The method for producing vegetables in the past two years has been to assign personnel specially for growing them and to assign some supplementary labour from the official organizations and schools. Each year we have on average been self-sufficient for three to six months. According to the Rear Services statistics, in 1941 their various official organizations and schools planted 1,801 *mu* of vegetables consisting of 1,030 *mu* of potatoes and 771 *mu* of cabbage, beans, turnips and miscellaneous vegetables. In autumn, autumn cabbage and autumn turnips were planted on the 771 *mu*. Over the year 879,000 *jin* of vegetables were harvested equal to one-third of annual consumption on average. According to the Central Administration Bureau statistics, in 1942 the various official organizations and schools directly under central control assigned forty personnel for growing vegetables and planted 388 *mu* of river land and 1,941 *mu* of hill land. They harvested 745,000 *jin* of vegetables, being self-sufficient for five months on average. The Central Administration Bureau itself supplied nine months of its needs. Yan'an University and the Natural Sciences Institute both supplied eight months of their needs, and the Central Research Institute and the Chinese Writers Anti-Aggression Association [*Wen-kang*] both supplied seven months of their needs. The circumstances for vegetable production by the personnel in the various official organizations are very varied. For example, in Guanzhong sub-region they can only plant a little on account of the climate, and can only achieve three months' self-sufficiency on average. In the special military area they can only reach two or three months' self-sufficiency because of the scarcity of land. In some areas such as Huachi, Mudan and other counties they can achieve six months' or more because they have land and can farm in partnerships. Production of vegetables for their own use by official organizations and schools throughout the Border Region is estimated to be worth around 6 million *yuan*.

The problem here is to discern whether the method whereby the official organizations and schools assign production personnel to grow vegetables outside their permanent organizational structure is ultimately worthwhile or not. The experience of the various offices under central control shows that it is. The best land for growing vegetables is river land, where all kinds of green vegetables can be grown. On hilly land only potatoes and beans can be grown. One *mu* of river land growing vegetables can supply five people for a whole year, that is 0.2 *mu* per person. However, 1.5 *mu* of hill land is required to supply one person for one year. Furthermore, so long as a man specializing in growing vegetables has additional help when spreading manure, he can farm 6 *mu* of river land. This means that one man specializing in growing vegetables together with some supplementary labour can supply a year's vegetables for thirty people. The daily vegetable requirement per head is 12 *liang* and the annual requirement is 300 *jin*. For thirty people the annual requirement is 9,000 *jin*. At December 1942 Yan'an market-prices of 3 *yuan* per *jin*, the total value of this is 27,000 *yuan*. Allowing 6,000 *yuan* for the man specializing in growing vegetables, there is a surplus of 21,000 *yuan*. Taking the necessary incentive payments into account, the least return is 20,000 *yuan*. Therefore in future after each official organization and school has carried out a thorough drive for better troops and simpler administration, it should pay attention to arranging river land for growing vegetables, to assigning personnel for the work, to providing supplementary labour and to ensuring self-sufficiency in vegetables for more than half a year and even for a whole year.

Apart from grain and vegetables, raising pigs and sheep for meat is also an important part of agriculture.

Some people consider that raising pigs wastes grain. However, our experience proves that raising pigs does not waste grain and, instead, not raising them does. First of all, without pigs left-overs have to be thrown away, and there are quite a lot of left-overs in large official organizations and companies. Secondly, if little meat is eaten then greater quantities of other food is consumed, and if a lot of meat is eaten then less other food is consumed. Thus, raising pigs to increase meat supplies is not only necessary to maintain health but is also economically rational. The various official organizations and schools have developed many ways of raising pigs. For example, the Central Party School directed the pig slaughterhouse to send someone to the kitchen daily to collect the water in which the grain was washed and the vegetable waste to feed the pigs. The Central General Affairs Section [Zhongyang Zongwuchu] directed someone to collect as pig-food the waste left after husking the grain and also the leaves and roots left over in the vegetable plots when the vegetables were harvested. According to the Rear Services Department statistics, in the first half of 1941 its various official organizations got 56,814 jin of pork worth 170,440 yuan at the market-prices of that time. This was enough for each person to have 1 jin of pork a month. If we add the following six months, the value for the whole year was roughly 350,000 yuan. According to the statistics of the Central Administration Bureau, the various official organizations and schools directly under central control raised an average of 265 pigs a month up to October 1942. Over the ten months this gave an estimated 23,330 jin of pork worth 700,000 yuan in Border Region currency. Another example is the top-level official organizations in Yan'an county, which in the first ten months of 1942 earned 10,000 yuan from pig-raising. According to these figures the total value of animal husbandry by the official organizations and schools of the whole Border Region is more than 4 million yuan.

As well as raising pigs, raising sheep is also profitable where there is pasture.

After a thorough drive for better troops and simpler administration in 1943, we can adopt the method used by 359 Brigade whereby they assign one cook for every forty people and reduce the service personnel. The remaining cooks and service personnel are sent to work on the production front where they can do many things such as growing grain and vegetables, and raising

219

pigs and sheep. Running large-scale animal husbandry on large livestock farms should be given greater prominence in 1943.

Apart from the grain, vegetables and animals, there is also charcoal-burning and labour done outside working hours, both of which have provided examples worth looking at. All the charcoal used in the winter of 1942 by the various official organizations and schools in Yan'an was provided by teams of people from those institutions sent up into the hills. If it had been bought, a substantial sum of money would have been involved. In September the Central General Affairs Section organized a charcoal-burning team of forty-two people made up of service personnel, cooks and grooms to spend three months up in the hills making charcoal. Altogether they prepared 145 pits of charcoal completing their task of making 140,000 jin. At 1.20 yuan a jin this was worth 168,000 yuan. If during the four winter months the 30,000 people in the official organizations and schools of the Border Region on average made 1 jin of charcoal per head per day, this would provide 3,600,000 jin of charcoal worth 3,600,000 yuan. If we do not make the charcoal ourselves, where shall we find such a large amount of money?

There is also the labour done outside working-hours by the miscellaneous duties personnel of the official organizations and offices of the Border Region. For example, the Central General Affairs Section this year mobilized them to repair buildings, to build surrounding walls, to make bridges, to build roads and to cut horse-fodder. This saved the government over 110,000 yuan. Similar labour done by miscellaneous personnel of the Central Party School saved the government over 139,000 yuan; and 359 Brigade did not employ outside workers for any of its repairs or new construction. All official organizations and schools should strive to do the same. Mobilize all the people in an official organization or school to do all the work they can do. If we only consider the labour done after working hours by miscellaneous duties personnel, the amount from all the official organizations and schools of the Border Region could be surprising. We should give rewards to all people who make achievements in production, and this should also apply to labour outside working-hours.

The above is a summary of the experience of the various

official organizations and schools of the Border Region in self-sufficient production during the period 1939–42.

According to the comrades doing economic work, in the two years 1941 and 1942 the agricultural, industrial and commercial capital of the Central Administration Bureau and the Rear Services Department rose from 1,281,917 *yuan* to 11,690,000 *yuan*. (much of this increase was due to the fall in the value of the currency and it was not all due to increased production). The production suplus of the year 1942 was 23,810,000 *yuan*. Except for the 2,330,000 *yuan* retained to increase production capital in 1943, the remaining 21,480,000 *yuan* was all used to supplement food, clothing, bedding and office expenses for the various official organizations and schools. In terms of the type of enterprise, agriculture accounted for 17 per cent, industry 8 per cent, salt 7 per cent and commerce 69 per cent [*sic*]. In terms of the official organizations, the enterprises directly under the control of the Rear Services Department got 8,400,000 *yuan*, those directly under the Central Administration Bureau 3,500,000 *yuan*, those jointly run by the above two 800,000 *yuan*, and those run by the various official organizations and schools individually 11,100,000. If we compare the amount of self-supporting production and the amount supplied by the people, the former is 57.5 per cent and the latter 42.5 per cent. The comrades at county level estimate that the monthly running-expenses for Party and government at county level is roughly 10,000 *yuan*. Their own production is around 9,000 *yuan* and the upper levels only issue around 1,000 *yuan*. The proportion is thus 90 per cent to 10 per cent and is an even greater achievement.

In sum, the self-supporting production work of the official organizations and schools of Yan'an and of the whole Border Region has had some success. It has not only supplied the greater part of daily running-expenses and solved urgent financial problems but has also laid a secure foundation for the public sector of the economy. Relying on this base, we can continue to develop production and solve future problems.

What is particularly important and worth raising is that we have gained experience in running economic enterprises. This is a priceless treasure that cannot be reckoned in figures. We should not only be able to manage political, military, Party and cultural affairs, but should also be able to manage economic affairs. If we could do all the others but not economic work, we would be a useless bunch of people. We would be overthrown by our enemies and decline until we collapsed.

In the light of our experience of the past five years and particularly the past two, production by official organizations and schools must henceforth improve, expanding its achievements, overcoming its weak points, developing towards greater consolidation and completing even greater production tasks. In 1943 we should adopt the following policies.

(1) Implement the policy of taking agriculture as the chief sector.

(A) According to the actual circumstances in the official organizations and schools, in each system adopt the following methods of running agriculture: (i) Those with no foundations in agricultural stations should at once set-to to prepare ploughs and tools, and separately or in partnership with the people grow grain and vegetables. (ii) Those with agricultural stations, as well as continuing production, should expand the scope of operations and arrange for surplus personnel to do more subsidiary work such as raising pigs, sheep, chickens and ducks, sawing planks and so forth. They should also form partnerships with the ordinary people and open new farms. With these methods grain production in 1943 will be greater and better than in 1942. Agriculture must not be considered backward and must not be neglected.

(B) All official organizations and schools, large and small, must allocate the necessary personnel to specialize in growing vegetables, supplemented by light work done by working personnel and students. According to the area and climate become self-sufficient in vegetables for six or more months of the year, and strive to become entirely self-sufficient. This is one of the most important steps in improving livelihood.

(2) Coordinate and develop the various kinds of handicrafts. According to the area, system and the principle of better troops and simpler administration, join the existing handicrafts of a similar nature run by each section into partnerships. At the same time, according to the needs of each area and each system, set up new handicraft workshops, such as oil-pressing workshops, places to make soya sauce and condiments, charcoal pits and so

forth. The principles for running these handicrafts should be first that the workshop itself must be self-supporting, and second that it can make a profit.

(3) Develop animal husbandry. All official organizations and schools both large and small should raise pigs and strive to equal 359 Brigade's rate of one pig for every five people, so as to increase the supply of meat. Treat increasing the supply of meat, improving living-standards and raising health-standards as extremely important matters. In addition, each large official organization and school, and particularly the army, should set aside capital and without harming the interests of the people select areas in Sanbian, Longdong, Jinpenwan and so forth to run livestock farms. They should raise large numbers of cows, sheep, donkeys and horses, preparing for the time after victory in the War of Resistance when the Border Region's salt trade declines and it has to be replaced by animal exports.

(4) Develop transport undertakings. After a thorough drive for better troops and simpler administration, keep only a small number of animals to ensure the transport of grain and straw needed by each official organization and school itself. All surplus animals together with animals specially purchased should be organized into transport teams to transport salt or goods. These transport undertakings can be run by area and system as the best way of reducing costs.

(5) Regulate commerce. Following the policy of commerce playing a supplementary role and the principles of not going against trading polices nor doing speculative business, run shops in partnerships or individually according to the circumstances in the various systems and units after the drive for better troops and simpler administration. Eradicate commerce which goes against policy and close unprofitable shops. The various systems should transfer the proportion needed from commercial capital to agriculture, animal husbandry, handicrafts and transport. Do not hesitate to lay secure foundations in the work of becoming self-supporting through agriculture, industry, animal husbandry and transport.

(6) Treat improving the livelihood of the working personnel, miscellaneous duties personnel and students in the official organizations and schools as an important matter. Responsible

people in these institutions should think of all kinds of ways of doing so. Under the principle of voluntary participation, they should encourage and direct miscellaneous duties personnel, working personnel and mothers with children to carry out some handicraft or agricultural production in ways which do not hinder their work, study or health. However, they should not run commerce. This work can be carried out in large production cooperatives, in small production groups or individually as the people involved wish. The government should provide loans for capital and the earnings should belong to the people who take part in the labour. All responsible people who run this very well and have the best successes should get rewards. All those who are not good at running their official organizations and schools and hence make the life of the working personnel, miscellaneous duties personnel, students, mothers, children, the sick and the convalescent too harsh, or those who improve livelihood through ways which are wrong, hinder work and study, or sabotage policies and orders should be criticized and taken to task.

(7) Implement unified leadership. Firmly carry out the principle of unified leadership and dispersed operation. The top-levels of the Central Committee, the Border Region, the special regions [zhuanqu] and the counties should all set up strong leadership organizations concerned with unifying all production undertakings. According to the system and level, unify the policies for running enterprises, unify the coordination between the enterprises, and unify the ways of inspecting the running of each enterprise. Furthermore, under the condition of permitting each production unit to retain a suitable profit for itself, within a suitable area and according to the nature of production and operation, unify the distribution of the profits from production. This is necessary to avoid the great evils of lack of coordination, of inequalities in profits and losses, and of disparities in hardship and comforts.

(8) All agriculture, industry, animal husbandry, transport and commerce must be run as proper enterprises [qiyehua], using the system of economic accounting. The food, bedding, clothing and payments for the working personnel and employees in each enterprise should be supplied by the enterprise itself. They must not be provided at public expense.

(9) All production organs (factories, shops, etc.) should be 'popularized' no matter whether they belong to the government, the troops or the official organizations and schools. With the exception of the allocation of production tasks, the administration and supervision of production and the disposal of the results of production, everything else is under the leadership of the local Party and government, even including branch life. All personnel in production organizations must carry out policies, be law-abiding and pay taxes, take off their uniforms and put on ordinary clothing, join in the activities of the local masses and be model citizens of the Border Region.

(10) In accordance with the concrete circumstances, the Finance and Economy Office and the financial and economic committees of the sub-regions should issue specific production tasks for 1943 to the official organizations and schools in each county system. They should investigate and examine the production plans, and enter all the results of production completed within the plan by these production units into the financial accounts. Surplus production beyond the plan should be retained by the production unit for itself as a means of improving livelihood. Upper levels should issue supplements to units whose production is not enough. Those that made a loss in 1942 should be quickly examined to find ways of making up the deficiency.

(11) The four shortcomings pointed out in Chapter 8, 'On the Development of the Productive Undertakings of the Troops',[1] also apply to the official organizations and schools. All official organizations and schools committing similar abuses should pay attention to correcting them.

(12) It must be clearly explained to all personnel engaged in agriculture, industry, animal husbandry, transport, commerce and labour outside working-hours (including the ordinary people working as hired labour or in partnerships) that their work is for the revolution and they are part of a very glorious cause. Setting aside a portion of the income from their labour to hand over to the government all helps our own, glorious and sacred revolutionary cause. It does not increase the assets of any individual. If publicly employed personnel working in the

[1] See above. pp. 195–9.

public sector of the economy plot to make special profits for themselves, they are guilty of immoral conduct within our ranks and crimes of corruption before the law. Those who are entirely free of corruption and waste, and work loyally for the Party and the country, are considered noble and moral, and should receive praise and rewards from the Party and the government. This point should be explained to the troops.

(13) All people doing economic, financial, supply and general-service work, so long as they are not corrupt, do not waste, are loyal and work for the Party and the country, should be honoured. All people who treat their work lightly or with disdain should be criticized and rebuked.

10

ON GRAIN WORK

We have now completed our discussion of economic work. Our economy is divided into the two large private and public sectors. The private sector of the economy includes agriculture, animal husbandry, handicrafts, cooperatives and salt undertakings. The public sector consists of the undertakings run by the government, the army, and the official organizations and schools. We have looked at all these things. We have not discussed commerce in the private sector since we still lack the necessary information. For the moment we have to ignore it. Now we must discuss the problems of finance. However, we shall not look at all of its aspects but just look at three questions: (i) the question of grain, (ii) the question of taxation, and (iii) the question of economizing.

Our finances depend on two sources, the people and ourselves. Financial work for the portion supplied by ourselves is basically distribution and supply work when the process of production by the three elements of the public sector of the economy is completed and becomes a process of distribution. The public sector of the economy is the primary foundation for our finances and supplies. It provided three-fifths of all finances and supplies during 1942. Thus our primary financial work consists of properly carrying out the distribution of the fruits of production in the public sector. We have already discussed this question at length as a supplementary factor when dealing with the public sector of the economy and there is no space to say more about the details here. It can wait for further studies later. Now we must discuss the second foundation for our finances and supplies – the portion obtained from the people, namely grain and tax. There is also the question of economizing. This is related to what we get from the people and what we supply ourselves. It is a question related to the whole of the resources we already possess and to the correct distribution and use of the funds for running our undertakings. Therefore it is an important financial problem. The grain question referred to here is the grain tax alone and not all grain problems. This is part of the tax system. However, since it is related to all the needs of the army and government, and to the relationship of 80 to 90 per cent of the people of the Border Region with the Party, the Eighth Route Army and the government, it is worth specially setting it aside from the general question of taxation and dealing with it first.

More than 90 per cent of the 1,400,000 people in the Border Region are peasants. Landlords and merchants make up less than 10 per cent. Over half of these peasants have obtained a share of land and the other half have not yet done so. Why are we striving to the utmost to enable the peasants to develop agriculture? In the first place our aim is to enable the peasants to grow richer and improve their life. Secondly, we want the peasants to be capable of paying grain tax to help meet the needs of the War of Resistance. There is also a third reason which is that we want the peasants, after obtaining a reduction in rent and in interest rates, to develop agricultural production in order to be able to pay part as land rent to the landlords, and thus to unite the landlords with ourselves in the War of Resistance. We must only do one thing to achieve these three aims and that is strive to the utmost to enable the peasants to develop agriculture. The more agricultural production develops and the greater the amount of agricultural and subsidiary products the peasants harvest each year, then the less the amount of grain tax paid to the government becomes as a proportion of their total harvest. We propose to levy an annual grain tax of 180,000 dan beginning in 1943. We intend to keep this amount as fixed in the following few years even if as a result of agricultural development the total amount of grain produced in the Border Region increases from its present level of around 1,500,000 dan. (Many comrades estimate that with better use of existing labour power, we can raise the total production of the Border Region to 2 million dan.) All increases will thus accrue to the peasants, making them keen to work hard to develop their own production, and enabling them to improve their own livelihood and to dress and eat well.

All comrades throughout the Border Region must learn from the way the comrades of Yan'an county strive to work in the interests of the peasants, so that the peasants rapidly get richer. The richer the peasants become, the less they take exception to handing over a fixed amount of grain tax and the more they feel close to and inseparable from the Communist Party, the Eighth Route Army and the Border Region Government. The peasant Wu Manyou of Yan'an county is clear proof of this. On 30 April 1942, the *Liberation Daily* carried the following report on him.

THE MODEL RURAL LABOUR HERO, WU MANYOU EXCELS IN OPENING NEW LAND AND HARVESTING GRAIN FOR SEVERAL YEARS RUNNING, AND INFLUENCES THE MASSES TO TAKE PART ACTIVELY IN SPRING PLOUGHING.

(Our special report.) Rural labour heroes appear one after another in the spring ploughing movement. In order to express their deep devotion to the Border Region, to consolidate the Region and to improve their own life, they display the spirit of labour to a high degree. Among them, Wu Manyou from Liulin district in Yan'an county is especially respected by most peasants. Every year his harvest of grain exceeds that of others by one-sixth. The two labour powers in his family farm over 120 mu of land. This year they opened up 35 mu of uncultivated land. He is already publicly recognized as a model labour hero by the peasants of the township. According to late news last night, the Reconstruction Department of the Border Region Government has decided to give him a special award.

(Our report from Yan'an.) For successive years the peasant Wu Manyou of Wujiacaoyuan in Second township, Liulin district, Yan'an county has been active in spring ploughing and grown good crops. Usually people get an average of 5 dou from every 3 mu; he gets 6 dou. Thus when the government issued the call for great efforts in spring ploughing he said: 'I have benefited from the revolution and I can never forget it. I truly love the Border Region and at the same time I work to improve my own life'. He redoubled his efforts at opening up new land and influenced the masses. He created an enthusiastic spring ploughing movement in his own village. All the peasants in Yan'an county know that Wu Manyou's township did the best farming this year. Wu Manyou originally planned to open up 35 mu. He had already opened up 15 mu before it rained, and he was even more active afterwards. He said: 'I can finish clearing the new land in ten days, and if there is time I'll exceed the plan'. As for his other 100-odd mu of cultivated land, some parts have already been seeded and some parts have already been turned over. All the inhabitants of Wujiacaoyuan, the village head, the head of the township, and the head of the district unanimously praise him as 'a model hero in spring ploughing'. Now the district government has applied to higher levels to reward him. On hearing this the Border Region Government also decided after practical investigation to give him a suitable reward as an incentive.

(Our report from Yan'an county.) During the spring ploughing movement many labour heroes have appeared, but in the final analysis who is best at growing crops? To clear up this question our reporters spent a month visiting various villages. Now they have found the model labour hero generally recognized by the masses. This model hero's name is Wu Manyou. This year he is forty-nine. He is well built and strong. Before the land revolution he was a tenant farmer. At that time he had to eat leaves and husks. He 'suffered hardship' [worked for others] by cutting firewood. The money he earned he had to pay as taxes to the local bad officials and rich gentry, and he himself usually went hungry. After the land revolution, he joined the revolution. He was given a share of land on the hills, roughly 40 shang equal to 120-odd mu. Apart from this private land, he has actively opened up and sown uncultivated land in successive years, and he raises cows and sheep. Now all the hill land is cultivated and he has two bullocks, three cows and more than a hundred sheep. His prospects grow brighter and brighter. He has got married, and eats and dresses well. Last year after government examination his family status was raised from poor peasant to middle peasant. He often says: 'When I think of the past and then of the present, how can I forget the benefits of the revolution and of the Border Region?'

(Our report from Yan'an county.) Model labour hero, Wu Manyou, plants crops like any other peasant. Why does he reap more grain than others? According to the peasants in his village there are several reasons. First, he gets up earlier than anyone else and goes to bed later. Before the sky grows light he has fed his cows and gone up the hill. He only comes back from his land when the sky is dark. He can really endure hard work. Second, in winter when there is no work to do, he diligently collects manure. As he also can raise sheep and cows, he has more manure than others. On average he applies seven pack-loads of manure to every 3 mu. Third, when the crops begin to shoot, some peasants are afraid to go up into the hills. They do not hoe the weeds or only hoe once at the most. He hoes twice at least, so his millet naturally grows well. Fourth, he ploughs deeply. Other households plough down 5 inches, he ploughs down 7 inches at least. Fifth, when breaking up the earth, he breaks it finely and is not careless. Sixth, he always ploughs and sows at the correct time, neither early nor late. Because of these fine qualities, he harvests a top yield per 3 mu of 12 dou on the old scale (18 dou on the market scale) and a lowest of 4 dou (6 market dou). The average is 6 dou (9 market dou). The average for other peasants is

5 *dou* (7 market *dou*). In terms of averages, he is one-sixth better than others.

(Our report from Yan'an county.) Model labour hero, Wu Manyou, is not only a model at growing crops but is also a model citizen. Last year he harvested 18 market *dan* of wheat (*xiaomai*) and 27 market *dan* of grains (equivalent to 16 *dan* 2 *dou* of hulled grains). He paid 14 *dan* 3 *dou* in grain tax, 1,000 *jin* of hay tax, contributed two lots of 150 *yuan* to government bonds, and paid 665 *yuan* cash substitute for the salt tax. The villagers said to him: 'Old Wu, you pay out too much, cut down a bit!' He said 'During the revolution, the Eighth Route Army protects our Border Region. People at the front loose blood. All we have to do is sweat a little more. How can you say "Too much"?' Afterwards everyone respected his opinion and enthusiastically gave grain to the State. This year the upper levels moved some refugees to live in the village. He lent grain and hoes to them and helped them find uncultivated land. He also often encouraged them materially and in spirit to open up and plant land. Usually he is also the most fair person in the village. His prestige among the ordinary people is very high and everyone trusts him. In May last year he was elected a member of the township council and director of the township's work in supporting families with dependants fighting in the War of Resistance. He has a younger brother who is a soldier with the Eighth Route Army, so he himself belongs to such a family but he declined public support. He said: 'Fighting is the duty of the Chinese people, there is nothing strange about it. I've enough to eat, what other support do I need?' However, he is extremly correct towards other families in the township with dependants at the front. At the same time he is very fair in his distribution of labour duties. There are twelve families in the township with dependants fighting in the war. This year he arranged substitute farming for 220 mu and all the families were grateful to him. No one in the township says he is not good.

(Our report from Yan'an county.) There are fourteen peasant households in Wujiacaoyuan with fourteen heads of family. When you raise the question of whether Wu Manyou is worthy of being called a model labour hero, everyone raises his thumb and says 'What else can be said about old Wu. He is the best at enduring hardship. If he isn't a hero who is fit to be?'

On 2 June there was another report in the *Liberation Daily*.

Because of the influence of the labour hero, Wu Manyou, Wujiacaoyuan which originally planned to open up 147 mu of uncultivated land, had already opened up 225 mu. Wu Manyou himself opened up 15 mu. After Wu Manyou was rewarded the whole township (Second township, Liulin district) opened up 540 mu.

On 29 October, the *Liberation Daily* carried a further report.

This year the harvest of coarse millet is very good. In Wu Manyou's village the yield per 3 mu is in general 5 to 6 dou but he has got 8 dou (each dou is the large kind equivalent to 45 jin). Most peasants get 3 or 4 dou of hulled grain from husking 1 dan of coarse grains. He always maintains the official standard for the equivalent amount of hulled grain. Wu Manyou often puts on a propagandistic air and says to others: 'If you want to get your crops as good as mine, learn from me! I have no secret, I am simply willing to labour'.

Wu Manyou is already a rich peasant. Because he got benefits from the soviet government in the past and the Border Region Government now, he has united his destiny with that of the Communist Party, the Eighth Route Army and the Border Region Government. All empty words are useless, we must give the people visible material wealth. The minds of many of our comrades have still not fully turned into the minds of communists. They only know how to do one kind of work, asking the people for this and that, for grain, for hay, for taxes and for mobilization for various kinds of work. They do not know how to do the other kind of work, striving to the utmost to help the people develop production and to improve their cultural level. It is entirely rational for us to ask things of the people for the sake of the revolution and the War of Resistance. It is good that our comrades consider that in doing this work they are doing the work they should do for the revolution. But it is only doing one aspect of work and it is not the primary aspect. The primary aspect of our work is not to ask things of the people but to give things to the people. What can we give the people? Under present conditions in the Shaan-Gan-Ning Border Region, we can organize, lead and help the people to develop production and increase their material wealth. And on this basis we can step-by-step raise their political awareness and cultural level. To these ends we must endure all discomforts and night and day, diligently and thoroughly look into the people's problems in their livelihood and production, including such important matters as plough-oxen, agricultural implements, seeds, manure, water conservancy, animal fodder, agricultural credit, immigration, opening up new land, improving agricultural methods, female labour, labour by loafers, plans for setting up households,

232

cooperatives, exchange-labour teams, transport teams, textiles, animal husbandry, salt industry and so forth. Moreover, we must concretely help the people to solve these problems and not use empty words. This work is the primary work for all Communist Party members working in the countryside. Only after we have done this aspect of work and achieved real results can we get the people's support when we do the second aspect of our work which is to ask them for things. Only then will they say that our requests are necessary and correct. Only then will they understand that if they do not give grain, hay and other things to the government, their life cannot be good and cannot get better. Only in this way will our work not be done through coercion. Only in this way will things run smoothly, and only in this way will we be truly united with the people. This is the basic line and policy of our party. Every comrade (including those in the army) should study this thoroughly. Only when our comrades understand and carry out the complementary nature of these two aspects of work, can we call ourselves all-round, communist revolutionaries. Otherwise, although we do revolutionary work and although we are revolutionaries, we shall still not be all-round revolutionaries. Furthermore, some comrades are still bureaucrats remote from the masses. Because they only know how to ask the masses for things and do not know how to or are unwilling to give things to the masses, the masses detest them. This question is extremely important. I hope everyone will pay great attention to it and propagandize the principle throughout the whole Party.

In what follows we shall sum up our past experience in grain work and point out the policy for 1943.

From 1937 to 1939, the grain tax levied in the Border Region covered only a part of supplies. The deficiency each year was made up by purchase using funds issued by the government. With the exception of particular areas and periods when there were grain difficulties, there were no insurmountable problems in the whole of grain supply for the four years. During that time we actually enabled the people to build up their resources. The burdens of grain tax were heavy on the rich peasants and landlords, very light on the middle peasants and most poor peasants had none at all. In 1940 outside aid was cut off and the government had no resources to buy grain. We had to turn to raising all of it in tax. However, the principle of 'calculating tax on the basis of income' had not yet changed. Also the grain tax for 1940 was raised to only 90,000 *dan* and the policies for collection were not altered. For supplies in the following year (1941) we put forward the policy of 'strengthening grain administration and ensuring grain sufficiency'. However, we could not provide all supplies since we had not levied much grain in 1940. There was also the related matter of achieving self-sufficiency in running costs in 1941, in connection with which the various army units and official organizations paid careful attention to grain in order to solve problems in livelihood. Another factor was that since the organizational structure of the departments doing grain work was not yet strong and the quality of the cadres was not good enough, the various regulations were not well established and we could not fully control grain income and expenditure in all places. At the time the problems of making excessive returns and rash leadership were very serious, personnel was constantly changing, increasing and decreasing, and there was too much occasional expenditure outside the set amount. The grain tax levied in 1940 provided supplies until March 1941, when some places already had nothing to eat. Before long there was a panic over grain everywhere. It was only by successively buying grain once and borrowing twice that we lasted until November. In order to guarantee supplies for 1942 and to repay loans taken in 1941, it was estimated that a levy of 200,000 *dan* was essential. At this time the problem of grain had already become the most serious financial problem. After repeated study by the Party and government and under the new principle for collection of 'calculating tax first on the basis of our expenditure and second on the basis of income', it was decided to levy 200,000 *dan* of grain and 26 million *jin* of hay. To ensure collection of this amount of grain and taking the interests of all social strata into account, the base for collection was expanded. The burden on the middle peasants was increased and the poor peasants began to bear some of it. We corrected the earlier phenomenon of bias towards the minority of wealthy.

The grain accounts at the various county granaries were not clearly kept in the past, and the great muddle in the formalities for buying and borrowing grain during 1941 had increased the difficulties of sorting them out. The Grain Office was deeply afraid that the lack of clarity over the old grain would influence the new. Therefore 'grasp the new grain, ensure supplies' was made the strategy for work in 1942. Events during the year showed that although there were deficiencies in implementation, the policy itself was entirely correct. Grain tax for 1942 was reduced to 160,000 dan and hay tax to 16 million jin. The policy for collection also reduced the burden on the poor peasants slightly. Furthermore, we are preparing to implement a unified progressive agricultural tax in 1943 in place of the grain-tax method. In order to raise the peasants' enthusiasm for production, we lent them some of the grain and hay during 1942 to help them solve problems during spring ploughing. In supply work the main thing is to concentrate on grain and hay.

As regards the work of collection, we only levied 10,000 dan in 1937 and 1938. The burden on the masses was very light and everyone was willing to pay. In 1939 the amount was raised to 50,000 dan. The government proclaimed new regulations for collecting the grain. Work groups were sent down to the countryside to make surveys and to collect tax according to the regulations. However, in reality, 50,000 dan was still a very slight amount of grain tax for the masses to bear. The cadres were used to the method of democratic apportionment of taxes and the survey work was very perfunctory. The so-called collection according to regulations remained a theory. In 1940 it was just the same. Only in 1941 when the grain-tax burden suddenly increased to 200,000 dan did the government again seriously revise the regulations. The Finance Department sent large numbers of work groups to the counties to work with the county and district governments in carrying out fairly thorough-going surveys so that the masses' burdens were made rational. This grain collection emphasized 'thorough-going surveys' and 'carrying out the regulations'. Summing up collection in 1941, there is clear proof that if good survey work is done, it is easy to carry out the regulations. For example, Ganquan county was very conscientious in making surveys and then implemented the regulations and the rates for collection. Quzi county carried out three surveys and was able to ensure a fair and rational distribution of the burden. In Baima district of Huachi county the requirement was not filled after two allocations. Eventually the head of the grain collection work group, Comrade Wang, himself surveyed one township to get experience. As a result the whole district over-fulfilled its quota by several tens of *dan*. In places where survey work was poorly done, such as in the special military area, the regulations could not be carried out. In general county cadres still treated survey work too lightly. Only a minority of them carried out thorough-going surveys for grain collection in 1941. The majority still used the old method of democratic apportionment of taxes. In 1942 the grain collection gained from the experience of the previous year. The regulations were revised again to bring them more in line with reality. More thorough surveys were undertaken on the basis of the surveys carried out in 1941. The Finance Department issued instructions that the cadres collecting the grain had to follow the regulations. In cases where carrying out the regulations meant that the task could not be completed, they could also use the method of democratic apportionment of taxes. At the same time, during this collection the cadres were given ideological education which overcame their previously crude work-style and backward conduct such as following personal preferences and holding things back. According to recent reports from Longdong there is once again proof of the importance of thorough-going surveys for the implementation of regulations. One district in Qingyang county carried out a thorough survey, and because much new land was cultivated during the year and production increased, it was able to exceed the original collection target by several hundred *dan* in line with the regulations.

A further point to consider is that for several years the figures set for the grain collection have been achieved and exceeded, but the work of putting the grain into the granaries has been too muddled. Many cadres involved in grain collection think that they only have to meet the target. They do not consider quality or investigate delayed payments. As a result on one hand the quality is not good enough with 15 to 20 per cent consisting of husks in some cases, and on the other there are instances where the masses delay in paying their grain. There is a difference between the amount collected and the amount put into the granaries. In the 1941 collection, although the quality was a bit better, there were still a lot of husks mixed with the grain. The slogan 'Grain to the Granary and Hay to the Cellar' was put forward to overcome the problem of late payment but there was still too much of it. In addition, because the 1941 collection was much bigger than any previous year, the difficulties of getting it into the granaries were much greater. As a result over 3,900 *dan* of the grain collected did not go into the granaries. This was nearly 2 per cent of the total. During the 1942 collection the problem of getting the grain into the granaries was specially emphasized. According to the latest examination this work has been done a little better this year. However, the question of whether the full total had been put in the granaries or not awaits a final summary before it can be answered.

Another point is that for several years the Finance Department has assigned work groups to help the county and district governments in the grain-levy work. Where county and district cadres are too weak, this method is of great help. Its shortcoming is that it easily creates dependency in the lower levels of government, and every time there is a mobilization, the upper levels have to send people. The cadres have to go back and forth, spending much time on the road, which leads to waste of manpower and of time. Since collection in 1942 had the good foundation of work done in 1941, the Finance Department adopted the principle of 'fewer and better' in its assignment of work teams. It sent fewer cadres to each county and increased the responsibility of the county and district government. In 1941, 150 people were sent down. On this basis they are preparing to move towards not sending down anyone at all, handing all the grain collection work over to the county and district governments.

As regards supply work, because general income and expenditure was not firmly controlled in 1941 so that grain had to be bought once and borrowed twice, and because mobilization was hurried and almost cruel, the masses were not satisfied. This was a great shortcoming. In 1942 we were able to control income and expenditure. We also had the 200,000 *dan* of grain levied in 1941 as a guarantee to ensure supplies until December. However, since the drive for better troops and simpler administration was not thorough, the budget could not be strictly implemented. Occasional expenditures combined with unpaid grain tax came to over 18,000 *dan*. In addition, troop movements influenced the relationship between supply and demand in various places, and grain balances in the first half of 1942 could not be maintained as allocated. Therefore, after July places like Yan'an, Nanniwan, and Linzhen one after another became short of grain. Afterwards, the Finance Department issued supplementary funds of 2 million *yuan* to buy grain and a summer collection was made. Only in this way was a grain panic avoided during 1942, and there was no bad effect on the masses. Next, for the grain in 1941 we adopted the method of 'allocation as a whole and divided administration'. Although this saved the bother and waste of transport to and fro, it brought about cases of uncontrolled selling of grain, which also entailed a lot of waste. There was still a gap between the amount collected and the amount needed for supplies, which also led to many shortcomings. For example, the grain and hay allocated to the various counties in 1941 was biased towards the harvest situation and neglected the supply and demand situation. The grain requirement in Sanbian for the year was over 10,000 *dan* but only 1,600 *dan* was collected. A supplement of 9,000 *dan* had to be transported from Longdong, Ansai, Zichang, Zhidan and so forth. Not only was the year's grain transport work excessive for the masses of these counties, but the masses in Sanbian were also very busy handling transshipment. They called out that 'this way is not as good as collecting more from us'. It is now estimated that just the 4,000 *dan* of grain moved to Sanbian from Longdong cost 7 million *yuan* to transport, which is more than the cost of buying grain in Sanbian. Another example was the grain collected in Yanchuan. Originally it should have supplied Yan'an. However in 1941 grain from Dongyang district was collected at the Majiapan granary which is on the opposite side of the county near the Yellow River. As a result it took an extra three days to transport the grain to Yan'an. Quite a few similar situations arose in other counties. Again, the plan for the 1941 hay collection was not thoroughly researched. It was decided everywhere to collect the hay after the grain and no attention was paid to supply and demand. As a result some places kept hay for which there was no use and it was allowed to go rotten which dissatisfied the masses. In other places which needed a lot of hay there was an exceptional shortage and supplies were only enough for eight months. Another example was the 1941 grain collection in Guanzhong. Millet was made the unit instead of wheat. The peasants had to go out of the Border Region to sell wheat and buy millet in order to pay the tax. As a result too much millet was collected, the troops were not used to eating it and there were many disputes. After summer begins, millet rots easily which added to the troubles. Again in 1941 the relative proportion between regular and miscellaneous grains was generalized, and not reckoned according to the grain production circumstances or the relationship between supply and demand in each place. As a result some places (such as the special military area) collected a lot of miscellaneous grain which could not be issued. Some places (such as Yan'an) needed horse fodder but could not get miscellaneous grains. The official organizations had to lower the relative proportions and exchange hulled grain for miscellaneous grain which in turn led to waste of grain. The above shortcomings illustrate that grain work is very concrete and meticulous, practical work. If it is done crudely and in a way divorced from reality then the results will disturb the people and disrupt the government. In 1942 after the grain collection work was handed over to the Grain Office, the management of grain collection and supplying was united. At the same time as a means of balancing resources, it was decided to accept a money substitute for the hay tax according to the different supply-and-demand situation in each place. As for the relative proportions of grains, the earlier way of generalized application was changed into a system of deciding according to the concrete situation in each place, thus overcoming the previous shortcoming.

Next, from the winter of 1941 up to the present quite large successes have been achieved in setting up and consolidating systems for grain supply. As regards the budget system, for example, in 1942 most official organizations were able to draw up their budgets at the correct time. They have got rid of the bad practices of claiming excess grain and eating double rations, and corrected the situation where counties approved budgets haphazardly and spent grain without control. In particular they have grasped the policy of 'the final account must not exceed the budget'. During 1942 they have conscientiously cut down on all irrational expenditure, economizing on over 19,000 *dan* of grain. As regards the system for paying out grain, most army units and official organizations have honoured the regulations that grain cannot be paid out without a grain payment document. The responsible comrades in the counties have also paid attention to this regulation. They have not indiscriminately permitted loans from tax grain. At the same time during 1942 all the counties have used the official *dou* measure which considerably reduced the number of disputes. As for the granary regulations, because of the cadres' limitations, these could only be strengthened first in the central granaries and then gradually generalized to all granaries. For keeping accounts, the Finance Department drew up two standard account-books (one new-style and detailed, the other very simple) which were adopted by the cadres according to their ability. In 1942 most granaries, good and bad, had account-books. Gradually we can reach the goal of being able to obtain at any time statistics for grain income, expenditure and the amounts and kinds of grain in store. As for the grain coupon regulations, there was much corruption in 1941 because we issued large numbers of coupons. In 1942 we abandoned the old grain coupons and issued three kinds of meal-ticket which were only supplied for circulation among personnel in the official organizations to cover meals. This was a step forward.

However, there were still many defects in the grain-supply work. For example, a minority of large units still could not draw up their budget at the stipulated time. A comparison of the actual personnel totals and the budgets of various large units showed that there was still quite a proportion of figures without foundation. Some instances of taking double rations still occurred. The ratio of livestock was not clearly laid down, which in some cases led to quite a lot of waste. Instances of individual troop units insisting on grain loans from granaries because they had wasted grain and overspent could still not completely be avoided. As for the storage system, most granaries still only managed to do the work of receiving and paying out grain and of

administration. They were not good enough at supervising collection, safe-keeping, submitting accounts and other duties. The
meal-tickets could not be circulated among the people, which
caused problems for personnel sent to do outside tasks. This too
was a shortcoming. Finally, there was a great defect in building
up and consolidating all regulations which was that the Grain
Office only emphasized its own regulations and difficulties. It
could not comprehensively and concretely concern itself with
solutions to the problems and difficulties facing each official
organization.

In 1942 the official organizations in charge of grain were very
successful in the work of clearing up the granaries' old grain
accounts. For several years the county grain accounts had not
been examined and reckoned up, so that the Grain Office's
accounts were no longer any use. For example, according to the
Office's accounts, in the winter of 1941, Ansai should have had
over 2,900 *dan* in store. In fact it had less than 100 *dan*. Again,
the account for the grain taken from the granary by the
sanitorium had not been worked out for five years. It was discovered in 1942 that it had collected over 100 *dan* too much.
There were many cases like these. Compounded by the muddle
over purchases and loans in 1941, many counties had no
accounts to be examined. As a result the Grain Office sent cadres
down to each place to work out the accounts, and adopted all
kinds of accounting methods. The old granary accounts were
only cleared up after six months' hard work. Now the Grain
Office is able to work out how much grain is actually held by the
granaries and can keep a hold on grain income and expenditure.
The counties' administration of grain was also previously very
poor with losses due to a combination of rats, insects, rotting and
so forth. In addition there was serious corruption among the
cadres. During grain collection in 1941, there were more than
ten cases. It had even gone so far that individual special agents
had infiltrated granary work. For example, Zhang Bingquan, the
director of the granary of Taile district in Fuxian, was a special
agent. In February 1942 he embezzled over 10 *dan* of public
grain and fled from the Border Region. This shows that previously the Grain Office's supervision of granary cadres was
too lax and its inspection work too infrequent. Since the granary

accounts were cleared up in 1942 and the leadership of the granaries by the five sections of government at county level was strengthened, corruption and waste have been reduced and many active and hardworking cadres have been discovered.

In carrying out collection policy in the two years 1939 and 1940, the regulations were fixed so that the tax threshold began at 1.2 *dan* (that is, peasant families whose harvest per person was less than 1.2 *dan* were not taxed). Tax was progressively applied to a top level of 36 per cent (that is, the tax rate increased until it levied 36 per cent of the harvest and thereafter the percentage did not increase). The failing here was that the tax burden was biased towards the minority of the well-off. At the same time the method of collection was that of democratic apportionment of taxes and not that laid down by the regulations. As a result, there were cases of 'going for big households' and 'ignoring everything but the target'. Also the collection policy was influenced by excessive 'leftism'. In 1941 the regulations were revised. The tax threshold was fixed at 0.5 *dan* (for example, a family of five whose annual harvest of regular grain was less than 2.5 *dan* was not taxed). Taxation was progressively applied up to 30 per cent. The implementation of these regulations resulted in a broadening of the base for collection. Apart from Huanxian which suffered natural disasters, the tax burden in all other counties was carried by over 80 per cent of the people and in Yan'an county it reached 95 per cent. In terms of caring for the interests of all classes and strata, with the exception of Yan'an, Yanchang and Ansai, the burden in other counties did not exceed 30 per cent of the harvest. However, there were still shortcomings. For example, the counties were not entirely rational in their allocations to meet the total collection. The special military area lowered the tax threshold to 0.3 *dan* and reduced the number of steps in the tax progression. As a result the poor and middle peasants suffered and the richer middle peasants and above were let off too lightly. Also, during grain collection in 1941 we only paid attention to collecting grain and not to reducing rents and interest rates at the same time. Some new immigrants who should not have paid tax had to do so. Family dependants of troops in the War of Resistance should have received special assistance but this was stopped in some cases. Some cotton-growers should not have been taxed for grain but were. All these things contravened the government's policies. Other policies such as caring for the interests of all strata, raising the enthusiasm for production of the peasants and so forth merely remained general slogans. Actual implementation was very deficient. With the experience of 1941, the grain collection in 1942 made some advances. However, we still did not pay enough attention to the cotton-growing policy. For example, the allocation of a quota for grain tax to the cotton-growing areas in the three eastern counties was the same as that allocated to other counties. When it came to collection, problems arose. If grain tax was not collected on the cotton fields the requirement could not be fulfilled. Yet if it was collected, it would conflict with government orders. Ultimately they had to make accommodations and reduce the collection by half. This still damaged the authority of the government.

In any work, going beyond policies depends on whether the cadres are good or bad. Grain work is no exception. The most hardworking people doing grain work are the granary cadres. The easiest corrupted are also the granary cadres. Therefore we shall here specially quote examples of typically good and typically bad granary cadres, so that everyone can learn from the good and be warned by the bad.

Good examples

(A) Comrade He Chungao, director of Panlong granary is an old fellow of fifty-two. He does not say much but is very careful and thoughtful, enthusiastic and hardworking. In 1939 he was assigned to work in the Zhenwudong granary of the Grain Office. In 1940 he was transferred to be director of the Panlong granary, concurrently responsible for the grain-market balancing station [diaojizhan] and the transport station. He is responsible for the work of three men. In the past he has been secretary of a district Party committee and has been trained at the Border Region Party School. Initially he was one of seven people including Jia Zhicai and Ren Shengbiao who were assigned from the Border Region Party School to do grain work but of these he alone remains at his post today. His cultural level is not among the lowest of the granary directors. He can write simple letters and keep clear accounts. He is very conscientious in studying the newly adopted account books and learns quickly. In 1941 when the 'monthly report tables' were issued to the granaries, some directors could not understand after three days of explanation. After hearing once he was able to raise questions and opinions. After a few questions like 'What should be filled in on this section?, Would it be all right to fill in that section like this?', he could complete and send in his 'monthly report tables' on time. Many fine qualities are expressed in his work. The first is meticulous attention to detail. When receiving grain he writes a receipt for the amount and makes up his accounts every evening. When paying-out he double-checks on the abacus. The second is a deep sense of responsibility. He takes great care of the granary. One storage bin was a little damp and he paid special attention. He often had the grain spread out to dry in the sun, and when paying-out grain he always paid from this bin first. Eventually he dug a ditch behind the bin and dug the surface of the earth around the bin lower than the bin, making it a little drier. When the granary needs minor repairs he does not hire workers but sets-to himself to carry bricks and plaster (under his influence the personnel in charge of moving the grain also work hard and help). As administrator of the transport depot, every time a transport team arrives he helps to cut grass, draw water and prepare food. His third quality is his friendly attitude to others. Some of the personnel in leading official organizations get in a bad temper when the grain is paid-out, but he patiently finishes the job and does not get into arguments. Sometimes some of the masses send bad grain when paying-in. He just encourages them to take it back. When buying grain to balance the market, he can discuss things and get close to the masses. But he also has his own opinions. Once when it was raining and the grain in the market could not be sold, he took the opportunity to purchase it. The price was fairly low and the masses were still pleased. For these reasons he enjoys some prestige among the masses of Panlong. When receiving tax grain in 1941, a peasant from Yongping district in Yanchuan county offered him bribes. He got angry and sent the man and the goods to the district government. His fourth quality is a plain and simple way of life. He raises very few questions about his own life and he expresses concern about receiving welfare expenses. In 1942 he was responsible for collecting 4,000 *dan* of tax grain and everyone was concerned that he might not manage since he is old and has few helpers. But every time he wrote a letter to the Grain Office, he said that he could manage.

(B) Comrade Bai Heming is director of the Tianzhuang granary in Suide. He is a graduate of upper primary school. He had worked in the old *baojia* office.[1] His qualities include first a deep sense of responsibility. When receiving grain he compares receipts and invoices every evening to make sure that there has been no mistake. He also makes out clear accounts for households owing grain, and supervises the districts and townships, encouraging them to send in their grain. Before receiving grain, he himself lays stones and boards in the storage bins, spreads dry straw and puts straw mats over the straw so as to guard against dampness. After the grain is in store, he himself seals up the bins which will not be opened soon, using bricks and plaster and covering-up holes which let in the wind, with broken mats. Secondly, he is friendly towards others. When receiving grain he inspects conscientiously. However, to those who send in bad grain he simply says: 'Look everybody, can you feel easy about sending grain like this for the troops?' He has never raised his voice in abuse. If someone from the army came to collect grain not in accordance with official procedures, he always courteously and patiently explained things. On the one hand he would lend some grain to prevent shortage, and on the other asked them to make good the procedures. Before long if anyone from the troops stationed in Suide went to collect grain from old Bai's granary, they always went through the procedures to avoid difficulties for old Bai and embarrassment for themselves. Thirdly, he is very hardworking. He gathers firewood and draws water himself. He is careful over operating and food costs. He reports excess expenditure to the fifth government section at county level. He does not indiscriminately take grain and sell it for the cash to make up deficiencies. Now Comrade Bai Heming has been promoted to be head of the fifth section of Suide county government.

[1] The local security office used in traditional times and by the Guomindang.

Bad examples

(A) Hu Dianchang was director of the granary of Fourth district Xinning. When receiving grain in the winter of 1941, he sold 3 *dan* privately, took 1.3 *dan* home, and lent 3.92 *dan* to his relatives and friends. He himself and his relatives and friends, Hu Diangong, Hu Qingrong and Liu Zixiao should have paid 7 *dan* of grain tax. They did not hand over a single grain but he still issued tax-grain receipts. When receiving grain he did not allow the masses to sweep up the grain on the floor, but swept it up himself and shared it with the personnel helping him to receive the grain. After he had finished issuing tax grain for deposit in citizens' homes, he was 0.2 *dan* short but he falsely reported 1 *dan* to the fifth section of the county government. After the fifth section found him out, he was sent to court, sentenced to prison and ordered to return the embezzled grain.

(B) In September 1939 after grain was sold from the Shuifan district granary in the Huachi county, 14.7 *dan* of tax grain was missing. The granary director, Wang Wenbin reported to the upper levels that rats had eaten 12.7 *dan* and another 2 *dan* had been contaminated. In 1941 when the grain collection work group went to investigate, they discovered that Wang Wenbin had gone to the county town for a meeting during the time when the grain was sold. His place had been taken by the district secretary Mao Yupeng. During the grain sales Mao Yupeng had lived exceptionally richly. He had bought a flock of sheep and two skin coats. He had also bought cloth. There was suspicion of embezzlement. However, at the time the county government did not investigate. Afterwards Mao Yupeng was transferred to work elsewhere. This affair is still going on.

Above we have summed up our experience in grain work during the past five years. Below are the policies for work in 1943.

(1) Implement the unified progressive agricultural tax. In the past we have used the method of levying national salvation grain tax. It is not an entirely satisfactory method of taxation. If it is well done it can only achieve the aim of being fair and rational in its burden on the people. It cannot give any effective encouragement to the peasants' feelings towards production. Therefore

we must actively prepare to implement the unified progressive agricultural tax. How should our preparatory work be done? (i) Under the leadership of the Finance Department set up a specialist research team consisting of five to seven cadres selected for their experience in political work and their good understanding of land and financial problems. This team should gather, study and arrange materials concerning progressive taxation, and plan the work for introducing it. In addition, directed by the Border Region Government, responsible comrades from the relevant official organizations led by the head of the Finance Department should organize a planning committee to take charge of policy, to solve major problems and to regularly lead the work of the research team. (ii) Carry out survey work. A detailed summary of grain collection work in 1942 should be supplied to the progressive taxation research team as concrete source material. The research team should first study some counties with different situations, whose collection in 1941 and 1942 was comparatively good. They should draw up an initial survey plan, and first carry out trial surveys. Afterwards they should revise the plan, draw up a format and carry out a general survey. In the light of the materials from the survey they should determine the regulations and methods. Counties with good successes who complete the work early can carry out a trial run during 1943. (iii) Carry out land registration at the same time as the surveys. (iv) Strengthen the government organization at township level, build up sound clerical records and survey thoroughly.

(2) Grasp grain and hay, ensure supplies. Supplying grain and hay is complex and detailed work. Grain and hay resources are widespread and not easily grasped. If we are unable to pay full attention at all times and cannot suitably adjust the relationship between supply and demand, it will be hard to make a good job of it. If we want to be able to grasp grain and hay and ensure supplies, we must do the following. (i) We must first ensure that all the 160,000 *dan* enters the granaries, and improve the quality so that 100 per cent is grain. Do not allow adulteration with husks. At the same time, call on all counties to eliminate evasion of payment. We must build up thorough regulations for the administration of grain and hay. Pay attention to the running and inspection of granaries. Set up central granaries. Gradually

improve equipment. Prevent damage through contamination and rotting, and corruption and theft. Strictly carry out the budget system. Completely eradicate excessive claims and taking double rations. Set up grain accounts in accordance with the cultural level of the cadres in each place. Do not be too elaborate but require that receipts, issues and stocks of grain are clearly recorded. Next, the regulations for paying-out grain are even more important and must be carried out. The reason for building up regulations soundly is to ensure supplies and to prevent corruption and waste. All instances of not adhering to discipline must be strictly corrected. However, a mechanical viewpoint which one-sidedly emphasizes regulations without concern for the concrete facts must also be guarded against. (ii) To ensure supplies, we must first handle the relationship between supply and demand of grain and hay. Prepare supplements for areas deficient in grain through transport, adjustment of distribution and so forth. In 1943 we should organize any unused animals owned by the official organizations to transport grain and hay, improve the work efficiency of every transport team (on average our animals each carry 1 dou less than those of the common folk and we need three days to go as far as they do in two) and lay down precise transport tasks so as to economize on manpower and animal power which can then be used for production. We must depend on the grain transported by the people, making plans early and using the slack agricultural periods and unused porters and animals. Except in special circumstances, mobilizing transport in the busy agricultural seasons is not allowed. Long-distance transport must also be avoided as much as possible. In areas where the distribution of grain can be adjusted, coordinated plans should be made by the Grain Office. Grain should be sold or bought at the right times so as to supplement supplies, save on transport and avoid waste. In areas where official organizations and schools are excessively concentrated such as Yan'an, we should consider the situation, and disperse men and horses to ease the distribution of grain and straw.

(3) Carry out the drive for better troops and simpler administration, store grain to prepare for famine. For successive years the Border Region has overdrawn its tax grain and has not got the slightest reserve. If natural disaster occurred, grain supplies for

the army and people would become an extremely serious problem. Everyone should be warned by this to take the following steps. (i) Resolutely carry out the new reorganization plan of the Party and government and the drive for better troops and simpler administration. Through simplification and strict economy ensure a balance between grain income and expenditure in 1943. (ii) Collect 180,000 *dan* of tax grain in 1943 so that we have a chance to retain some as reserve against need. (iii) During 1943 the troops, official organizations and schools should put developing agriculture in first place. Growing grain should form a considerable proportion of farming work so that there will be an even greater surplus in 1944 and we will be prepared against disaster. The troops, official organizations and schools certainly may not relax their own grain production because we are preparing to levy 180,000 *dan* during 1943.

(4) Strive to economize, strictly prevent waste of grain. There is a serious waste of grain among the official organizations and troops. Thus, mounting a campaign to economize should be one of our central tasks for 1943. Recently in Yan'an some official organizations and schools have inspected the amount of waste and carried out economy campaigns with great success. For example, the administrators of a training squad in the supply department of the garrison forces were diligent and responsible. When issuing grain and flour, they did the weighing themselves. Thus their food supply was just right and they were often able to eat buns and noodles. The Central Party School has large kitchens. Recently administration of food has been strict. Grain-cooking has been supervised. Left-over grain has been kept and eaten the following meal. After this was done, only 1 *jin* of millet was consumed per head per day. Before a month was up more than 5 *dan* of millet was saved. Another example was the collective meals at the nursery. In the past when the people there took meals in separate groups, the nursery consumed 150 *jin* of flour a meal. After collective meals were introduced, they only consumed 100 *jin* saving one-third. You see, comrades, what a surprising amount this is. Similarly the central departments and committees have implemented collective mess-halls and have also got good results. The Central Party School planned in the first half of the year to raise 2,000 chickens which required 300

bowls of millet a day. The waste was quite large. Afterwards they killed most of the chickens and only sixty were left. This saved quite a lot of grain. In addition, it is necessary to foster the habit of using meal-tickets. It can reduce the issue of large amounts of grain. In sum, in order to ensure that there are absolutely no shortages of grain, on the one hand we must levy and produce it and on the other we must seek to economize. This is the work for leading comrades and it is a mass-movement. Everyone must pay attention and complete the task given by the Party.

Two chapters on taxation and economizing originally planned for this book could not be written in time because the Senior Cadres' Conference closed. They had to be left out.

the Author

GLOSSARY OF SPECIAL TERMS

an huozi	安夥子	to take on tenants
an zhuangjia	安庄稼	to take on share-cropping tenants
baicao	白草	white grass
baipiao	白票	national currency
bao'an budui	保安部队	peace preservation corps
baogu	包谷	maize
biangong	变工	exchange-labour teams
bingcao	兵草	bing grass
Caijing Banshichu	财经办事处	Finance and Economy Office
Caiting	财厅	Finance Department
candou	蚕豆	broad beans
chengben kuaijizhi	成本会计制	cost accounting system
chuxupiao	储蓄票	savings bonds
culiang	粗粮	grain (unhulled)
da maifu	打埋伏	to hold something in reserve
da shenfen	打身份	to assign personal shares
daigengzhi	代耕制	the system of substitute cultivation
daxian	打线	threaders
diao fenzi	调分子	to hire help
diaojizhan	调济站	grain-market balancing station (used to regulate the market)
er liuzi	二流子	loafer
er qian	二钱	two ounces

251

fenfang	粉房	flour mill
Gonghe	工合	Chinese Industrial Cooperative
gongjijin	公积金	public accumulation fund
gongtou	工头	foreman
gongyijin	公益金	public welfare fund
gongyixin	公益心	public welfare centre
gongzhaiquan	公债券	government bonds
gu(zi)	谷（子）	spiked millet
gu changgong	催长工	to hire long-term labourers
guoliushui	过流水	turnover
Guomin Jingjibu	国民经济部	National Economy Department
heidou	黑豆	black beans
Houqinbu	后勤	Rear Services Department
huoshi danwei	伙食单位	provisions unit
huozhong	夥种	to farm in partnership, share-cropping tenants
Jianting	建厅	Reconstruction Department
jiaodao dadui	教导大队	instruction brigade
jiguanhua	机关化	to organize along the lines of a government organ (i.e. subject to budgetary rather than cost accounting procedures).
jijian jiangli zhidu	计件奖励制度	piecework incentive system
jijian leijin gongzizhi	计件累进工资制	progressive piecework wages system
jingbeiqu	警备区	special military area
jingji hesuanzhi	经济核算制	economic accounting
Jingjianbu	经建部	Economic Construction Department
jiuguo gongzhai	救国公债	government bonds for national salvation
kang	炕	brick bed
ke	科	section (of the county government)

lan gong	揽工	to contract short-term labour
lao mazi	老麻子	sesame(?)
Liushouchu	留守处	Garrison Office
luoxian	络线	thread joiners
luwei	芦苇	reed grass
magan	马干	horse feed
malancao	马兰草	malan grass
meitan	煤炭	coke, charcoal
meizi	糜子	coarse millet
musu	苜蓿	alfalfa
ningtiaozi	宁条子	*caraguna korshinskii*, a local variety of the Siberian pea-tree
nongchang	农场	agricultural station
pingyizhi	评议制	assessment method
qiyehua	企业化	to run as an enterprise, enterprization (contrasted with *jiguanhua*)
Shaangong	陕公	North Shaanxi Public School
shaliu	沙柳	sand willows
shitan	石炭	coal and charcoal
Shuili Ju	水利局	Water Conservancy Bureau
shuimandi	水漫地	water-logged land
su	粟	millet
tanpai	摊派	to apportion out (taxes)
tanyang	滩羊	*tanyang* sheep
Tewuying	特务营	Special Duties Battalion
tian gou	天沟	deep gully
tun tian	屯田	'camp-field system' used to describe military units doing their own farming
Wen-kang	文抗	Chinese Writers' Anti-Aggression Association
Wuzi Ju	物资局	Commodities Bureau

253

xiaodou	小豆	adzuki beans
xiao mazi	小麻子	hemp seeds
xiaomai	小麦	wheat
Xibei Ju	西北局	Northwest Bureau
Xibei Junwei	西北军委	Northwest Military Committee
xiliang	细粮	hulled grain
yangyu	洋芋	sweet potatoes
Yanye Gongsi	盐业公司	Salt Company
yiyuanhua	一元化	unify, united
youfang	油房	oil-pressing shop
yumai	玉麦	oats
zhagong	札工	contract-labour teams
zhameng	蚱蜢	locusts
zhigonghui	职工会	workers' congress
Zhong-cai xitong	中财系统	The system under the Central Committee Finance and Economy Office
Zhongyang Bangongting	中央办公厅	Central Work Department
Zhongyang Guanliju	中央管理局	Central Administration Bureau
Zhongyang Xuanchuanbu	中央宣传部	Central Propaganda Department
Zhongyang Zongwuchu	中央总务处	Central General Affairs Section
Zhongyang Zuzhibu	中央组织部	Central Organization Department
zhongyuan	中原	the eastern areas of Shaanxi province
zhuanqu	专区	special regions
zhuanshu	专署	special offices
ziweijun	自卫军	self-defence army

GLOSSARY OF PLACE NAMES

Anding	安定	Goumenshang	沟门上
Ansai	安塞	Guanzhong	关中
Baima	白马	Gulin	固临
Bao'an	保安	Guoxian	崞县
Changcheng	长城	Hancheng	韩城
Chengguan	城关	Henan	河南
Chishui	赤水	Hengshan	横山
Chuankou	川口	Heshui	合水
Chunhua	淳化	Huachi	华池
Chunyao	淳耀	Huai	淮
Dingbian	定边	Huanxian	环县
Donghenanzhen	东河南镇	Huluhe	葫芦河
Dongyang	东阳	Jiangxi	江西
Dufuchuan	杜甫川	Jianjuntaicun	监军台村
Erjiachuan	二家川	Jiaocheng	交城
Fengfu	丰富	Jiaxian	葭县
Fucunchuan	傅村川	Jingbian	靖边
Fugu	府谷	Jinpen	金盆
Fuxian	鄜县	Jinpenhe	金盆河
Ganguyi	甘谷驿	Jinpenwan	金盆湾
Ganquan	甘泉	Jiulishan	九里山
Gaomaowan	高茆湾	Laiyuan	涞源
Gaoyang	高阳	Lannipo	烂泥坡

255

Liangzhuang	梁庄	Qingyang	庆阳
Lijiabian	李家砭	Quzi	曲子
Lijiaqu	李家渠	Sanbian	三边
Lingqiu	灵邱	Sanlimiao	三里庙
Linzhen	临镇	Sanshilipu	三十里铺
Liugen Shui	柳根水	Shaan-Gan-Ning	陕甘宁
Liujiaping	刘家坪	Shanxi	山西
Liulin	柳林	Shanxi-Chahar-Hebei	山西
Longdong	陇东		察哈尔 河北
Loufan	娄烦	Shaoshan	梢山
Luanshitouchuan	乱石头川	Shenfu	神甫
Lüfengpo	吕凤坡	Shenmu	神木
Lujiajiao	芦家角	Shuifan	水泛
Luochuan	洛川	Sichuan	四川
Majiapan	马家畔	Songshulin	松树林
Malan	马栏	Suide	绥德
Mashichuan	马市川	Sui-Mi	绥米
Mizhi	米脂	(Joint reference to Suide and Mizhi counties)	
Mudan	牡丹	Sunkeyaoxian	孙克要险
Nanguan	南关	Taile	太乐
Nanniwan	南泥湾	Taiyuan	太原
Nanyigou	南义沟	Tianjiagelao	田家圪垎
Nanzhuanghe	南庄河	Tianzhuang	田庄
Ningwu	宁武	Tongguan	同官
Ningxia	宁夏	Tuwan	兔湾
Ningxian	宁县	Wenshui	文水
Panlong	盘龙	Wubao	吴堡
Qilipu	七里铺	Wujiacaoyuan	吴家枣园
Qinghai	青海	Wuliwan	五里湾
Qingjian	清涧	Wuqi	吴起

256

GLOSSARY OF PLACE NAMES

Wuyang	乌羊	Yijun	宜君
Wuyasi	乌鸦寺	Yongping	永坪
Xiaguanzhen	下关镇	Yongsheng	永胜
Xi'an	西安	Yuju	禹居
Xinning	新宁	Yulin	榆林
Xinzheng	新正	Yunshansi	云山寺
Yan'an	延安	Zhangcunyi	张村驿
Yanchang	延长	Zhangjiacha	张家岔
Yanchi	盐池	Zhangjiahe	张家河口
Yanchuan	延川	Zhangjiakou	张家口
Yangqiaopan	杨桥畔	Zhengning	正宁
Yangwu	阳武	Zhenwudong	真武洞
Yaodian	姚店	Zhenyuan	镇原
Yaoxian	耀县	Zhidan	志丹
Yichuan	宜川	Zichang	子长
Yihezhen	义合镇		

257

GLOSSARY OF PERSONAL NAMES

Bai Da	白 大	Liu Jianzhang	刘 建 章
Bai Fenyu	白 粉 玉	Liu Shichang	刘 世 昌
Bai Heming	白 合 明	Liu Zhidan	刘 志 丹
Cao Yucheng	曹 玉 城	Liu Zixiao	刘 子 孝
Chang Degong	常 德 功	Lu Zhongcai	魯 忠 才
Dong Zhongshu	董 仲 舒	Mao Kehu	卯 克 呼
Du Fafu	杜 发 福	Mao Keye	茆 克 业
Du Hai	杜 海	Mao Yupeng	毛 羽 鹏
Gao Kelin	高 克 林	Ren Shengbiao	任 生 彪
Gao Wu	高 武	Shen Hong	沈 鸿
He Chungao	何 纯 高	Sun Shenghua	孙 生 花
He Weizhong	何 维 忠	Wang Pi'nian	王 丕 年
Hu Dianchang	胡 典 长	Wang Shengming	王 生 明
Hu Diangong	胡 典 功	Wang Tianjin	王 天 金
Hu Qingrong	胡 清 荣	Wang Wenbin	王 文 斌
Huang Baozhong	黄 保 中	Wang Yaoming	王 耀 明
Hui San	惠 三	Wang Yuxian	王 毓 贤
Jia Zhicai	贾 志 才	Wu Manyou	吴 满 有
Kong Zhaoqing	孔 照 庆	Xiang (Duke)	相 公
Li Dejin	李 德 金	Yan Fenghe	阎 凤 和
Li Maolin	李 茂 林	Yang Wanbao	杨 万 保
Li Shengcai	李 生 彩	Yang Yingcheng	杨 应 成
Li Shenghai	李 生 海	Zhang Bingquan	张 秉 权
Li Shengzhang	李 生 章	Zhao Zhankui	赵 占 魁
Liu Guai	刘 拐	Zhu De	朱 德

BIBLIOGRAPHY

Alley, R. *Fruition: The Story of George Alwin Hogg*, Caxton Press, Christchurch, New Zealand, 1967

Benton, G. 'The Second "Wang Ming Line" ', *The China Quarterly*, No. 61, March 1975, pp. 61–94

Benton, G. 'The Second "Wang Ming Line" ' – Comment, *The China Quarterly*, No. 69, March 1977, pp. 145–54

Buck, J. L. *Land Utilization in China*, University of Nanking, 1937

Carrère, H. and Schram, S. *Marxism and Asia*, Allen Lane, 1969

Chen Boda *A Study of Land Rent in Pre-Liberation China*, Foreign Languages Press, Beijing, 1966

Chen, J. 'Defining Chinese Warlords and their Factions', *Bulletin of the School of Oriental and African Studies*, Vol. 31, Pt. 3 (1968), pp. 563–600.

Close, U. and McCormick, E. 'Where the Mountains Walked', *The National Geographic Magazine*, Vol. 41, No. 5, May 1922, pp. 445–64

Compton, B. *Mao's China: Party Reform Documents 1942–1944*, University of Washington Press, 1952

Ding Wang (ed.) *Peng Dehuai Wenti Zhuanji*, Zhong-gong Wenhua Da Geming Ziliao Huibian, Vol. 3, Mingbao Yuekan Chubanshe, Hong Kong, 1969

Foreman, H. *Report from Red China*, Book Find Club, New York, 1945

Gittings, J. *The World and China, 1922–1972*, Eyre Methuen, 1974

Gray, J. 'The Two Roads; Alternative Strategies of Social Change and Economic Growth in China', pp. 109–57, in Schram (ed.) 1973

Harrison, J. *The Long March to Power*, Macmillan, 1972

Hsiao, T. L. *The Land Revolution in China 1930–1934*, University of Washington Press, 1969

Johnson, C. *Peasant Nationalism and Communist Power*, Stanford University Press, 1962

Kangri Zhanzheng Shiqi Jiefangqu Gaikuang, Renmin Chubanshe, Beijing, 1953

Mao Zedong Jingji Wenti Yu Caizheng Wenti, Xin Minzhu Chubanshe, Hong Kong, 1949

261

Mao Zedong *Mao Zedong Sixiang Wansui* 2 vols., reprinted by Institute of International Relations, Taibei, 1967 and 1969

Mao Zedong *Mao Zedong Xuanji*, 5 vols., Beijing, 1951, 1952, 1953, 1960, 1977

Mao Zedong *Miscellany of Mao Tse-tung Thought (1949–1968)* 2 parts – Joint Publications and Research Service 61269–1, 61269–2, 1974, distributed by the National Technical Information Service of the US Department of Commerce

Mao Zedong *Mō Takutō Shū* (Mao Zedong Ji), 10 vols., Hokubosha, Tokyo, 1970–2

Mao Zedong *Selected Works of Mao Zedong*, 5 vols., Beijing, 1964–77

Myrdal, J. *Report from a Chinese Village*, Signet Books, 1966

Schram, S. (ed.) *Authority, Participation and Cultural Change in China*, Cambridge University Press, 1973

Schram, S. *Mao Tse-tung*, Penguin, 1967

Schram, S. 'Mao Tse-tung and Secret Societies', *The China Quarterly*, No. 27, July–September 1966, pp. 1–13

Schram, S. (ed.) *Mao Tse-tung Unrehearsed*, Penguin, 1974

Schram, S. *The Political Thought of Mao Tse-tung*, Penguin, 1969

Schran, P. *Guerrilla Economy: The Development of the Shensi-Kansu-Ninghsia Border Region, 1937–1945*, State University of New York, 1976

Schran, P. *The Development of Chinese Agriculture 1950–1959*, University of Illinois Press, 1969

Selden, M. 'The Guerrilla Movement in Northwest China: the Origins of the Shensi-Kansu-Ninghsia Border Region' (2 parts), *The China Quarterly*, No. 28, October-December 1966 and No. 29, January–March 1967

Selden, M. *The Yenan Way in Revolutionary China*, Harvard University Press, 1971

Shaan-Gan-Ning Bianqu Canyihui Wenxian Huiji, Renmin Chubanshe, Beijing, 1958

Shaan-Gan-Ning Bianqu de Laodong Huzhu, Jinan Shudian, 1946

Shaan-Gan-Ning Bianqu Zhengfu Gongzuo Boagao 1939–1941, Yan'an, 1941

Shaan-Gan-Ning Bianqu Zuzhi Laodong Huzhu de Jingyan, Huabei Shudian, 1944

Sheridan, J. *Chinese Warlord: The Career of Feng Yu-hsiang*, Stanford University Press, 1966

Shum, K. K. 'The Second "Wang Ming Line" ' – Comment, *The China Quarterly*, No. 69, March 1977, pp. 136–45

Snow, E. *Red Star over China*, Gollancz, 1937

Snow, E. *Scorched Earth*, Gollancz, 1940

Stein, G. *The Challenge of Red China*, Pilot Press, 1945

BIBLIOGRAPHY

Tanaka, K. *Mass Mobilization: The Chinese Communist Party and the Peasants*, Unpublished Ph.D. thesis, Australian National University, 1972

Teichman, E. *Travels of a Consular Officer in North-West China*, Cambridge University Press, 1921

Tian Jiaying *Mao Zedong Tongzhi Lun Kangri Shiqi de Zhengfeng Yundong he Shengchan Yundong*, Beijing, 1953

Tregear, T. R. *A Geography of China*, University of London Press, 1965

Wilson, D. (ed.) *Mao Tse-tung in the Scales of History*, Cambridge University Press, 1977

Young, A. *China's Wartime Finance and Inflation 1937–1945*, Harvard East Asian Series, 20, Harvard University Press, 1965

Zagoria, D. S. *The Sino-Soviet Conflict 1956–61*, Atheneum, 1967

263

INDEX